Race, Curriculum, and the Politics of Educational Justice

Wayne Au

Teachers College Press
Teachers College, Columbia University

Published by Teachers College Press,® 1234 Amsterdam Avenue, New York, NY 10027

Library of Congress Cataloging-in-Publication Data is available at loc.gov

ISBN 978-0-8077-8718-2 (paper)
ISBN 978-0-8077-8719-9 (hardcover)
ISBN 978-0-8077-8314-6 (ebook)

Printed on acid-free paper
Manufactured in the United States of America

MULTICULTURAL EDUCATION SERIES

JAMES A. BANKS, Series Editor

Race, Curriculum, and the Politics of Educational Justice
WAYNE AU

Fostering School-Family Relationships in Multicultural Communities
MATTHEW KNOESTER, MAURA G. ROBINSON, & TOUORIZOU HERVÉ SOMÉ

Affirming Student Ethnic Identities: How Teachers Can Create Welcoming Classrooms
ANDRÉ J. BRANCH

Critical Theory, Methods, and Design in Educational Research
LOIS WEIS & MICHELLE FINE

Critical Ethnic Studies and the Global Pursuit of Justice
JAMES WRIGHT

Let's Talk About DEI: Productive Disagreements About America's Most Polarizing Topics
SHAUN HARPER

Why Historically Black Colleges and Universities Matter: 25 Years of Historical Research for Justice
MARYBETH GASMAN

Hidden in Blackness: Being Black and Being an Immigrant in U.S. Schools and Colleges
CHRYSTAL A. GEORGE MWANGI & ADAURENNAYA C. ONYEWUENYI

"To Remain an Indian": Lessons in Democracy from a Century of Native American Education, 2nd Ed.
K. TSIANINA LOMAWAIMA AND TERESA L. MCCARTY

From Foster Care to College: Navigating Educational Challenges and Creating Possibilities
ROYEL M. JOHNSON

Achieving Equal Educational Opportunity for Students of Color: Disrupting Structural Racism—An American Imperative
RICHARD R. VALENCIA

Critical Multicultural Education: Theory and Practice
CHRISTINE E. SLEETER

Race and Media Literacy, Explained (or Why Does the Black Guy Die First?)
FREDERICK W. GOODING, JR.

Whiteness in the Ivory Tower: Why *Don't* We Notice the White Students Sitting Together in the Quad?
NOLAN L. CABRERA

Culturally Sustaining Policymaking in Indigenous Communities: Partnering to Promote Lasting Change
APRILLE J. PHILLIPS

Educating for Equity and Excellence: Enacting Culturally Responsive Teaching
GENEVA GAY

Speculative Pedagogies: Designing Equitable Educational Futures
ANTERO GARCIA & NICOLE MIRRA, EDS.

Seeing Whiteness: The Essential Essays of Robin DiAngelo
ROBIN DIANGELO

Becoming an Antiracist School Leader: Dare to Be Real
PATRICK A. DUFFY

The Hip-Hop Mindset: Success Strategies for Educators and Other Professionals
TOBY S. JENKINS

Education for Liberal Democracy: Using Classroom Discussion to Build Knowledge and Voice
WALTER C. PARKER

Critical Race Theory and Its Critics: Implications for Research and Teaching
FRANCESCA LÓPEZ & CHRISTINE E. SLEETER

Anti-Blackness at School: Creating Affirming Educational Spaces for African American Students
JOI A. SPENCER & KERRI ULLUCCI

Sustaining Disabled Youth: Centering Disability in Asset Pedagogies
FEDERICO R. WAITOLLER & KATHLEEN A. KING THORIUS, EDS.

The Civil Rights Road to Deeper Learning: Five Essentials for Equity
KIA DARLING-HAMMOND & LINDA DARLING-HAMMOND

Reckoning With Racism in Family-School Partnerships: Centering Black Parents' School Engagement
JENNIFER L. MCCARTHY FOUBERT

Teaching Anti-Fascism: A Critical Multicultural Pedagogy for Civic Engagement
MICHAEL VAVRUS

Unsettling Settler-Colonial Education: The Transformational Indigenous Praxis Model
CORNEL PEWEWARDY ET AL., EDS.

Culturally and Socially Responsible Assessment: Theory, Research, and Practice
CATHERINE S. TAYLOR, WITH SUSAN B. NOLEN

LGBTQ Youth and Education: Policies and Practices 2nd Ed.
CRIS MAYO

For a complete list of series titles, please visit www.tcpress.com/MCE

(continued)

Multicultural Education Series, *continued*

Transforming Multicultural Education Policy and Practice
James A. Banks, Ed.

Critical Race Theory in Education
Gloria Ladson-Billings

Civic Education in the Age of Mass Migration
Angela M. Banks

Creating a Home in Schools
Francisco Rios & A Longoria

Generation Mixed Goes to School
Ralina L. Joseph & Allison Briscoe-Smith

Indian Education for All
John P. Hopkins

Racial Microaggressions
Daniel G. Solórzano & Lindsay Pérez Huber

City Schools and the American Dream 2
Pedro A. Noguera & Esa Syeed

Measuring Race
Robert T. Teranishi et al.

Transformative Ethnic Studies in Schools
Christine E. Sleeter & Miguel Zavala

Why Race and Culture Matter in Schools, 2nd Ed.
Tyrone C. Howard

Just Schools
Ann M. Ishimaru

"We Dare Say Love"
Na'ilah Suad Nasir et al., Eds.

Teaching What *Really* Happened, 2nd Ed.
James W. Loewen

Culturally Responsive Teaching, 3rd Ed.
Geneva Gay

Music, Education, and Diversity
Patricia Shehan Campbell

Reaching and Teaching Students in Poverty, 2nd Ed.
Paul C. Gorski

Deconstructing Race
Jabari Mahiri

Is Everyone Really Equal? 2nd Ed.
Özlem Sensoy & Robin DiAngelo

Transforming Educational Pathways for Chicana/o Students
Dolores Delgado Bernal & Enrique Alemán Jr.

Un-Standardizing Curriculum, 2nd Ed.
Christine E. Sleeter & Judith Flores Carmona

Global Migration, Diversity, and Civic Education
James A. Banks et al., Eds.

Reclaiming the Multicultural Roots of U.S. Curriculum
Wayne Au et al.

We Can't Teach What We Don't Know, 3rd Ed.
Gary R. Howard

Diversity and Education
Michael Vavrus

Mathematics for Equity
Na'ilah Suad Nasir et al., Eds.

Race, Empire, and English Language Teaching
Suhanthie Motha

Black Male(d)
Tyrone C. Howard

Race Frameworks
Zeus Leonardo

Class Rules
Peter W. Cookson Jr.

Achieving Equity for Latino Students
Frances Contreras

Literacy Achievement and Diversity
Kathryn H. Au

Understanding English Language Variation in U.S. Schools
Anne H. Charity Hudley & Christine Mallinson

Latino Children Learning English
Guadalupe Valdés et al.

Asians in the Ivory Tower
Robert T. Teranishi

Diversity and Equity in Science Education
Okhee Lee & Cory A. Buxton

Forbidden Language
Patricia Gándara & Megan Hopkins, Eds.

The Light in Their Eyes, 10th Anniversary Ed.
Sonia Nieto

The Flat World and Education
Linda Darling-Hammond

Educating Citizens in a Multicultural Society, 2nd Ed.
James A. Banks

Culture, Literacy, and Learning
Carol D. Lee

Facing Accountability in Education
Christine E. Sleeter, Ed.

Talkin Black Talk
H. Samy Alim & John Baugh, Eds.

Improving Access to Mathematics
Na'ilah Suad Nasir & Paul Cobb, Eds.

Beyond the Big House
Gloria Ladson-Billings

Improving Multicultural Education
Cherry A. McGee Banks

Transforming the Multicultural Education of Teachers
Michael Vavrus

Learning to Teach for Social Justice
Linda Darling-Hammond et al., Eds.

Learning and Not Learning English
Guadalupe Valdés

Multicultural Education, Transformative Knowledge, and Action
James A. Banks, Ed.

Contents

PART II: RACIAL (IN)JUSTICE AND NEOLIBERAL EDUCATION REFORM

PART III: ASIAN AMERICAN RACIALIZATION AND EDUCATION

Series Foreword

In this compassionate, compelling, and timely book, Wayne Au draws on his experience as a classroom teacher and social activist to argue that a pedagogy and a curriculum of insurgency are essential to reform schools and to actualize racial and social-class equality. A pedagogy of insurgency consists of "bravery and risk, allyship and solidarity across communities of struggle, organizing and protest, critical analyses of power, curriculum of insurgency, contradictions of schooling and reimagining education, and connection to broader struggles and social movements" (p. 26).

Au argues that the pedagogy and curriculum in most schools reinforce the racialized and social-class stratification within society writ large. However, schools can be "powerful sites of resistance and rebellion, spaces for building critical consciousness and fostering collective action for justice" (p. 29). Au depicts vivid examples of how schools can reinforce existing equalities as well as resist them. He describes how one of his 9th-grade teachers contradicted the major tenets of multicultural education by marginalizing the voices of students, including Au's, which taught him that multicultural education must involve dialogue with multiple voices—inclusive of students' own voices. In another teacher's class, Au learned that effective multicultural education is a critique of Eurocentric school knowledge as well as an envisioning of action to make society more equitable and just. Activism, Au maintains, is a required goal of a pedagogy and curriculum of insurgency. In his most recent work, Au rarely uses the term "multicultural education" because "the struggle around these issues has developed sharper language that is aimed at anti-racism, fighting white supremacy, and settler colonialism, among other intersectional framings" (p. 3).

Au's discussion of the ways in which standardized testing reinforces the racial and social-class stratification within schools and society writ large is ingenious and visionary. He explicates how standardized testing obscures racial and social-class inequality by using the ideology of individual meritocracy. Standardized testing has enhanced inequality in many ways, including giving credence to the idea that African Americans, Mexican Americans, other students of color, and low-income students are less intellectually capable because of their lower IQ scores, which often results in these students being tracked into classes that are less intellectually challenging, which actualizes the self-fulfilling prophecy. Standardized testing has also given a boost to charter schools because of the ways test results have been used to judge regular public schools, a practice that often benefits profit-making corporations (Ravitch, 2025).

The ways in which standardized testing and ability grouping have been used to victimize and marginalize African Americans, Mexican Americans, and other students of color has a long and sordid history in U.S. schools and in the testing industry, which dates back to when the Stanford-Binet IQ test came into use in 1932. Arthur R. Jensen (1969) argued, in an article published in *Harvard Educational Review*, that Head Start and other compensatory programs designed to increase the academic achievement of low-income and minority students failed because of their inferior genetic characteristics. Jensen (1969) discussed "evidence which suggests that social class and racial variations in intelligence cannot be accounted for by differences in environment but must be attributed partially to genetic differences" (p. 2). Jensen's article was highly influential because he was a professor at a prestigious university (University of California, Berkeley) who published the article in a prestigious journal, which devoted an entire issue to his article. In its second 1969 issue, *Harvard Educational Review* published articles that described the problems and limitations of Jensen's article (Hunt, 1969; Kagan, 1969). However, when the issue with the critiques was published, the harm caused by the Jensen article had already been done. Two decades after the publication of the Jensen article, sociologist Jane R. Mercer (1989) described the detrimental consequences of standardized testing and proposed alternative paradigms for assessment that are culturally sensitive and responsive.

Au provides a searing and trenchant critique of the Model Minority stereotype of Asian Americans. The idea of Asian Americans as the Model Minority originated in 1966 when the *New York Times* published an article by William Petersen, "Success Story: Japanese-American Style." Petersen argued that in terms of good citizenship, Japanese Americans were better than any other group, including native-born whites. Au illuminates in sometimes touching ways how destructive the Model Minority stereotype is for both Asian Americans and other groups of color. He maintains that the Model Minority stereotype is embedded in racism, white supremacy, and anti-Blackness. The message conveyed to African Americans and groups of color is to stop complaining and to emulate the experience of Asian Americans. A poignant consequence of the Model Minority stereotype is that many Asian Americans have internalized it and believe that if they are not academically successful they are not authentic Asian Americans, which results in many Asian Americans experiencing "Model Minority stress." Writes Au, "Clearly, the Asian American Model Minority stereotype comes at a cost: It supports anti-Black racism and deficit views of Black people, subjects Asian Americans to white supremacist fears and violence, and Cut on p. 119. damages the Asian American psyche" (p. 119).

The description and illustration of a pedagogy and curriculum of insurgency, the elucidation of the harmful effects of standardized testing, and the critique of depicting Asian Americans as the Model Minority make this book a significant and prescient contribution to the Multicultural Education Series. The major purpose of the Multicultural Education Series is to provide preservice educators, practicing educators, graduate students, scholars, and policymakers with an interrelated and comprehensive set of books that summarizes and analyzes important research, theory, and practice related to the education of ethnic, racial, cultural, and linguistic groups in the United States and the education of mainstream students about diversity. The dimensions of multicultural education, developed by Banks (2004) and described in the *Handbook of Research on Multicultural Education, The Routledge International Companion to Multicultural Education* (Banks, 2009) and the *Encyclopedia of Diversity in Education* (Banks, 2012), provide the conceptual framework for the development of the publications in the Series. The dimensions are *content integration, the knowledge construction process, prejudice reduction, equity pedagogy*, and an *empowering institutional culture and social structure*.

The books in the Multicultural Education Series provide research, theoretical, and practical knowledge about the behaviors and learning characteristics of students of color (Darling-Hammond & Darling-Hammond, 2022; Conchas & Vigil, 2012; Lee, 2007), language-minority students (Gándara & Hopkins, 2010; Valdés, 2001; Valdés et al., 2011), low-income students (Cookson, 2013; Gorski, 2018), and other minoritized population groups, such as students who speak different varieties of English (Charity Hudley & Mallinson, 2011), LGBTQ+ youth (Mayo, 2022), and students with disabilities (Waitoller & Thorius, 2022).

An important goal of a pedagogy and curriculum of insurgency is to reduce institutional and structural racism in schools, colleges, and universities. A number of books in the Multicultural Education Series focus on ways to lessen racism in educational institutions. These books include *Is Everyone Really Equal?: An Introduction to Key Concepts in Social Justice Education* (Second Edition) by Özlem Sensoy and Robin DiAngelo (2017); *We Can't Teach What We Don't Know: White Teachers, Multiracial Schools* (Third Edition) by Gary Howard (2016); *Deconstructing Race: Multicultural Education Beyond the Color-Bind* by Jabari Mahiri (2017); *Race Frameworks: A Multidimensional Theory of Racism and Education* by Zeus Leonardo (2013); *Racial Microaggressions: Using Critical Race Theory to Respond to Everyday Racism* by Daniel G. Solórzano and Lindsay Pérez Huber (2020), and *Seeing Whiteness: The Essential Essays of Robin DiAngelo* by Robin DiAngelo (2023).

The incisive and powerful discussion of a pedagogy and curriculum of insurgency, the penetrating critique of standardized testing, and the description of the detrimental effects of the Model Minority stereotype make this a timely, informative, and valuable book in these challenging and contentious times for diversity, equity, and inclusion. I hope this caring and inspirational book will be seriously read and stimulate action to create more humane and just classrooms and schools.

—James A. Banks

REFERENCES

Banks, J. A. (2004). Multicultural education: Historical development, dimensions, and practice. In J. A. Banks & C. A. M. Banks (Eds.), *Handbook of research on multicultural education* (2nd ed., pp. 3–29). Jossey-Bass.

Banks, J. A. (Ed.). (2009). *The Routledge international companion to multicultural education*. Routledge.

Banks, J. A. (2012). Multicultural education: Dimensions of. In J. A. Banks (Ed)., *Encyclopedia of diversity in education* (vol. 3, pp. 1538–1547). Sage Publications.

Charity Hudley, A. H., & Mallinson, C. (2011). *Understanding language variation in U.S. schools*. Teachers College Press.

Conchas, G. Q., & Vigil, J. D. (2012). *Streetsmart schoolsmart: Urban poverty and the education of adolescent boys*. Teachers College Press.

Cookson, P. W. Jr. (2013). *Class rules: Exposing inequality in American high schools*. New Teachers College Press.

DiAngelo, R. (2023). *Seeing whiteness: The essential essays of Robin DiAngelo*. Teachers College Press.

Darling-Hammond, K., & Darling-Hammond, L. (2022). *The civil rights road to deeper learning: Five essentials for equity*. Teachers College Press.

Gándara, P., & Hopkins, M. (Eds.). (2010). *Forbidden language: English language learners and restrictive language policies*. Teachers College Press.

Gorski, P. C. (2018). *Reaching and teaching students in poverty: Strategies for erasing the opportunity* gap (2nd ed.). Teachers College Press.

Howard, G. (2016). *We can't teach what we don't know: White teachers, multiracial schools* (3rd ed.). Teachers College Press.

Hunt, J. M. (1969). Has compensatory education failed? Has it been attempted? *Harvard Educational Review*, *39*(2), 278–300.

Jensen, A. R. (1969). How much can we boost IQ and scholastic achievement? *Harvard Educational Review, 39*(1), 1–123.

Kagan, J. (1969). Inadequate evidence and illogical conclusions. *Harvard Educational Review*, *39*(2), 274–277.

Lee, C. D. (2007). *Culture, literacy, and learning: Taking bloom in the midst of the whirlwind*. Teachers College Press.

Leonardo, Z. (2013). *Race frameworks: A multidimensional theory of racism and education*. Teachers College Press.

Mahiri, J. (2017). *Deconstructing race: Multicultural education beyond the color-bind*. Teachers College Press.

Mayo, C. (2022). *LGBTQ youth and education: Policies and practices* (2nd ed.). Teachers College Press.

Mercer, J. R. (1989). Alternative programs for assessment in a pluralistic society. In J. A. Banks & C. A. M. Banks (Eds.), *Multicultural education: Issues and perspectives* (pp. 289–304). Allyn and Bacon.

Petersen, W. (1966, January 9). Success story, Japanese-American style. *The New York Times*, 21, 33, 36, 38, 40–41, 43.

Ravitch, D. (2025). *Their* kind of indoctrination. *The New York Review of Books*. https://www.nybooks.com/online/2025/01/11/their-kind-of-indoctrination/?srsltid=AfmBOorqzUt7EtnVnxNk0rH_QLn1FX6KNkPwWKtgZvYof3jToo85S9br

Sensoy, Ö. & DiAngelo, R. (2017). *Is everyone really equal? An introduction to key concepts in social justice education* (2nd ed.). Teachers College Press.

Solórzano, D. & Huber, L. P. (2020). *Racial microaggressions: Using critical race theory to respond to everyday racism*. Teachers College Press.

Valdés, G. (2001). *Learning and not learning English: Latino Students in American schools*. Teachers College Press.

Valdés, G., Capitelli, S., & Alvarez, L. (2011). *Latino children learning English: Steps in the journey*. Teachers College Press.

Waitoller, F. R. & Thorius, K. A. K. (2022). *Sustaining disabled youth: Centering disability in asset pedagogies*. Teachers College Press.

Acknowledgments

I am indebted to Dr. James Banks for inviting me to contribute this book to his series, and for his overall support of my work over the years. I also have to thank Rethinking Schools, not just for the permission to reprint my articles, but also for the help that the entire editorial team plays in shaping the quality of the content. Pieces included here were supported and influenced by too many folks to name, but some of them are (in no particular order): E. Wayne Ross, OiYan Poon, Anthony Brown, Benji Chang (Rest in Power, my brother), Nolan Cabrera, Leigh Patel, Alex Means, Michael Apple, Michael Dumas, Julie Fain and Haymarket Books, Jesse Hagopian, Edwin Mayorga, and David Stovall. Of course, everything I do is buoyed by the grounding, love, learning, and intellects of my family, Mira Shimabukuro and Makoto.

Acknowledgments

Introduction

In 9th grade, I remember turning to a friend in my world history class at Garfield High School in Seattle, and we both agreed we would become teachers to hopefully do better than what we were experiencing (Au, 2009a). While my friend and I took different paths, we both did achieve our goal of becoming teachers. I began my journey to teaching at The Evergreen State College in the early 1990s, where I worked with tribal and urban youth across the South Puget Sound region as a staff member for an Upward Bound program serving low-income high school students who would be the first generation in their families to attend college. I continued on to get my Master in Teaching degree at Evergreen, and eventually ended up as a high school teacher at a program for "dropouts" in the Seattle Public Schools. Seemingly to follow through with my 9th-grade plan, I then returned to Garfield High School to teach history (my friend became a teacher in the Oakland Unified School District in California), and soon after I moved on to teach at Berkeley High School in Berkeley, California. Dealing with a combination of burnout and frustration with being laid off due to state budget cuts, I left Berkeley High, pursued my PhD at the University of Wisconsin, and became an assistant professor at California State University, Fullerton. After a few years there, I was fortunate enough to able to come back home to Seattle when I took a job at the University of Washington Bothell, where, as of this writing, I am now a dean and professor.

Across this time, I have always been a radical teacher (Au, 2018), someone guided by an understanding of classrooms as gardens to nurture critical consciousness about society and help students understand themselves as potential activists—or, in Freire's (1974) terms, acting within the world as subjects of their own histories. Teaching "dropouts" in Seattle, we regularly used *A People's History of The United States* (Zinn, 1995) and *Open Veins of Latin America* (Galeano, 1998) as core history texts to aid students in understanding how current social, economic, and cultural relations and systems are grounded in a past that was steeped in capitalism and settler colonialism. At this time the era-defining protest against the World Trade Organization took place in Seattle, and so we took the historical moment as an opportunity to teach about globalization and the perils of "free trade" for people and the planet, while also taking part in the protests as part of the organized labor contingent (Au, 2000). When I returned to Garfield High School as a history teacher, I was fortunate to inherit the responsibility of teaching the very same Black History course that had shaped my political, racial, and cultural consciousness as a student some 10 years earlier (Au, 2009a). My educational radicalism continued at Berkeley High School, where I not only taught 9th-grade Ethnic Studies courses, but also had the privilege of teaching both an Asian American History class and an Asian American Literature class. My university teaching has been much of the same, as I am constantly incorporating a politics of justice into my curriculum and teaching—including developing classes on critical education policy studies and critical pedagogy.

Importantly, activism has also been a part of my personal and professional life every step of the way. In my earlier teaching years in Seattle, I helped co-found a Puget Sound Rethinking Schools group to organize meetings and begin hosting local social justice educator events. Eventually, and following our friends and comrades in the San Francisco Bay Area, we connected with the Portland Area Rethinking Schools group to start jointly planning and co-hosting an annual Northwest Teaching for Social Justice Conference. At our pre-pandemic peak, our entirely volunteer-run conference was drawing over 1,200 educators, mostly from around the Pacific Northwest region, but also some nationally. Later, teaching in Berkeley, I was a co-founder of Education Not Incarceration, a community-based coalition that organized against the State of California's budget priorities, which at the time was cutting education spending while increasing monies for prisons. I also became involved with the National Coalition of Education Activists (now defunct), ultimately joining their board, around this time as well.

When I was working on my PhD at the University of Wisconsin, Madison, I deepened my relationship with Rethinking Schools,—a national leader in supporting justice-centered education located in nearby Milwaukee. This not only allowed me to formally join a community of K–12 teachers connected with *Rethinking Schools* magazine, it also enabled me to further build relationships with education activists nationally. Once I returned to the Seattle area as a professor, I found myself plugging back into my old networks of social justice educators, where I became deeply involved in community-based struggles against high-stakes testing (Au, 2013; Hagopian, 2014d) and charter schools (Au, 2012a, 2016c; Au & Ferrare, 2014). Additionally, as a parent of a school-aged child, I engaged in struggles over Black Lives Matter in schools (Au & Hagopian, 2017; Hagopian, 2016; Watson et al., 2018), and supported K–12 Ethnic Studies in Seattle schools and beyond (Au, 2020).

I understand that *Race, Curriculum, and the Politics of Educational Justice* is not officially a biography, but I could not work on this collection without considering how it maps my development and evolution as a scholar and writer, cataloguing different threads of my work and life. This was one of the most personally rewarding aspects of writing *Race, Curriculum, and the Politics of Educational Justice*, because it thrust me into reflecting across the last 2 decades of my published work (and 3 decades of working in education) to not only look for different themes, but also to attempt to integrate and synthesize my own identity as an academic, an activist, a parent, and a teacher—all while also trying to (imperfectly) navigate the academy, institutions of higher education, rightist political movements, state and local politics, community and familial relations, and my own personal identity as a gendered, classed, and racialized being.

What I was happy to see in my own work is the constant struggle to not just connect practice and theory, but to embody this praxis in who I am. The pieces I've included here hopefully illustrate this theory-practice dialectic, albeit on the page. Part of this is found in writing for different audiences, sometimes translating scholarly prose that was published in an academic journal and distilling the ideas down into writing that is livelier and more accessible for a much wider audience of teachers, parents, and students. Another part of this is writing about activism for audiences of both scholars and teachers, helping us (myself included) continue to feel and understand the power that communities can harness through organizing and solidarity. As I put this collection together, I enjoyed seeing these pieces of writing, transported across time and space, and recontextualized next to each other here.

THE CHAPTERS IN CONTEXT

All the chapters in *Race, Curriculum, and the Politics of Educational Justice* have been published elsewhere, some within very different contexts. Part I, "Curriculum and the Politics of Knowledge," gathers a group of four chapters that look at how school curriculum always carries with it deep struggles over specific sets of knowledge politics, with different groups literally fighting about not only who should have power to decide curriculum, but also what knowledge will be validated within the curriculum. Chapter 1, "Decolonizing the Classroom: Lessons in Multicultural Education," was first published in the 2008/2009 winter issue of *Rethinking Schools* (Au, 2009a). However, it is an article that reaches back to my days as a student at Garfield High School in Seattle, as well as when I returned to Garfield as a teacher. While I think this piece stands on its own (and has held up well over the years), I must note two things. First, I basically never use the term "multicultural education" anymore, mostly because I feel like the struggle around these issues has developed sharper language that is aimed at anti-racism, fighting white supremacy, and settler colonialism, among other intersectional framings (Au, 2024a). Second, I wrote this piece before substantial critiques had arisen around using the term "decolonizing" too loosely (Tuck & Yang, 2012). While I think I write within the spirit of decolonization, I probably would have used different framing had I written this piece today.

Chapter 2, "A Pedagogy of Insurgency: Teaching and Organizing for Radical Racial Justice in Our Schools," was originally published in *Educational Studies* (Au, 2021), but it grew partially out of a keynote addresses I delivered in 2017 and 2019, and partially out of 2017 activism around the Black Lives Matter movement in Seattle Public Schools. The backdrop for all of it was the first Trump administration, as well as the surge in attacks on racial, gender, and sexual justice that were amassing. Activism is critical here, as this chapter highlights how a single action at a single elementary school can not only ignite a district-wide movement (Au & Hagopian, 2017), but also inspire a national Black Lives Matter at School movement as well (Anderson et al., 2020; Au & Hagopian, 2021). Chapter 3, "It Is All Indoctrination: Power and the Impossibility of Apolitical Social Studies Curriculum," was more recently in *The Social Studies Curriculum* (Au, 2024b). Like the previous chapter, in this one I specifically address the anti-CRT, anti-DEI, anti-anti-racist, anti-trans, and anti-queer education movements that have risen to prominence around the United States, and I argue that no knowledge is ever neutral. Apropos of it all, as of this writing we are preparing for even more of these attacks, and with more intensity, with the second Trump administration. As such, I fear that these chapters are as relevant now as ever.

Part I closes out with a deep dive into curriculum theory, where in Chapter 4, "The Long March Toward Revitalization: Developing Standpoint in Curriculum Studies," I essentially offer a theoretical argument and conceptual framing for not only why all curriculum/knowledge is political, but also why those from more marginalized subject positions can potentially see the "truth" of social relations more clearly than those with more power—essentially outlining an epistemology of the oppressed. This chapter was originally published as a paper in *Teachers College Record* (Au, 2012b), and was written around the same time I was putting together my own thinking for my book, *Critical Curriculum Studies* (Au, 2011a). In an important way, Part I of *Race, Curriculum, and the Politics of Educational Justice* is illustrative of my conceptual approach to the book: The sections effectively spiral out from the concrete toward the more abstract. In this case, the first chapter is entirely grounded in my life experience, with Chapters 2 and 3 offering different mixes of theory and practice, and finally Chapter 4 provides a more theoretical view of how I understand the politics of knowledge in the curriculum. This and the other parts follow this pattern of moving from the specific to the general, moving inductively from practice toward theory.

Part II, "Racial (In)Justice and Neoliberal Education Reform," in some ways marks a turn away from curriculum theory but also doesn't. Here I gather pieces that look at how dominant education reforms, particularly high-stakes testing and charter schools, have mainly operated as tools of racial injustice. Of course, curriculum is implicated in these reforms because policy tools shape the kinds of resources allocated to schools and, perhaps most importantly, influence the curricular decisions being made by teachers, schools, districts, and states (e.g., teaching to the test). This reality is highlighted concretely in Chapter 5, "Racial Justice Is Not a Choice: White Supremacy, High-Stakes Testing, and the Punishment of Black and Brown Students" (Au, 2019), first published in *Rethinking Schools*. In this piece I synthesize several analyses from my ongoing work on high-stakes testing (Au, 2023b) for a broader audience, addressing the myriad ways that such testing has been detrimental to the educational, emotional, and physical experiences of working-class Black and Brown students in particular. Because I always want us to see possibilities for a different world through models and activism, this chapter also offers a framing for what more liberatory forms of assessment might look like.

Chapter 6, "Dispossession and Defiance: A Race and Class Political Economy of Neoliberal Education Reform," was first published as a chapter in my book, *A Marxist Education* (Au, 2018). It offers a lengthier treatment of the structures of neoliberal education reforms, outlining exactly how both high-stakes testing and charter schools ultimately serve the same, exploitative agenda. Again, resistance is important here, and this chapter ends with examples of how communities of color have resisted the colonizing, neoliberal policies being advanced by politicians, the wealthy, and educational leaders. Chapter 7, "Meritocracy 2.0: High-Stakes, Standardized Testing as a Racial Project of Neoliberal Multiculturalism," was originally published in *Educational Policy* (Au, 2016a) and has more recently become one of my most cited articles. In this chapter I take a slightly different angle on my critiques of high-stakes testing by using the lenses of meritocracy and neoliberal multiculturalism (Melamed, 2011) to reframe the foundational racism of the tests. I found this useful because meritocracy provides an underlying theory of how the tests are used ideologically to support neoliberal education reforms, and in turn neoliberal multiculturalism helps us understand how a false politics of racial justice gets used as a justification for those same reforms. As with Part I, Part II moves from concrete to abstract, from practice to theory, as it opens with a more grounded *Rethinking Schools* chapter, moves through a chapter that is grounded and uses theory, and ends with a more theoretically complex chapter.

Part III, "Asian American Racialization and Education," highlights my more recent turn in critical education analysis, where I've been trying to better understand Asian American racialization relative to other racial groups as well on its own terms, particularly within educational history and politics (Au, 2025a). Some of this turn grew out of the spike in anti-Asian hate and acts of violence in and around 2020. Some of it has come from my own need to regularly explore and understand my own identity. Some of it was generated out of what I perceived as a significant gap in our discourse and analyses of Asian American education generally, even among my more progressive and radical activist friends. As with almost all my writing, it certainly was driven by a felt *need* for folks around me to better understand Asian Americans and Asian American education. Importantly, Part III is about curriculum and policy as well: The racialization of Asian Americans as a Model Minority gets used regularly to advance particular policies like high-stakes testing and opposition to affirmative action, and, as I argue here, one antidote to this use/misuse of Asian Americans is a curriculum built toward solidarity.

Chapter 8, "'Superachievers' vs. 'Super Predators': How the Racist Love of the Model Minority Is Weaponized Against Black and Asian American Students"

(Au, 2025b), first published in *Rethinking Schools*, is the most recent of the works collected here. This chapter offers an accessible analysis of the origins of the Model Minority stereotype, its connection to anti-Blackness, and how it damages Asian American students. Chapter 9, "'Isn't That What the Case Is About, the Discrimination Against Asian Americans?': Conservatives Use Racial Wedge to Attack Affirmative Action" (Au, 2023a), also published in *Rethinking Schools*, uses the U.S. Supreme Court ruling against race-based affirmative action in higher education admissions policies to highlight how conservative whites successfully leveraged conservative Asian Americans to advance a fundamentally white supremacist attack on a racial equity program. This chapter very concretely highlights how Asian Americans, framed as the Model Minority, get weaponized to attack other racial groups, Black and Brown students in particular. Chapter 10, "Asian American Racialization, Racial Capitalism, and the Threat of the Educational Model Minority" (Au, 2022), first published in the *Review of Education, Pedagogy, and Cultural Studies*, then offers a deep theoretical treatment of why and how Asian American racialization positions us to be used and weaponized in such ways.

It is important to recognize that *Race, Curriculum, and the Politics of Educational Justice* is not just a gathering of my work. Rather, this is a curated group of slightly edited, previously published papers, essays, and chapters that fit certain parameters like book length (short), specific series (Dr. Banks's series on multicultural education, broadly defined), and coherence of content. As noted previously, I also wanted this collection to reflect my own development across time, and I was committed to linking my writing for *Rethinking Schools* with my more academic, scholarly papers and chapters, both as a model for others to think about how to speak to multiple audiences and as a chance to illustrate a more grounded and activist academic practice.

Indeed, this is one of the main reasons readers will notice some brief overlap of content between chapters. For instance, I used the same examples of anti-immigrant sentiment expressed by some particularly racist teachers in different chapters, just as I explain the definition of neoliberal education reform in two different pieces. I also recap the history of the Model Minority stereotype and the psychological effects of this stereotype in more than one chapter. Additionally, in multiple chapters I explain the white supremacist history of high-stakes testing, the negative impacts that high-stakes testing has on working-class Black and Brown students, and the use of civil rights discourse to try to justify the uses of high-stakes testing to support racial equity. However, while there are some shared histories, examples, analyses, and points of argument here in *Race, Curriculum, and the Politics of Educational Justice*, it is also important to recognize that there are different levels of discussion throughout. For example, while the discussions of neoliberalism that exist in Chapters 6 and 7 do overlap, they differ greatly in detail. Chapter 6 offers a much deeper, much more complex explanation of neoliberal education reform than Chapter 7. This makes sense given that Chapter 6 offers a much lengthier treatment of how these reforms have played out concretely in schools and communities, whereas Chapter 7 is a shorter, more academic chapter that only required a brief discussion of neoliberalism in service to the specific theoretical arguments that I make there. The same could be said of my discussion of the use of civil rights discourse in support of arguments for high-stakes testing and racial equity. While I use this discourse to make a particularly sharp and quick point in Chapter 5, and I touch ever so briefly on it again in Chapter 6, it is actually central to some of the analysis of neoliberal multiculturalism in Chapter 7—and so it gets a more thorough and complex treatment there. Some of this is just the reality of writing about similar issues while addressing different audiences, as well as making specifically different arguments built around similar foundations of knowledge or history.

Finally, I want to make it clear that the chapters in *Race, Curriculum, and the Politics of Educational Justice* should not be viewed as a linear development in my work. Even though it is true that my turn toward a more substantial analysis of Asian American racialization and education is most recent, I have in fact touched on Asian American education at different points since early in my career (B. Chang & Au, 2007). Similarly, while the beginning of my academic career focused on high-stakes testing, my work in that area has been ongoing since then, including the more recent publication of the second edition of my book, *Unequal By Design: High-Stakes Testing and the Standardization of Inequality* (Au, 2023b). Of course, curriculum has always been present in my thinking, teaching, and writing as well (Au, 2011a; Au et al., 2016). So, rather than viewing the chapters here in a linear fashion, I personally see them more as spiraling in development, with each iteration and "next" piece illustrating different, sometimes more complex, thinking and analysis.

Part I

CURRICULUM AND THE POLITICS OF KNOWLEDGE

CHAPTER 1

Decolonizing the Classroom

Lessons in Multicultural Education

When I was in 9th grade, I had Mr. Anderson for honors World History. Mr. Anderson was one of those teachers that all the honors and AP-track parents wanted their kids to have. He had a reputation for academic rigor, for preparing teenagers for their stratospheric climb toward being a National Merit Scholar slated to attend an Ivy League college.

Like many history teachers, Mr. Anderson talked about his trips to places we studied. During our unit on China, I remember him telling us stories about his trip there, including the exciting fruit he ate, something he called "lee-chee." Now, my 14-year-old self knew what he was talking about. I loved lychee. Available only about six weeks a year and costing up to $8 a pound, lychees were a rare treat in my family. After my parents divorced, my Chinese American father would take me to San Francisco's Chinatown during my summer visits with him. He would buy bunches of the fruit with rough red skin and syrupy sweet, smooth, translucent flesh. Sitting in the park, cracking the lychee's firm skin and feeling its juices drip down our chins and fingers, my father told me stories of his childhood in Hawai'i, about how he would sneak into the lychee groves to get the precious fruit at the risk of getting shot by farmers guarding their precious crops.

But in my family, we said it differently than Mr. Anderson. We pronounced it "LIE-chee." Knowing that the translation between Chinese and English is difficult and imprecise, I raised my hand and tried to tell my teacher how my family pronounced it. Mr. Anderson wasn't having it. This white teacher had been to China and knew better. So, he told me (and the class) that I was simply wrong, that I didn't know what I was talking about. Never mind my memories of lychee, never mind my father's stories, and never mind that my Chinese grandmother, aunts, uncles, and cousins all pronounced it "LIE-chee."

Now that I have been both a high school teacher and a teacher of teachers, when I reflect back on his class, I see that Mr. Anderson taught me some basic lessons about multicultural education, albeit by negative example. For instance, in Mr. Anderson's class, student knowledge about communities, cultures, and

---

Previously published as "Decolonizing the Classroom: Lessons in Multicultural Education," *Rethinking Schools*, *23*(2), 27–30, 2009. Reprinted by permission of Rethinking Schools.

diversity didn't matter, especially if it contradicted his own. Further, Mr. Anderson's contempt for student knowledge revealed no sense of curiosity about the experiences and stories that might lead to a different perspective than his. The lesson to learn here is that multicultural education should be grounded in the lives of students, not only because such a perspective provides a diversity of viewpoints, but also because it honors students' identities, cultures, and experiences.

Another related lesson I took away from Mr. Anderson's negative example is that multicultural education should seek to draw on the knowledge, perspectives, and voices of the actual communities being studied. In Mr. Anderson's class, my own authentic cultural knowledge and perspective as a Chinese American had no value, and he actively disregarded my own lived experiences. Again, Mr. Anderson was contemptuous of student knowledge, and he disregarded the importance of building from kids' lives and prior experiences.

Mr. Anderson's example also taught me that because it is deeply connected to students' lives, multicultural education has to be based on dialogue—both among students and between students and teachers. As students in Mr. Anderson's class, we were always on the outside looking in, and he and the textbooks were the sole authorities. There was no dialogue only monologue. The final lesson I drew from Mr. Anderson is that, when classes are not grounded in the lives of students, when they do not include the voices and knowledge of communities being studied, and when they are not based in dialogue, they create environments where not only are white students miseducated, but students of color feel as if their very identities are under attack.

MULTICULTURAL EDUCATION ON THE DOWN-LOW

In high school I had to get my real multicultural education on the down-low, outside of classes like Mr. Anderson's. I went to Garfield High School, located in Seattle's historically African American neighborhood, the Central District. Garfield has traditionally been Seattle's Black high school, and back in the 1970s there was a strong Black Panther Party presence both in the neighborhood and in the school itself. Garfield, always a basketball powerhouse, also boasts a rich connection to African American culture and music, with names like Quincy Jones and Jimi Hendrix still haunting the hallways. This tradition continues today, when in more recent years, Garfield has been a site for organizing around Black Lives Matter in schools.

By the time I got there in the late 1980s, Garfield had become a flagship for the Seattle Public Schools. It housed the district's Advanced Placement program, maintained a world-renowned jazz band, was the district's science magnet high school, and provided a model of Seattle's desegregation busing system (of which I was a part). Totaling around 1,600 students, Garfield's student body hovered at about 50% African American and 50% white, with a few Latine and Asian Americans like myself sprinkled in.

Given Garfield's history, position in the community, and commitment to racially integrated education, you might think that real multicultural education took place in most classes. Sadly, it didn't. Fortunately for me, there was one teacher, Mr. Davis, who taught two "secret" classes at my school: one section of a Harlem Renaissance language arts class and one section of an African Studies world history class. To get into Mr. Davis's classes, you first had to learn (by word of mouth) the true content of his classes, which were listed plainly in the schedule as Language Arts 10b and Social Studies elective. Second, you had to convince your counselor that yes, you really did want to be in Mr. Davis's class, that yes, you really knew that you were taking "regular" track courses.

For the first time in my schooling experience, I was one of only two non–African American students in a class. In Mr. Davis's classes we looked at the politics of Blackness through the poetry and literature of the Harlem Renaissance and hashed through segregation, desegregation, and African American identity in U.S. history. We read about how Greek civilization was built upon a legacy of knowledge that had already existed in Egypt. And then we learned that Egypt wasn't really "Egypt." From an African-centric standpoint it was actually called Kemet, with its own rich cultural worldview, symbolism, and creation stories.

I sat in this decidedly African-centric, predominantly African American cultural space, trying to sort through my own cultural identity as a mixed white and Chinese American young man, my own connection with African American culture, and my own sense of education and the politics of race. And I'm sure my presence also left many of my African American classmates questioning. I mean, what was this Asian American kid doing in the Black Studies classes anyway? Why does he care? Isn't race and racism mainly about Black and white? Do Chinese Americans even count as people of color? Struggling with these questions (and many more), all of us were asked to stretch.

To be sure, an African-centric course cannot be "multicultural" in and of itself. African-centered is just that, African-centered. But in the real-life context of a school like Garfield, Mr. Davis's classes embodied multicultural education; it was grounded in the lives, identities, and histories of students; it provided critical and alternative perspectives on history that we were not getting in our other classes; and it openly addressed the issue of racism.

Again, now having worked with very diverse populations of students of my own as both a high school and a university teacher, I see that Mr. Davis's classes also taught me about multicultural education. For instance, his class illustrated how multicultural education is fundamentally based in a critique of school knowledge that has historically been Eurocentric. For example, it was in his class that we learned that "civilization" did not start in Europe, that other nations and cultures had great civilizations that pre-dated their Western counterpart. Challenging such Eurocentrism also spoke to the cultural and political imperative to resist Eurocentric curriculum, as Mr. Davis saw his course as a positive and supportive intervention in the identity development and self-esteem for the students in his classes. Finally, inherent in Mr. Davis's instruction was the lesson that it is important to critically question what textbooks and teachers say about the world.

Mr. Davis's classes also offer a lesson on how multicultural education invites students to engage with real social issues. In his courses, my classmates and I connected our burgeoning historical understandings of race and racism to contemporary issues. We argued about interracial dating, Black nationalism, racism, and education. In this way, multicultural education inherently connects learning to the world outside of our classrooms.

Another lesson to be gained from Mr. Davis's example is that multicultural education creates a space for students to meaningfully engage with one another. It was through such struggle over social and political issues that I developed substantive relationships with my African American classmates—relationships that I do not think could have developed in my other, more Eurocentric classes that were either populated predominantly by white kids or simply did not create the space to really engage students of color. Finally, it is crucial to acknowledge that Mr. Davis's classes helped me learn that multicultural education is rigorous. In African Studies and Harlem Renaissance, we read serious texts like George G. M. James's (1954/1995) *Stolen Legacy* to learn about ancient Egypt's effect on ancient Greek civilization, or Joel Augustus Rogers's (1917/2015) *From "Superman" to Man* to gain historical perspectives of U.S. race relations.

MULTICULTURAL EDUCATION AND RIGOR

The connection between multicultural education and rigor is important because one of the consistent critiques against multicultural education is that it isn't "real" education, that it isn't rigorous. However, the idea that multicultural education represents a lowering of standards or represents a neglect of academic rigor is false.

Let's compare Mr. Davis's and Mr. Anderson's classes. As with most "rigorous," upper-track classes, the central pieces of rigor I remember from Mr. Anderson's "honors" World History class consisted of an immense amount of textbook reading, chapter questions, and a research paper. And such courses are rigorous in particular ways. Certainly they have formal and strict requirements, and Mr. Anderson's class, like most others of its kind, was demanding in terms of workload. We were always kept busy. Now as a professor of education, when I critically reflect on these types of "honors" or "advanced" classes, I think that although they require significant amounts of work, they are not necessarily intellectually rigorous. Instead they often require memorization and textbook reading comprehension, not critical analysis. Knowledge is multifaceted, and simply reading tough books does not mean that students are engaged in understanding the complexities of any particular historical episode or time period.

Take teaching about the U.S. war with Mexico, for instance. A typical class would focus solely on the actions of governments—U.S. and Mexican alike. A multicultural perspective asks about the Irish American soldiers, Mexican women in conquered territories, Black and white abolitionists who opposed the war, soldiers who embraced and also rejected the war, Mexican cadets who jumped to their death rather than surrender to invading U.S. troops, and so forth. A multicultural perspective is not only inherently more interesting, it is also more complex—and more fully truthful, if we dare use that word. Further, academic rigor is impossible without the multiple perspectives that multicultural education provides because without it, we miss huge pieces of history, culture, and society—leaving huge gaps in our knowledge about the world.

Mr. Anderson's class miseducated us about the world, too. For instance, in addition to the textbook readings for our unit on Africa, Mr. Anderson had us watch the movie *The Gods Must Be Crazy*. In this movie an African San is befuddled by Western technology and makes a buffoon of himself. Through my 9th-grade eyes, I saw the colonizers' view of the African-native-as-primitive, of darker peoples as idiotic and childlike.

Mr. Anderson didn't really teach about this film. He just showed it as an "entertaining" way for 14-year-olds to learn about Africa. So we never learned how such a film could justify the system of apartheid in South Africa by portraying the San people as incompetent and unable to be incorporated into a democratic society. We never learned how such a film might rationalize the idea that the San needed "benevolent" white rulers to take care of them.

My African Studies course with Mr. Davis, however, was different, and despite its tag as being "regular," its perspective made it more intellectually rigorous than my "honors" history classes because, as all good multicultural education should do, we were asked to consider the variety of our own experiences and relate them to the complexities of history and society.

I remember struggling to write a paper for Mr. Davis that explained the relationship between race, poverty, and education in the United States. While in many ways this topic was probably beyond my mid-teen reach, in many ways it wasn't; the relationship between race, poverty, and education was something I was trying to understand (and still am), and writing a paper about it pushed me in my writing and my thinking. Assignments like this made me think hard in my "regular" African Studies class, whereas my "honors" World History class asked for very little thinking at all—just lots of work. More importantly, this assignment illustrates how a multicultural curriculum honors the experiences and curiosity of students so that their own questions about these issues are encouraged and honored as a way of fueling their academic inquiry.

This rigorous need for multicultural perspectives raises another critical lesson: Multicultural education cannot be relegated to individual classes. Mr. Davis's classes were important because they existed within a context where most other classes were Eurocentric, so they became spaces of multicultural resistance. But ideally all classes at Garfield—social studies, language arts, math, science, art, etc.—should have taken multicultural education seriously if they really wanted to be rigorous and if they really wanted to engage all students in learning. For that matter, all classes for all students, from prekindergarten on, should take multicultural education seriously. Then, students would generally be in a position to more actively and collectively resist classroom colonization and would be smarter in that they could take up a more critical analysis of all course content.

THE STRUGGLE FOR MULTICULTURAL EDUCATION

Sadly, college-bound students at Garfield certainly didn't fight to get Mr. Davis's classes on their transcripts. Instead they would forego Harlem Renaissance and African Studies in order to stay in AP and on the honors track. Things haven't changed all that much since I was in high school, because in today's context of high-stakes education, multicultural education is still viewed as not academically rigorous, not "real" education, and not worthy of being included in the curriculum in its own right. The lowly status of multicultural curriculum has also meant a constant fight to justify its existence. Take again, for instance, the African Studies class at Garfield. Ten years after I had walked the halls as a student, I returned to Garfield as a teacher. To my great pleasure, African Studies was given to me as part of my teaching load.

Not surprisingly, I found that many teachers in the Social Studies department openly sneered at the African Studies course, and the department chair—seeing that Mr. Davis had left to become a principal—thought it would be a good chance to get rid of the class. In his mind, it had no value. What the department chair couldn't see, and what I knew as a legacy student of that very same class, was that African Studies created an irreplaceable space to engage in the politics of Blackness that existed nowhere else at Garfield. Further, African Studies was an irreplaceable space where students' cultures were respected, where students learned to think in terms of multiple social experiences, where traditional narratives and explanations were complicated by race and culture. After a protracted and sometimes nasty fight, the African Studies course survived (and I enjoyed teaching it), but there shouldn't have been a fight to begin with. My experience fighting for African Studies taught me another lesson: Multicultural education is rooted in an anti-racist struggle over whose knowledge and experiences should be included in the curriculum.

THE NEED FOR MULTICULTURAL EDUCATION

I think the biggest lesson in multicultural education I've learned from my experiences as a student, teacher, and teacher educator is that it is a valuable and necessary orientation toward teaching and learning that needs to be embraced by all educators. Every institution I've ever worked in has been resistant to multicultural education in some way, shape, or form, and I'm tired of having to justify it, tired of having to prove its worth. As a person of color I take offense at the idea that my history, my perspective on the world as an individual and a representative member of a community, does not matter.

As a teacher educator I encounter on a daily basis the consequences of schooling that is not multicultural. Many of my students know little of the histories and cultures of the students that they will end up teaching. What's more, they don't know that they don't know, and I fear that many of them will enter communities of color as an army of Mr. Andersons, damaging the young people they're trusted to educate. Hopefully, the lessons in multicultural education they learn in my classes will help them become more like Mr. Davis, teachers who can lead a struggle against racism in their classrooms.

CHAPTER 2

A Pedagogy of Insurgency

Teaching and Organizing for Radical Racial Justice in Our Schools

INTRODUCTION

We understand the terrors of this historical moment: rising white nationalism and white supremacist violence, xenophobia, homophobia, sharpening economic inequality, homelessness and underemployment, neoliberal assaults on workers and the environment, Islamophobia, attacks on immigrants, and kids in cages, among others (Beirich, 2019; Costello, 2016; Fraser, 2017; Kirchner, 2017; Lane, 2016). While schools are guilty of perpetuating some of these terrors, they have also been sites of significant movements for justice (Apple, 2013). Teachers, as key forces in shaping human consciousness and as intellectual and emotional laborers in institutions that touch most young people, are uniquely positioned to take a stand and decide just what kind of education they think is necessary given the terrors of our current context.

In this chapter I argue that in the face of such sharp injustice and ongoing crisis in the United States and around the world, teachers can and should organize for racial justice and actively resist the oppressive politics and policies being used to attack so many of our communities. Specifically, drawing on the organizing for Black Lives Matter in schools in Seattle, Washington, I discuss the power of teachers, school communities, and professors to organize against white supremacy through activism and teaching. In doing so, I suggest that, given the tenor of our times, we must be committed to what I'm calling a "pedagogy of insurgency." I start with a story of bravery and resistance of a single elementary school in southside Seattle. I then detail the political context of the rise of white supremacy in the United States and the ways that some educators and schools have worked to maintain racist and supremacist politics. I go on to relate how what started at one elementary school grew into a Seattle, citywide Black Lives Matter at School Day, which itself became the initial inspiration for

---

Previously published as "A Pedagogy of Insurgency: Teaching and Organizing for Radical Racial Justice in Our Schools," 2021, *Educational* Studies, *57*(2), 109–123. https://doi.org/10.1080/00131946.2021.1878181.

the National Black Lives Matter at School Week of Action. Using the educator organizing around Black Lives Matter at School as an illustrative example, I discuss how these teacher, union, and community activists embody aspects of what I define as a "pedagogy of insurgency."

BOMB THREATS AND BLACK LIVES MATTER AT SCHOOL

Early on the morning of September 16, 2016, amidst increased police presence in the neighborhood, John Muir Elementary in Seattle was emptied of all school personnel as bomb-sniffing dogs checked the building. No bombs were found, and the all-clear was given for school to carry on as usual for the day (Au, 2017; Au & Hagopian, 2017). But obviously, this day was anything but usual. In the weeks preceding that momentous September morning, DeShawn Jackson, a John Muir Elementary staff member, had planned an event titled "100 Black Men Uniting to Change the Narrative." The idea was to get 100 Black men to line up outside of the school to greet the students of John Muir as they came through the doors, giving students high-fives, accolades, and cheers for their school day. Mr. Jackson's plan was to publicly and purposefully shift the constructed narratives around Black males not caring about, supporting, or being successful at education, in addition to pushing Seattle Schools to take the education of Black children more seriously (Cornwell, 2016b).

DeShawn Jackson's concern about the educational success of Black students in Seattle Schools is important and real. In 2017, despite only 16% of the total student population being Black, reported data show that Black students represent 38% of Seattle Schools' suspensions and 50% of the district's expulsions (Groeger et al., 2018). These disparities on discipline rates have consistently been a part of the Seattle Schools' landscape, where a federal education inquiry in 2012 into the district's disparities also found that Black high school students were suspended or expelled at 3 times the rate of other students, and at 3½ times that of other students in middle school (Myers, 2013). Additionally, as of 2018, Black students in Seattle Schools graduated at a rate of nearly 14% less than their white peers (Office of Superintendent of Public Instruction, 2019).

John Muir Elementary sits in the Rainier Valley neighborhood of Seattle, and despite recent, rapid gentrification, its student population matches that of this historically poorer and less-white neighborhood; during the 2016–2017 school year, 68% of Muir's students qualified for free and reduced lunch (granted, an imperfect marker of poverty), 33% were officially designated as transition bilingual, and 50% of the students were African American (Office of Superintendent of Public Instruction, 2017a)—a mix of African immigrant families and historic Black American multigenerational families that once lived in the neighborhood. In this regard, DeShawn Jackson was merely expressing his deep care for the children in his school and their community.

As the event was being organized, teachers and other school staff decided that they wanted to express their solidarity with not only the spirit of Jackson's event, but also the education of Black children. It is important to recognize the broader national context at this moment. This happened in the autumn of 2016. Nationally, the Black Lives matter Movement had been intensely in full swing across the country, with several major protests and police shootings of Black women and men happening during the summer of 2016—one of which included the police killing of Philando Castile, a school employee in Minnesota (ABC, 2018).

Over the previous couple of years, the staff at John Muir Elementary had also been focusing professional development on issues of racial justice in education, including having the staff explore their own racial identities and start to look at how their own biases influence decisions about curriculum, pedagogy, and discipline (Au & Hagopian, 2017). Additionally, the city's teachers' union, the Seattle Education Association, had gone on strike the year before, and as part of that strike, they successfully bargained for racial equity teams to be formed at dozens of schools across the district to increase the capacity and commitment for racial justice in Seattle Schools (Whelan, 2015). In the context of both the #BlackLivesMatter movement and the school's outward commitment to teaching for racial justice, the John Muir Elementary staff made a decision to design t-shirts that read, "Black Lives Matter: We Stand Together: John Muir Elementary" (D. Taylor, 2016), and to wear them on the same day as the "100 Black Men Uniting to Change the Narrative" event organized by Jackson.

Soon after the John Muir Elementary staff made their decision and designed their t-shirts, the local Seattle media somehow learned about both the shirts and the planned act of solidarity (D. Taylor, 2016). The story was then picked up by conservative, right-wing, and, ultimately, white supremacist news outlets like Blue Lives Matter and Breitbart (see, e.g., K. Rodriguez, 2016), who were outraged that an entire public school staff would dare wear t-shirts that said "Black Lives Matter." An avalanche of racist, hateful emails, phone calls, and other messages soon piled onto both the Seattle school district and Muir staff and administration, and, eventually, in a blog chatroom somewhere on the Internet, someone made a bomb threat against John Muir Elementary, causing the district to officially cancel the "100 Black Men Uniting to Change the Narrative" event (Cornwell, 2016a).

It is important that we do not lose sight of the callous and racist power of the bomb threat made against John Muir Elementary. Here we have a school of roughly 350 children from the ages of 5 years old to 11 years old, 80% of whom are students of color, half of whom are Black/African American, and most of whom are poor (Office of Superintendent of Public Instruction, 2017a). These are immigrant and U.S.-born kids, all from the neighborhood. They have families of brothers and sisters, moms and dads, aunts and uncles, elders and teachers, and cousins and friends whom they love. They want to play and learn and smile and laugh and grow. These are children. And because of a simple affirmation of Blackness and solidarity, white supremacist terrorists threatened to kill these children and the staff at their school.

THE STATE OF THE NATION

Sadly, the contemporary fact of white supremacist terrorism simply does not surprise us anymore. Particularly dangerous strands of white, male, Christian nationalism have become either more popular or more public than in previous decades (Beirich, 2019). It is a kind of authoritarian populism that, as Hall (1979) so astutely observed, is

> . . . an exceptional form of the capitalist state—which, unlike classical fascism, has retained most (though not all) of the formal representative institution in place, and which at the same time has been able to construct around itself an active popular consent . . . It has entailed a striking weakening of democratic forms and initiatives, but not their suspension. (p. 15)

This rise of authoritarian populist power has constructed itself around a violent mix of toxic masculinity, homophobia, xenophobia, anti-trans and queerness, anti-Semitism, anti-immigration, Islamophobia, anti-environmentalism, anti-socialism, pro-capitalism, hyper-individualism, pro-imperialist, pro-war, pro-settler colonialism, and pro-racism and white supremacy (Apple, 2006). This shift in politics perhaps signals that we are witnessing the end of the era of neoliberal multiculturalism, where diversity has been used to try to sell us on the supposed progressive plurality of capitalism and capitalist democracy while simultaneously pasting over capitalism's rampant destruction of people and planet through hyper-exploitation and hyper-resource extraction (Fraser, 2017; Lane, 2016; Melamed, 2011). Instead, in the current era, the niceties of inclusion have in many circles been ditched entirely, and those of us who live outside of any part of the white, hetero, male, Christian, capitalist, U.S. citizenry are potentially the enemy, all potential targets of violent attacks carried out with either explicit or implicit state sanction.

Seattle, a city considered by many to be quite liberal, has not been immune to these regressive politics. Reports of hate crimes in Seattle have increased 400% since 2012, and from 2017–2018 alone, the Seattle Police Department reported a 25% increase in hate crimes. In November 2018, the FBI reported a 17% increase in hate crimes nationally and a 25% increase in Washington state (Kroman, 2019). These are just the officially reported hate crimes, and, given that such crimes are under reported, we can safely assume that the actual numbers of experienced hate crimes are much higher (Kirchner, 2017). These trends are also nationally consistent with various hateful policies advanced during the Trump administration. From children in cages, to deportations, to attacks on the rights of immigrants, to anti-LGBQTIA forces gaining institutional power, to threats against programs that support working-class students, to the coming storm against higher education (Beirich, 2019), the list of policy travesties of the Trump administration has been as long as it has been depressing. It is important to note that, even though Trump lost the 2020 election, 46.8% of voters, or over 74 million U.S. citizens, voted for Trump (Lindsay, 2020). That means over 74 million people in the United States were either actively supportive of or at least open to the nationalist, white supremacist, and patriarchal politics of his administration. So while the figurehead may have been voted out of office, the movement remains: Trump's presidency merely rendered the true politics of millions of Americans explicitly public.

The actions of the educators at John Muir Elementary and their honoring of Black lives directly challenged the authoritarian populist politics and were simply too much for the white supremacists to rationally handle. Predictably, the threats against the school were just a part of a larger trend of the changing climate in schools as well as nationally. A 2016 Southern Poverty Law Center report of a survey of over 2,000 K–12 U.S. teachers found a rise in anti-immigrant and anti-Muslim sentiments since the beginning of the 2016 presidential campaign (Costello, 2016). Labeling this phenomenon "The Trump Effect," the study relayed stories of Latinx students in Tennessee who every day worriedly asked, "Is the wall here yet?" (p. 5), and a teacher in New Hampshire commenting that "A lot of students think we should kill any and all people we do not agree with. They also think that all Muslims are the same and a threat to our country and way of life. They believe all Muslims want to kill us" (p. 5). In 2016 U.S. teachers also reported a drastic increase in post-election hate speech (Wallace & Lamotte, 2016), with some reporting that they had children in their classrooms crying out of worries and fears about their families being deported (Kamenetz, 2017). Additionally, a 2017 report from the Institute for Democracy, Education, and Access at UCLA found that high school students, particularly high school students of color in the United States, were feeling increased levels of stress and hostility in their school environments. The study found that predominantly white schools in particular were becoming increasingly hostile environments for non-white students and students who were not Christian (Rogers et al., 2017).

Schools are both producers and transmitters of broader social relations (Au, 2018), so it should come as no surprise that some of these regressive politics can be carried into classrooms by teachers as well. As an example, during the February 16, 2017, "Day Without Immigrants" national protest in support of immigrant rights, several teachers across the United States were put on leave for their remarks on social media. Teachers at Rubidoux High School in Jurupa Valley, California—a school that is 90% "Hispanic" (Education Data Partnership, 2025), were caught saying things like: "That's what you get when you jump on some sort of bandwagon cause as an excuse to be lazy and/or get drunk. . . . Best school day ever." Or, ". . . Small classes, trouble makers were gone fantastic day!" (Chasmar, 2017). On the same day, a teacher in Naples, Florida, in a district that is a little over 50% "Hispanic" (Collier County Public

Schools, 2017), tweeted, "The funny part about immigrants staying home is the rest of us who pay for them are here at work like we've always been. . . . So glad to hear about massive deportation. Let's make America great again. Thanks Donald Trump!!" (ABC10 News, 2017). In the state of Washington, an elementary teacher in the town of Prosser—a district that is over 50% "Hispanic" (Office of Superintendent of Public Instruction, 2017b)—was also placed on leave after she posted the following to Facebook:

> This [Day Without Immigrants] is a great idea narrows the search down . . .
> If you would like to report illegal aliens, please call Immigration and Customs Enforcement (ICE) at 1–866-DHS-2ICE (347–2423). They will need to know names, locations (either work place or residence) and any other specific information you can provide. Visit www.ice.gov for more information.
> If this offended you in anyway do me a favor and unfriend my American ass!!!
> . . . TRUMP all the way!!! (Probert, 2017)

These teachers' responses to the powerful "Day Without Immigrants" protest demonstrate the white supremacist coding of associating Brown kids with the subjectivities of being "bad," "illegal," and not welcome in schools. They also illustrate the sharp need for us to think about who should be teaching our children. We know from research and anecdotal evidence that varying levels of racism persist across our predominately white K–12 teaching force (Lurie, 2015), and unfortunately such views toward immigrant and English-language learner (ELL) students are more prominent than they should be (Walker et al., 2004). These examples also raise the question: Can someone who is fundamentally anti-immigrant (or anti-LGBQT, anti-Islam, anti-Black, anti-Semitic, for that matter) be trusted to care for immigrant students, let alone be an effective teacher? My answer, of course, is that they cannot be trusted to care for any students, especially Black and Indigenous students of color or immigrant students, let alone students from other marginalized communities. These teachers are dangerous to the well-being of all kids and to the well-being of our communities.

EDUCATORS ELEVATING THE FIGHT AGAINST WHITE SUPREMACY

Despite this rise in authoritarian populist politics of fascism and white supremacy, it is absolutely critical to understand that we can also take hope in the activism and power of insurgent educators rebelling against injustice. For instance, in the face of the cowardly and racist bomb threat, the staff and community at John Muir Elementary did something brave and important that September morning. After the police determined there was no bomb at school, the Muir administration gave everyone the all-clear. And, despite the Seattle school district officially canceling the "100 Black Men Uniting to Change the Narrative" event, we knew that Mr. Jackson and others had secretly organized for it to happen anyway (Au & Hagopian, 2017).

My family and I lived two blocks from John Muir Elementary, and at the time my son was a 2nd-grader there. I so vividly remember walking with my family down the block to school that morning, feeling excited and rebellious, knowing that our school community was going to stand against the white supremacists. As we approached the end of our block, we could hear the sounds of drums echoing off the neighborhood houses. As we made the right turn toward the school, we saw dozens of Black men lining the sidewalk leading into the school with staff and parents gathered around as well, many wearing their "Black Lives Matter: We Stand Together: John Muir Elementary" t-shirts. Folks were singing and dancing (Au & Hagopian, 2017). It was a beautiful celebration of resistance and a lesson about the importance of a pedagogy of insurgency in these times. It was even more beautiful to watch this insurgency spread throughout the district.

Once the initial bomb threat against John Muir was made and the event was officially canceled, and after meeting with some of the teacher-leaders at Muir, members of the Social Equity Educators (SEE), a Left caucus of the Seattle Education Association teachers' union (SEA), decided to stand in solidarity with the Muir teachers, students, and community by organizing for a district wide Black Lives Matter at School event on October 19, roughly a month after Muir's "100 Black Men Uniting to Change the Narrative" event. As part of their organizing, SEE developed a three-point policy to support racial justice and the idea of making Black lives matter in schools. These points were as follows:

- Support Ethnic Studies in all schools
- Replace zero-tolerance discipline with restorative justice practices
- De-track classes within the schools to undo the racial segregation that is reinforced by tracking

SEE also submitted a resolution to the larger SEA, proposing that the union explicitly support the teachers at John Muir Elementary and endorse the district-wide Black Lives Matter at School Day. The SEA representative assembly voted to support this action unanimously (Au & Hagopian, 2017).

Soon after the SEA endorsement of the October 19 Black Lives Matter at School Day, community and parent groups began to also show their support. The Seattle chapter of the National Association for the Advancement of Colored People (NAACP) and the executive board of the Seattle Council Parent Teacher Association both endorsed the event, as did Soup for Teachers, a popular parent organizing group that came together to support the 2015 Seattle teachers' strike. National support for Seattle's Black Lives Matter at School Day also began to build as well, as almost 250 educational scholars across the United States signed a petition of support, and another statement of support was signed by nationally known figures such as Black Lives Matter co-founder Opal Tometi, former MSNBC anchor Melissa Harris-Perry, Pulitzer Prize–winning journalist

Jose Antonio Vargas, 1968 Olympic bronze medalist and activist John Carlos, dissident scholar Noam Chomsky, and noted education author Jonathan Kozol. In perhaps a surprising turn of events, without any explicit pressure from teachers, activists, or the larger community, Seattle Public Schools also officially endorsed the October 19 Black Lives Matter at School Day as part of the district's program to close opportunity gaps and promote accelerated learning for students of color (Archibald, 2016; Au & Hagopian, 2017). In many ways this was a historic moment in the educational politics of Seattle; the teachers' union, the PTSA, parent activists, community activists, and the school district were seemingly united in their support for making Black lives matter at school.

By the time the October 19, 2016 Black Lives Matter at School Day arrived in Seattle, over 2,000 of the Black Lives Matter t-shirts designed by SEE had been sold, and hundreds of other similarly designed shirts—with the individual flavor of each school—were also being sold and distributed by different elementary schools around the city. SEE and the parent activist group Soup for Teachers partnered to produce an informational handout for educators across the district, pointing them to resources to support making Black Lives Matter in schools. Reader boards at many schools were changed to say, "Black Lives Matter," and several schools set up informational tables for parents, sharing resources dedicated to helping them talk with their kids about race and racism. Multiple schools across the district worked together to develop some curriculum or share existing teaching resources. Some schools held Black Lives Matter at School rallies during lunch. The day culminated in a celebration through spoken word, dance, and music that drew several hundred attendees (Au & Hagopian, 2017). Importantly, the Seattle action soon inspired similar actions in cities like Philadelphia and Rochester, and the growing number of Black Lives Matter at School activists nationally eventually came together to develop the Black Lives Matter at School Week of Action (Anderson et al., 2020; Black Lives Matter at School, 2019; Corn, 2018).

A PEDAGOGY OF INSURGENCY

During a presidential regime that normalized violence, white supremacist nationalism, and toxic masculinity (Beirich, 2019), the staff at John Muir Elementary and many of the schools and communities across Seattle Public Schools (and eventually the across the nation) illustrated a pedagogy of insurgency from which we all can learn. To be an insurgent is to be a rebel, and an insurgency means rebelling against the current regime (Merriam-Webster, 2019). The concept of insurgency has not been wielded widely in the educational literature. Giroux (1993) uses the term "insurgent multiculturalism" in his argument for a more radical form of multicultural education he felt was needed in the aftermath of the 1992 rebellions in Los Angeles. DeLeon (2014) uses anarchist theory to argue for "insurgent social studies" that look beyond capitalism toward utopias while using anticapitalist sabotage along the way. Stovall (2016) discusses Critical Race Theory as an "insurgent" conceptual framework in his work analyzing neoliberal attacks on Chicago schools and the community organizing that arose in resistance. McCoy (2017), in their dissertation research on teaching for social justice in university literature courses, essentially coined the term "pedagogy of insurgency," and explored it across several chapters about their own teaching and curriculum in higher education.

All of these scholars clearly build on an ethos and legacy of insurgency as rebellion and resistance toward a new, more radically liberating future. In theorizing a pedagogy of resistance here, I am most definitely in broad alignment with the spirit of Giroux's (1993), DeLeon's (2014), Stovall's (2016), and McCoy's (2017) individual projects. However, my theorizing of a pedagogy of insurgency departs somewhat from my colleagues' in that the framework I advance here is more detailed in its articulation, with the express point of outlining what insurgency looks like in the practice of educational activism and radical teaching—a practice that links political insurgency both inside and outside of the K–12 classroom. Based on my observations and analysis as both a critical scholar-activist and someone who was directly involved in the local organizing with education activists in support of the Seattle Black Lives Matter at School Day, I articulate a pedagogy of insurgency as having several key aspects: bravery and risk, allyship and solidarity across communities of struggle, organizing and protest, critical analyses of power, curriculum of insurgency, contradictions of schooling and reimagining education, and connection to broader struggles and social movements. In what follows I discuss each in more detail.

BRAVERY AND RISK

The educators in Seattle embodied a pedagogy of insurgency that was first and foremost based on a kind of bravery required to fight back against educational injustice. A pedagogy of insurgency requires bravery because it is an act of rebellion, and as such, it also carries risk. In the case of the Seattle educators and organizers, there was real physical risk involved in acting in defense of our kids. Additionally, the educators in Seattle could not be sure what the fallout might have been with their actions across the district. So there was also longer-term risk in facing a more sustained backlash from white liberals in the city of Seattle, some of whom ultimately proved to be opposed to Black Lives Matter either inside or outside of schools. For instance, a series of district emails surfaced months after the day of action, where the liberal racism of Seattle parents came through rather loudly (Raftery, 2017). In this regard, a pedagogy of insurgency also compels us to call out liberal racism, which often verbally says it supports educational justice and racial equity but ultimately ends up supporting white supremacy and injustice through actions and decisions.

ALLIES, ACCOMPLICES, SOLIDARITY

With risk in mind, it is critical to understand that a pedagogy of insurgency also seeks out allies and accomplices, builds solidarities across identities, unites those who can be united, and moves through coalition and communities of struggle. In Seattle it was the power and strength first of the staff at John Muir Elementary, and then of the community of struggle that grew around them once the bomb threat came. Importantly, this community of struggle blossomed into an even broader solidarity that enveloped institutions like the teachers' union, community organizations, and even, if mainly symbolically, the school district. Eventually, Seattle became part of a coalition of cities involved in the national Black Lives Matter at School Week of Action (Anderson et al., 2020). In this way, a pedagogy of insurgency not only understands that we are stronger when we organize together against injustice, it is fundamentally centered around collective action as opposed to purely individual resistance.

ORGANIZING AND PROTEST

By extension, a pedagogy of insurgency values protest and demonstration as a form of teaching, which is taught both by example as we observe others in protest and through direct participation in protests ourselves. The Seattle Black Lives Matter at School action developed a myriad of concrete skills to so many involved, from communication, to handling media, to collective work, to self-education, to the spreading of critical perspectives, to curriculum development and pedagogy, to actual teaching and learning of Black Lives Matter at School content, to systematic and materialist thinking about the role of institutions in social change, to understanding the politics of whiteness and the cultural politics of Seattle as a city. Organizing and protest were at the heart of the Black Lives Matter at School movement in Seattle, with the movement itself serving as a classroom for many.

CRITICAL ANALYSES OF POWER

As part of the broader constellation of critical pedagogies that seek to use education to interrogate power and take action against oppression (Apple & Au, 2009; Freire, 1974), a pedagogy of insurgency moves us to foster critical analyses of structural power and inequality, while similarly fostering activism and organizing, among educators, students, parents, administrators, and members of the broader community. In this sense, a pedagogy of insurgency also recognizes that part of our duty and mission as insurgent educators is to spread rebellion and resistance to injustice. Again, the Seattle Black Lives Matter at School movement illustrates these principles. Even the initial affirmation of Blackness from the "100 Black Men Uniting to Change the Narrative" event that spurred the entirety of the organizing in Seattle was grounded in a deep and substantial systematic critique of racism and white supremacy in Seattle Schools. Then, each unfolding event leading up to the October 19th day of action, as well as the day itself, all provided opportunities for continuing the ongoing process of increasing everyone's critical understandings of how racism and white supremacy have been operationalized in our educational practices and policies. In this way, the Black Lives Matter at School movement embodied the development of critical consciousness consistent with the conceptions of both Freire and Vygotsky (Au, 2018), as varying individuals and groups worked with each other to move through zones of proximal development, learning more about organizing and more about white supremacy in schooling.

A CURRICULUM OF INSURGENCY

A pedagogy of insurgency also implies a curriculum of insurgency. As the Seattle Black Lives Matter at School Day developed, it became clear that teachers across the district needed an appropriate curriculum to support their teaching. The teachers' union, parent activists, and individual education activists quickly pulled together curriculum so that there was content to support the subject matter of honoring Black lives. Educators pulled together lessons on Black history and Black authors, lessons on policy brutality and the schools-to-prisons pipeline, and the power of Black resistance—with special emphasis on the organizing contributions of Black women in the struggle for liberation (Au & Hagopian, 2017; Black Lives Matter at School, 2019; Watson et al., 2018). A curriculum of insurgency is necessary because it aims to provide learners with the opportunity and space to engage with concepts related to oppression and liberation and makes sense of them relative to their own lives (Au, 2011a).

EMBRACES THE CONTRADICTIONS OF SCHOOLING AND REIMAGINES EDUCATION

By extension, a pedagogy of insurgency teaches toward, and embraces, the contradictions of schooling as part of a process of reimagining what education in a more just social order could and should look like. We know that schools generally reproduce all the inequalities that we see in society and capitalism (Apple, 1995; Au, 2023b), and we know that schools transmit cultural norms (Bernstein, 1977; Leonardo, 2009) and have been used as weapons of white supremacy against communities of color (Au et al., 2016). Indeed, Seattle Schools is just as guilty as every other major urban school district in its maintenance of whiteness and reproduction of a myriad of structural inequalities (Brazile,

2019; Groeger et al., 2018; Myers, 2013; Office of Superintendent of Public Instruction, 2019). But, as the Seattle day of action to demonstrate Black Lives Matter at School revealed, a pedagogy of insurgency also teaches us how, despite their overall reproduction of inequalities, schools can also be powerful sites of resistance and rebellion, spaces for building critical consciousness and fostering collective action for justice. Educators can and do have the power to challenge the "cop in the head" (Boal, 1990) as we self-police our own actions, to make the decision to break with the system and try to reorganize institutional norms. In this way, a pedagogy of insurgency holds that schools are not solely transmitters of the conditions of inequality, but also potentially the soil for sowing conscious seeds for breaking the conditions of inequality among teachers, students, and administrators as well.

CONNECTS TO BROADER STRUGGLES AND MOVEMENTS

Relatedly, a pedagogy of insurgence is grounded in, or connected to, broader contemporary and historical social movements for justice. The pedagogy of insurgency driving Seattle's Black Lives Matter at School Day was entirely and dialectically connected with the much larger Black Lives Matter movement that was happening around the United States. Indeed, and quite importantly, even as the Black Lives Matter movement has formally subsided in recent years, educators and activists are continuing to carry that movement forward nationally through the ongoing Black Lives Matter at School Week of Action (Anderson et al., 2020; Black Lives Matter At School, 2019; Corn, 2018; see also, Watson et al., 2018). This aspect of a pedagogy of insurgency holds true in other areas as well.

For instance, despite the decades-long decline in the power of unions overall in the United States, through statewide labor actions and strikes in several major metropolitan areas, the teachers' unions have taken the lead in reinvigorating the labor movement in this country (Blanc, 2019; McAlevey, 2019; A. Wong, 2019). Similarly, the movement for Ethnic Studies in schools, which was vibrant nationally in the late 1960s into the 1970s—mainly in higher education—has been reignited over the last 15 years by K–12 teachers and students, who have been successfully organizing for the implementation of Ethnic Studies at the state, district, and school levels across the country, as part of a broader struggle for racial justice in our schools (Au, 2020; Cuauhtin et al., 2019a; Gewertz, 2019). In addition to the Making Black Lives Matter at School movement, both the teachers' strikes and the movement for K–12 Ethnic Studies are examples of pedagogy of insurgence as well. While each may have their own specific set of politics and principles guiding their specific frameworks, paradigms, and organizing philosophies, all are broadly and deeply connected communities and social movements; all prize activism, protest, and demonstration as critical parts of teaching and learning; all seek to build critical understandings of structural inequalities; all embrace the contradictions of power in schooling; all embrace collectivity, solidarity, and community building as a source of power; and all require bravery and strength in the face of risk of symbolic and real violence.

CONCLUSION: LOOKING FORWARD

As we look forward, there is much for us to embrace and rebel against as part of a pedagogy of insurgency. We must be insurgent against high-stakes testing and the entirety of the standards and accountability movements. Those in power are using these tools to kill the love of learning in our children, as well as kill the love of teaching in our educators. They're trying to turn us into data points, dehumanize us, and alienate us from the act of learning—an act that should be the most human and most joyful of endeavors. We need to be insurgent against U.S. Immigration and Customs Enforcement (or ICE) as they terrorize our students, our families, and our communities. Similarly, we need to be insurgent against Islamophobia, white supremacy, toxic masculinity, homophobia, transphobia, anti-Semitism, and patriarchy. These ideologies and their adherents are enacting real violence against our friends, loved ones, and our communities in general. As educators in these times, our teaching needs to be driven by our commitments to justice. It must live at the heart of what we do as educators.

We also need to be insurgent against the militarization and policing of our schools and children. We cannot be in the business of preparing our poor kids and our Black and Brown kids to be fodder for U.S. imperialist wars of aggression or as disposable labor in our prison system. We also need to be insurgent against austerity funding of public education from K–12 through the university and social programs more generally, as well as insurgent against the privatization and financialization of education and society more generally. Our systems of support, the people working in them, and the people being served by them are all being strangled through a combination of neoliberal defunding and capitalist profiteering. Indeed, in this way we also need to be insurgent against capitalism and its exploitation of people and the environment. Ultimately, by calling for a pedagogy of insurgency, I am saying that it is time to openly rebel against it all, that we not only give ourselves permission to resist but understand that it is our duty to resist, and that only through engaging in collective struggle will we find a new path forward for the sake of all our peoples and our planet.

CHAPTER 3

It Is All Indoctrination

Power and the Impossibility of Apolitical Social Studies Curriculum

INTRODUCTION

It is an exciting time to be a social studies teacher. Tensions abound. Politically charged fights about what we should or should not be teaching in our schools seem to erupt everywhere we look. Conservative parents, mad about Critical Race Theory and protections of transgender students, are protesting and getting arrested at school board meetings (Ellis & Sanchez, 2021). Conservative state representatives are trying to ban the teaching of certain words or ideas in classrooms (Lieb, 2025; Vetterkind, 2021), while the Trump administration has issued a series of executive orders seeking to eliminate anything related to diversity, equity, or inclusion for being divisive and unpatriotic (U.S. Department of Education, 2025; White House, 2025). Meanwhile, there have been progressive movements pushing in opposite directions. The movement for K–12 Ethnic Studies and racial justice in education has made gains in multiple states (Au, 2020), and the Black Lives Matter at School movement has similarly grown among individual educators, schools, and districts across the United States (Au & Hagopian, 2021; D. Jones & Hagopian, 2020). Social studies teachers often serve as the arbiters of teaching current events and controversial topics in schools (Hess, 2009), and as such they are poised to both be stuck in the middle of these fights and play important roles in developing critical consciousness about these issues with students and communities (Au, 2009c; Ross, 1998).

These struggles over the politics of knowledge in the social studies have always existed. In this chapter, I take up this issue and ultimately contend that the oft-argued ideal that social studies should be sites of politically neutral curriculum and tell "both sides" is not only politically naïve, but also functionally impossible because all knowledge about society and history carries perspective with it. That is to say, all knowledge we engage in as social studies teachers,

---

Previously published as "It Is All Indoctrination: Power and the Impossibility of Apolitical Social Studies Curriculum," in E. W. Ross (Ed.), *The Social Studies Curriculum: Purposes, Problems, and Possibilities* (5th ed., pp. 31–48), 2024, SUNY Press.

regardless of politics, is in fact a form of indoctrination. To do so, I begin here by outlining some modern-day struggles over the politics of what should be taught in social studies within the context of the rise of particularly virulent right-wing conservativism. I then discuss the progressive movements for bringing Ethnic Studies and Black Lives Matter into K–12 schools, followed by a recounting of conservative backlash against racial justice movements in education. I follow with some arguments about how our social studies textbooks and standards were already terrible with regard to racial justice before the anti–Critical Race Theory backlash and link it all to the history of struggles over social studies and curriculum going back 100 years. I conclude this chapter by discussing Gramsci's concept of hegemony and how that helps us understand that since all education is a form of indoctrination, the real issue is indoctrination toward what kind of society.

THE RIGHTWARD TURN

Scholars have argued that our country has been experiencing a conservative modernization in the United States for several decades (Apple, 2006; Shor, 1986). More recently, we've experienced the rise of particularly dangerous strands of white, patriarchal, Christian nationalism that has constructed itself around a violent mix of toxic masculinity, homophobia, xenophobia, anti-trans and queerness, anti-Semitism, anti-immigration, Islamophobia, anti-environmentalism, anti-socialism, pro-capitalism, hyper-individualism, pro-imperialist, pro-war, pro-settler colonialism, and pro-racism and white supremacy (Beirich, 2019; Fraser, 2017; Kirchner, 2017). This shift perhaps signals the end of the era of neoliberal multiculturalism, where diversity has been used to try to sell us on the supposed progressive plurality of capitalism and capitalist democracy while simultaneously pasting over capitalism's rampant destruction of people and planet through hyper-exploitation and hyper-resource extraction (Fraser, 2017; Lane, 2016; Melamed, 2011). Instead, in the current era, the niceties of inclusion and diversity have been left behind, and those of us who live outside of any part of the white, hetero, male, Christian, capitalist U.S. citizenry are all potential targets of violent attacks carried out with either explicit or implicit state sanction.

The rightward political shift toward regressive conservative politics has had a significant impact on our schools as well, illustrated very concretely in the ways that the first Trump presidency served as kind of a lightning rod for these kinds of white nationalist politics. For instance, a 2016 Southern Poverty Law Center survey of over 2,000 K–12 U.S. teachers found a rise in anti-immigrant and anti-Muslim sentiments since the beginning of the 2016 presidential campaign (Costello, 2016). Labeling this phenomenon "the Trump Effect," the study relayed stories of Latinx students in Tennessee who worriedly asked, "Is the wall here yet?" (p. 5), and a teacher in New Hampshire commenting that, "A lot of students think we should kill any and all people we do not agree with. They also think that all Muslims are the same and a threat to our country and way of life. They believe all Muslims want to kill us" (p. 5). In 2016 U.S. teachers also reported significant increases in hate speech post-election (Wallace & Lamotte, 2016), with some saying they had children in classrooms crying out of fear their families would be deported (Kamenetz, 2017). A 2017 report from the Institute for Democracy, Education, and Access at UCLA found that high school students of color, in particular in the United States, were feeling increased levels of stress and hostility in their school environments. The study found that predominantly white schools became increasingly hostile environments for non-white students and students who were not Christian (Rogers et al., 2017). Teachers have carried these regressive politics into classrooms as well, evidenced by numerous instances of teachers being disciplined for posting blatantly racist and anti-immigrant sentiments on social media (see, e.g., ABC10 News, 2017; Chasmar, 2017; Probert, 2017). Now, during Trump's second term as president, we are seeing these kinds of politics embedded in federal, state, and school district policies through broad-based bans on the teaching of anything related to diversity, equity, or inclusion (Lieb, 2025; U.S. Department of Education, 2025; White House, 2025)

K–12 ETHNIC STUDIES AND BLACK LIVES MATTER AT SCHOOL

In the midst of this more recent rightward political turn (and perhaps *because* of), it is important to know that there have been significant and important, community-driven struggles for curriculum that specifically attends to racial justice in schools, much of which has lived in the area of social studies education. For instance, there has been a growing national movement for bringing Ethnic Studies into K–12 classrooms. Ethnic Studies started as an academic field in 1968 when Black, Latinx, Native American, and Asian American students, calling themselves the Third World Liberation Front, went on strike at San Francisco State University in California demanding an Ethnic Studies department and more faculty to teach Ethnic Studies courses. In turn, some K–12 schools around the country also started teaching courses in Asian American, Native Americans, African American, and Mexican American Studies (Au, 2020; Cuauhtin et al., 2019a). However, the current movement for K–12 Ethnic Studies blossomed in 2010 when the State of Arizona banned a well-established and academically successful Mexican American Studies program in Tucson, an action that included the censoring of specific books. Educators and activists around the country took note, and used Arizona's racist and draconian treatment of Ethnic Studies as a moment to organize and push for Ethnic Studies elsewhere. Since then, several major school districts around the country have either created Ethnic Studies courses, established departments, or made Ethnic Studies a graduation requirement. Since 2013 at least 24 states have passed various forms of K–12 Ethnic Studies laws or policies or introduced legislation in support of Ethnic Studies or multicultural history (Au, 2020).

Ethnic Studies in the K–12 context tends to be centered in the social studies as well as in the area of language arts. While there are different models and frameworks, K–12 Ethnic Studies tends to focus on issues of identity, history, and culture within broader frameworks of anti-racism, decolonization, activism, and cultural healing. For instance, K–12 Ethnic Studies courses might ask students to critically analyze U.S. history textbooks for omissions of marginalized groups or which U.S. presidents owned slaves, report on their findings, and reach out to textbook companies to try to spur them to make changes. Students in Ethnic Studies might also learn about the colonial myths of Thanksgiving and be challenged to understand those myths within the framework of colonization and the attempted genocide of Indigenous Peoples of North America. K–12 Ethnic Studies also takes pedagogy and student experiences seriously by focusing on dialogue and other more engaging approaches that allow students to draw on their own identities in the classroom (Au, 2020; Cuauhtin et al., 2019a). Between the pedagogy, content, and the movement for courses and requirements, K–12 Ethnic Studies has become a site of resistance against growing conservatism that the country has been experiencing generally.

Similarly, within the context of a much broader Black Lives Matter movement that saw massive nationwide protests in 2016 and 2020, there has been significant work with making Black Lives Matter at school through local and national campaigns (Anderson et al., 2020; Black Lives Matter at School, 2019; Hagopian, 2020). This movement was sparked by a group of public elementary school teachers in Seattle, Washington, who were doing anti-racist work at their school, and who decided to produce and wear t-shirts that said, "Black Lives Matter. We Stand Together. John Muir Elementary." Word of the t-shirts got to the local media, and the story was subsequently picked up by right-wing media outlets like Breitbart and Blue Lives Matter. Eventually, someone online made a bomb threat against the school, which galvanized educators and activists around the city and country in support of this work. What started as a Black Lives Matter at School Day in Seattle soon inspired similar actions in cities like Philadelphia and Rochester, and the growing number of Black Lives Matter at School activists nationally eventually came together to develop the Black Lives Matter at School national week of action (Au & Hagopian, 2021; Hagopian, 2020).

Now, for the last few years, thousands of educators across the country have participated in the Black Lives Matter at School national week of action. The national Black Lives Matter at School organization adapted the Black Lives Matter global network's 13 guiding principles to drive the curriculum:

Monday: Restorative justice, empathy, and loving engagement
Tuesday: Diversity and globalism
Wednesday: Trans affirming, queer affirming, collective value
Thursday: Intergenerational, Black families, Black villages
Friday: Black women, unapologetically Black (Hagopian, 2020, pp. 12–13)

Using these principles, educators have developed curriculum and resources that challenge the Eurocentric, white supremacist master narrative of history (Huggins, 1991) to not only teach about anti-Blackness in the United States, but also teach about Black resistance to oppression, Black joy, and Black identity (D. Jones & Hagopian, 2020; Watson et al., 2018). Akin to the movement for K–12 Ethnic Studies, the Black Lives Matter at School movement has helped to make classroom spaces sites of resistance to the growing tide of white supremacist nationalism in the United States.

THE ANTI-ANTI-RACISTS STRIKE BACK

However, even though we know that schools and education, especially social studies education, are important sites for building critical consciousness among students in the struggle for social justice, we would be foolish to think that schools alone are enough to move all of society (Apple, 2013; Au, 2010a, 2018). So it should come as no surprise that, despite the important gains made by the movements for K–12 Ethnic Studies and Black Lives Matter at School, we are also seeing a retrenchment of racist, nationalist, white supremacist politics of knowledge in the classrooms—mostly aimed at the social studies. A recent round of this racist retrenchment was sparked by *The 1619 Project*. Published by *The New York Times* in 2019, this collection of materials and essays was developed by journalist Nikole Hannah-Jones, and it centers the legacy of slavery and the influences of Black Americans in U.S. history. *The 1619 Project* quickly became a favorite target of right-wing conservatives, including Donald Trump, who claimed that the *Project* would teach children to hate America because it included how chattel slavery and anti-Black racism have been key aspects of U.S. history. Worried about left-wing indoctrination, several states subsequently sought to pass bills banning *The 1619 Project* from being taught in schools (Schwartz, 2021). Since then, conservatives have turned their sights on Critical Race Theory (CRT), in particular, as the educational bogeyman that threatens to ruin America. Multiple states have attempted to pass laws banning CRT as well as a slew of other ideas that, while not really part of CRT, are associated with racial equality and movements for justice generally (Lieb, 2025; Sanchez, 2021; Waxman, 2023; Zinn Education Project, 2021).

As an example, in June 2021, HB 3979 became law in Texas. While this law doesn't specifically use the term "Critical Race Theory," it bans teachers from teaching or discussing current events or a "widely debated and currently controversial issue of public policy or social affair" (as quoted in A. Kelley, 2021). It also bans teaching that anyone is "inherently racist, sexist, or oppressive, whether consciously or unconsciously" (as quoted in A. Kelley, 2021), and it specifies that schools cannot teach *The 1619 Project* (A. Kelley, 2021; K. McGee, 2021). Interestingly, and perhaps showing the struggle over racial politics in the state, the bill also requires that students be taught about "the history of white supremacy, including but not limited to the institution of slavery, the eugenics movement, and the Ku Klux Klan, and the ways in which it is morally wrong" (as quoted in K. McGee, 2021). A similar law proposed in Pennsylvania

> . . . bars teachers from teaching or using materials that describe the United States as "fundamentally racist," that say "merit-based systems are either racist or sexist," or that suggest an individual "bears responsibility for actions committed in the past by members of the individual's race or sex." (Sanchez, 2021)

As another example, in September 2021, Republican lawmakers in the Wisconsin Assembly passed a bill that would create a civic curriculum that all schools in the state would have to follow. This bill also banned a number of words/concepts that have been grouped together as representing Critical Race Theory. While the bill was ultimately vetoed by the governor, it is educative to see what kinds of language conservatives are fearful of appearing in classrooms. Some terms and concepts in this proposed ban are social and emotional learning, multiculturalism, anti-racism, diversity training, equity, social justice, "woke," abolitionist teaching, cultural competence, examine "systems," cultural awareness, intersection and intersectionality, conscious and unconscious bias, patriarchy, and culturally responsive teaching, among a long list of other terms (Vetterkind, 2021). Other states are attempting similar bans through state superintendents' offices or state boards of education (Lieb, 2025; Sanchez, 2021), and local school boards are becoming hotbeds for conservative activist protests against CRT and justice-oriented curriculum (Ellis & Sanchez, 2021; Kingkade et al., 2021).

TEXTS AND STANDARDS, ALWAYS A STRUGGLE

Scholars have long maintained that, despite conservative fears about what is being taught to children, social studies textbooks and standards have been—and continue to be—fairly regressive when it comes to how they handle historically marginalized populations, especially in terms of race. While the literature in this area is extensive, here are a few examples. Shear's (2015) study of how U.S. history textbooks treat the history of Native American boarding schools finds (a) whitewashing of cultural genocide by marginalizing Indigenous education, (b) treating cultural genocide as a peaceful educational reform, (c) erasing Indigenous education after 1900, and (d) not using Native voices to tell their own stories. Other research has found that state-mandated K–12 standards in U.S. history, civics, and government generally justify the logics of settler colonialism, erase Indigenous nationhood, or relegate Indigenous Peoples to history (Sabzalian et al., 2021; Shear et al., 2015). As another example, in their review of literature, King and Simmons (2018) highlight how research has consistently found that U.S. history textbooks purposefully omitted and/or distorted Black history with the intent of maintaining racist ideology and white supremacy, and generally cast Black Americans as racially inferior. In their study of how textbooks represent violence toward African Americans, Brown and Brown (2010) found that, despite the fact that such violence was portrayed in analyzed texts, the racial violence was largely explained as acts committed by individuals and were subsequently disassociated from racism as an institution. In a study of introductory American government textbooks, Takeda (2015) found that Asian Americans were largely not included in the texts, and Hartlep and Scott's (2016) comprehensive review of textbooks and teacher handbooks found that Asian Americans were either stereotyped or they were mentioned very little. Similarly, Cruz's (2002) study of U.S. history textbooks found that not only were Latinx peoples rarely mentioned, but when they were mentioned it was often through the eyes of U.S. imperialism, and they were portrayed as violent, lazy, and unwilling to assimilate into U.S. society.

These racist portrayals are deeply embedded in the history of social studies education, particularly with regard to Black and Indigenous peoples. Historians during the early 1900s, for instance, regularly maintained and propagated white supremacist beliefs, calling slavery a blessing because it would rescue Black people from being "savages" (King et al., 2012) and hailing manifest destiny as a way to civilize the "savage" Indian (Lomawaima, 1999). Fortunately, there was also significant resistance to such portrayals through history books. As Brown (2010) recounts, the important work on Black history textbooks by Carter G. Woodson and Charles H. Wesley in the early 20th century openly challenged the scientific racism of the time, offered in-depth narratives of Black history, upheld African cultures, and touched on Black resistance to chattel slavery in the United States. In addition to Woodson, King (2014) also discusses the work of Merly Epps, Edward A. Johnson, and Lelia Amos Pendleton as part of a legacy of Black "activist academicians" who all wrote social studies textbooks that challenged racial injustice.

George S. Counts and Harold Ruggs are two white early social studies progressives who wrote social studies textbooks that took aim at economic inequality during this same time period. While both of them were weak in their treatment of racism, and in Ruggs's case making contradictory and sometimes racist arguments along the way (Apple, 2013; King et al., 2012), both Counts and Ruggs challenged socioeconomic inequalities in schooling and advanced curriculum that encouraged economic equality. Their arguments proved to be particularly powerful—and dangerous—in the context of the Great Depression. As such, both Counts and Ruggs were attacked for being unpatriotic and un-American, and they were red-baited with accusations of being communists (Apple, 2013). In many ways, the struggles over the politics of knowledge in social studies is the same today as it was 100 years ago, with racial and economic inequalities being tied to public outrage and school knowledge being a site where battles around these issues have been waged.

NO NEUTRAL KNOWLEDGE

In social studies education, we often hear arguments that teachers should be neutral and objective, or that we need to teach "both sides" of any issue or history, and if we are not doing that, we are guilty of indoctrinating students (Gold, 2016; Ross, 2000, 2015). At the heart of those arguments are several presumptions about how much power teachers and curriculum have to sway students (do kids always listen to adults and automatically believe what we present them?), about how students take in and process what they are learning in classrooms (are they repositories that we just pour perspective into?), and about knowledge existing in a pure state, outside of context, culture, or history (does our understanding about something ever change, evolve, or shift as we see it in a different light or in new conditions?). Black educators from the early1900s like Woodson, Wesley, and others mentioned above (A. L. Brown, 2010; King et al., 2012) undoubtedly knew that social, historical, and political contexts shaped both our construction of knowledge and how people acted on that knowledge. Counts and Ruggs also knew this. Even as they differed in degree and method, both Counts and Ruggs understood that schools and school knowledge have a potential role in shaping society for the better, and if that we wanted things to improve in the world, then we needed teachers and curriculum aimed at that improvement (Apple, 2013; Ross, 2000).

What is key to understand about knowledge, and social studies knowledge in particular, is that there is no "neutral," unbiased entrée into anything. The lack of neutrality even comes down to the very language we use to teach. Language is an expression of culture (Ngũgĩ, 1986), and language derives meaning in use in context (Gee, 2008). By teaching (or writing, as I am doing here) in standard American English, our words carry cultural assumptions and norms built into both the history and structure of the language itself. This happens in a myriad of ways. One is that English, as a language, contains its own cultural logics of classifications and categories for communication (Gelman & Roberts, 2017). Another is that we know specific forms of English are treated as being superior to other forms. For instance, standard American English has long been associated with higher levels of education, smartness, higher socioeconomic status, and whiteness, and these same racist norms are in turn used to associate African American Vernacular English with being less educated, less intelligent, and poor (Smitherman, 1997). As another example, the fact that English is the standard institutional language used to teach in the United States immediately signals that it has been the language of colonization and is used to maintain settler colonialism here (Iyengar, 2014). No matter what language we are using, as soon as we speak or write, cultural norms, histories, and contextual power relations are already intruding upon whatever "neutral" or "unbiased" or "objective" social studies knowledge we are teaching. It is inescapable.

The issue of broader context of knowledge also looms large in discussions of neutral social studies knowledge. While there has been strong scholarship on the complexities of teaching controversial issues asking students to consider multiple perspectives on historical arguments (Hess, 2009), what counts as "controversial" and therefore warrants the teaching of multiple perspectives (or "both sides") of a historical issue is entirely dependent on the context in which you teach. As of this writing, a glaring, non-education example can be found in the fight over COVID-19 vaccines and mask mandates. Here in my community in Seattle, neither getting a COVID vaccine nor wearing a mask indoors is considered particularly controversial—and we likely would not teach either as being so. However, we know that in other communities in other parts of the state or country, major fights have erupted over both the vaccine and wearing masks (Hill & Dreher, 2021; J. S. Kelleher et al., 2021). What is not controversial here in Seattle is clearly controversial elsewhere.

We can say the exact same thing about the teaching of social studies. While all state social studies standards are problematic (see, e.g., Bigelow, 2010; Sabzalian et al., 2021), some states have become infamous for severely distorting history in favor of conservative politics. In Texas, for instance, their state standards have regularly downplayed slavery as a root issue of the Civil War, omitted Indigenous peoples, and challenged the constitutional separation of church and state, among others (Agarwal, 2019; Foner, 2010). As another example, the recent Texas House Bill 3979 in response to Critical Race Theory and *The, 1619 Project* requires teachers to teach controversial issues from "diverse and contending perspectives without giving deference to one perspective" (as quoted in Mockaitis, 2021). In implementing the law, an administrator in a Texas school district told teachers that if they were going to teach the Jewish Holocaust, then they had to make sure they had books with "opposing" views. After apologizing for what happened, the superintendent of the same district explained that they now know that House Bill 3979 does not require the teaching of opposing views on what are considered historical facts (Mockaitis, 2021).

My point here is not to pick on Texas. However, the Texas example does illustrate how geographic and political context shape what is considered acceptable as official knowledge in schools (Apple, 2014). Further, while I know that the Holocaust is always used as one of those extreme examples because there is no "both sides" when it comes to genocide, the fact that a school official anywhere in the United States felt like they could suggest the need to teach "opposing" views of the Holocaust as being anywhere within the realm of reason perfectly illustrates how commonsense truths—or what is considered controversial—absolutely depend on context. Hence, we have to recognize that apolitical, neutral knowledge doesn't exist, because all teaching and all curriculum, whether through language or political context, have politics and culture built directly into them.

HEGEMONY AND INDOCTRINATION

Gramsci's (1971) conception of hegemony is helpful in understanding that indoctrination exists in all of education. Gramsci theorizes that "social hegemony" is the

> . . . "spontaneous" consent given by the great masses of the population to the general direction imposed on social life by the dominant fundamental group; this consent is "historically" caused by the prestige (and consequent confidence) which the dominant group enjoys because of its position and function in the world of production. (p. 12)

He further discusses how social hegemony takes on a kind of universal consciousness in the ways that "[T]he development and expansion of the particular [dominant] group are conceived of and presented, as being the motor force of a universal expansion" (p. 182). Here Gramsci is addressing how those with power work to develop forms of consciousness among people so as to make dominant social relations seem natural, as part of a broader commonsense about how the world works. In turn, this also enables the masses of people to willingly grant consent to be ruled by those in power. While the concept of hegemony is used by many educational scholars (including me), it is often used as a shorthand to refer to the conservative hegemonic block that has power under capitalism. What is often missed is that Gramsci distinguished between capitalist bourgeois hegemony (that is, the hegemony of the ruling class under capitalism) and what he was striving for: proletarian hegemony (that is, the hegemony of the working class under socialism).

I raise this because Gramsci clearly understood that hegemony—the maintenance of forms of consciousness aligned with social order—was never neutral, that our broader commonsense understandings of the world and society are always bound and given direction by political commitments and processes. Based on the language we use, the texts we choose, the state standards we are supposed to teach toward, content we are compelled by state standards to exclude or simply choose to exclude by choice, what we teach as controversial or uncontroversial, what we teach as historical fact or what we teach as historical question, we are teaching with political directionality. We are participating (consciously or not) in a form of indoctrination. We are engaging in a socially and politically constrained process that communicates to students what is considered acceptable or unacceptable and what counts as official knowledge either in the interest of maintaining existing relations or in the interest of changing existing relations. This is the point for social studies educators to grasp: We are always educating toward a set of politics. The question is not whether it is good or bad to do so. The question is really, "Toward what politics are we educating?"

CHAPTER 4

The Long March Toward Revitalization

Developing Standpoint in Curriculum Studies

It has been over 55 years since Schwab (1969) declared the field of curriculum studies "moribund," and nearly 50 years since Huebner (1976) pronounced it "dead." The terminal prognosis made by both scholars was based on the same set of symptoms: a conceptual disunity and lack of practical application of curriculum studies to school practices. It has been a long, slow death, however, as curriculum scholars have expressed concern over conceptual disunity in the field in the decades since (Au, 2011a; Jackson, 1996; Morrison, 2004; Snaza, 2014), because curriculum studies is apparently mired in crisis of disarray and conceptual confusion that inhibits its growth and development (Miller, 2005; Slabbert & Hattingh, 2006). Importantly, it must be noted that others, such as Malewski (2009), argue that fretting about this disunity is based on normative assumptions about the field of curriculum studies itself, and that such epistemological and ontological diversity is instead desirable because it represents a proliferation of different ideas and approaches in the field.

In this chapter I enter this ongoing scholarly debate within curriculum studies with the intent of offering one potential conceptual resolution to this historical tension in the field. I begin here with a discussion of the current contours of conceptual struggle within curriculum studies, which revolves around what has been constructed as a lack of paradigmatic unity (due to a focus on subjectivities) versus a lack of pragmatic connection to real-world curricular issues (due to an overemphasis on theory). I then offer a critical analysis of some of the strengths and weaknesses found within this struggle, and, building upon the model offered by feminist standpoint theory, I elaborate an epistemological, methodological, and conceptual framework for standpoint in curriculum studies as a tool that offers a possible solution to tensions in the field. I conclude with a brief analysis of two lesson plans, using curricular standpoint as a lens.

Previously published as "The Long March Toward Revitalization: Developing Standpoint in Curriculum Studies," 2012, *Teachers College Record*, *114*(5), 1–30. https://doi.org/10.1177/016146811211400508.

THE CRITICAL TURN IN CURRICULUM STUDIES

In the mid-1970s, curriculum studies took a notable turn toward critical politics, with issues of equality and power within education highlighted as a focus in curricular research (see, e.g., Anyon, 1980; Apple, 1971, 1973; Rosenbaum, 1976). Pinar (1975, 1978) dubbed this critical turn as the "reconceptualization." In the decades since, a significant number of curriculum scholars have maintained research trajectories that use postmodernist-influenced theoretical orientations with the expressed intent of explicitly examining the positionality and subjectivity of both knowledge and educational actors (Kafala & Cary, 2006; Slattery, 2006). Specifically, to lesser and greater degrees, scholars have taken up postmodernist-influenced lenses such as feminism (see, e.g., Luke & Gore, 1992), cultural studies (see, e.g., Pinar, 2006), poststructuralism (see, e.g., Popkewitz & Fendler, 1999), disability studies (see, e.g., Erevelles, 2005), neo-Marxism (see, e.g., Apple, 1995), and post-colonial studies (see, e.g., Dimitriadis & McCarthy, 2001), among others, to analyze the politics of school knowledge and classroom practices. Although some of the curricular scholarship associated with these analyses maintained an overall focus on material reality (e.g., Anyon, 1980; Apple, 1995), what unites these postmodernist-influenced orientations is an overt recognition of the subjectivity of experience and epistemology (Benton & Craib, 2011) that acknowledges the complexity of social and material reality for multiple groups and communities (Fraser, 1995; Hartsock, 1998a). As such, critical scholarship in curriculum studies has made great strides in not only questioning relationships of power as they exist within school knowledge, but also in striving for curriculum that is more equitable, more inclusive of various perspectives, and more resistant to status quo relations.

Research on synoptic curriculum studies texts confirms a steady shift toward the recognition of those commonly associated with the "reconceptualization" of the field (P.-G. Kim & Marshall, 2006), such that, as Miller (2005) asserts,

> . . . [I]t now certainly is commonplace to view US curriculum studies as situated, always located within larger discursive frameworks, always part of US cultural, political, and educational moments of the day and place. American curriculum studies and curriculum design and development are seen as bound up in a wealth of local political, cultural, economic, social, historical complexities. Curriculum is taken as embedded in multiple local contexts of use, multiple contexts of construction and relationships. (p. 18)

Thus, between postmodernism's focus on the subjectivity of meaning and perspective (Benton & Craib, 2001), the increased presence of postmodern influenced critical theories in curriculum studies (P.-G. Kim & Marshall, 2006; Miller, 2005), and the fragmented and compartmentalized structures of schooling and curriculum generally (Slabbert & Hattingh, 2006), the existence of a fractured or balkanized field of curriculum studies is hardly surprising (Kafala & Cary, 2006; Malewski, 2009); scholars have been applying new paradigms and epistemologies in their attempts to more fully understand the complexity of what is taught in schools as well as the meanings that students, teachers, and communities subsequently construct in the process.

THE PRAGMATIC RESPONSE

The shift toward analyses that explicitly focused on politics and power in school knowledge associated with the reconceptualization did not happen without resistance within the field of curriculum studies itself. Weighing in on both the death of the field and the critical turn, Jackson (1980) asserted that perhaps the field of curriculum studies never really existed at all, going on to deride the critical politics associated with the reconceptualization. Hlebowitsh (1993, 2005) and Wraga (1998, 1999), both individually and jointly (Wraga & Hlebowitsh, 2003) have carried forward aspects of Jackson's critique, asserting that the field of curriculum studies has given too much credence to critical theorizing, overpoliticized the field, focused too much on theoretical exploration, and neglected practical curriculum design.

In response specifically to the critical turn in curriculum studies, Wraga and Hlebowitsh (2003) call for a "renaissance" in curriculum theory that specifically rejects paradigmatic orientations that they suggest have no place in the field, where ideology and "sound scholarship" are incompatible and where life experience should not be considered within the defined curriculum. Thus they advocate for a de-politicized field where "curriculum scholars shed ideological blinders, clearly delineate boundaries of the field, consciously build upon the field's constructive legacies, and foster a robust interplay between curriculum theory and curriculum practice" (p. 435).

There are three aspects of Wraga and Hlebowitsh's (2003) framing that are particularly important to highlight. First is their lamentation that curriculum studies does not have the same amount of power or effectiveness that it once leveraged in schools in the United States. Their renaissance thus hints at a return to a romantic past where districts and schools relied on university scholarship for curricular guidance. Second, and fundamental to their overall analysis, is a pragmatic push for curriculum studies to embrace school practice. This aspect serves the dual purposes of critiquing reconceptualist scholars for being focused on theory and increasing the relevance of the field in the day-to-day operations of schools. Third, and as an extension of their pragmatism, is their idea that by focusing more on practice (what works and what needs to be done), curriculum studies necessarily should not incorporate ideology, politics, personal experience, culture, and other forms of subjectivity that might be brought to analyses of school knowledge.

PRAGMATIC AND SUBJECTIVE CONSIDERATIONS

Despite the strengths offered by postmodern subjectivity in curriculum studies and the concrete practicality called for by curricular pragmatists, both positions suffer from some critical shortcomings. For instance, Wraga and Hlebowitsh's (2003) suggested curricular "renaissance" is extremely problematic. Most prominent is their push to focus on issues other than the existence of political, cultural, and ideological relationships between schools, the curriculum, and society—a position that seems ridiculous considering the sheer intensity of struggles over school knowledge (Apple, 2013, 2014; Au, 2023b, 2024b). The boundaries of our knowledge, including what comes to "count" as legitimate curricular knowledge, are intimately intertwined with social and political relations (Apple, 2014; Au, 2011a; Bernstein, 1999; Malewski, 2009). This is even true within the field of curriculum studies itself, which has developed its own canon of curriculum history imbued with racialized norms (Au et al., 2016; A. L. Brown & Au, 2014). Further, it seems equally impossible to deny the ideological nature of *all* scholarship and research (Patel, 2016; Smith, 1999), particularly when researchers themselves lay claim to ideological neutrality and, by extension, methodological objectivity, associated with the positivistic sciences (Benton & Craib, 2011). In this regard, Wraga and Hlebowitsh's (2003) call for curriculum studies to "shed ideological blinders" (p. 435) in search of some form of paradigmatic unity lends itself to a hegemonically defined, positivistic field of curriculum studies (Morrison, 2004). In this sense Wraga and Hlebowitsh's (2003) response to critical subjectivity in curriculum studies implies a call for a form of a normative pragmatism.

It is important to recognize that there is nothing inherently negative about the growth of criticality in curriculum studies associated with the reconceptualization, just as there is nothing inherently negative about a lack of paradigmatic unity in the field (Malewski, 2009). Indeed, one could argue that the diverse forms of critical analyses demonstrate the field's resilience, strength, and adaptability. Further, given the conservative modernization that has taken place socially and educationally (Apple, 2006, 2013) and the increasing institutional inequalities both nationally and internationally associated with neoliberalism (Au, 2018; K. Kelleher, 2019; Lipman, 2011), the critical political analyses in curriculum studies seem more than appropriate. Further still, the modern decline in the influence of curriculum studies in public education must be understood within the current context, particularly the shifting and diverse stakeholders involved in public school reform (Au & Ferrare, 2015a; Ball, 2012) and the increasing influence of tests and textbook publishers on the curriculum (Au, 2023b).

Despite the above criticisms, it is equally important to acknowledge an important issue within curriculum studies that Wraga and Hlebowitsh (2003) identify: Curriculum studies as a whole would be better served if it were more grounded in schools (Apple, 2010). In their assessment, however, Wraga and

Hlebowitsh charge reconceptualist and critical curriculum scholars with being particularly disconnected from actual curricular practice at the school and classroom levels. Such an assessment is curious because historically a significant body of the work done by such scholars specifically focuses on the politics of power and culture as it manifests in school knowledge at many levels, including the classroom (e.g., Anyon, 1980; Apple, 1986; Beyer & Liston, 1996; Sleeter, 2002). Indeed, the point of much reconceptualist and critical scholarship in curriculum studies is to influence practice by taking up real-world issues such as educational inequality as a focus.

Intent, however, does not always equate with outcome, and despite the focus of some scholars on practice, it is true that postmodern analyses can often be disconnected from engagement with material reality (Au & Apple, 2009). It is thus also important to reevaluate the influence of postmodern subjectivity in curriculum studies (Apple, 2010; Au, 2011a; Beyer & Liston, 1992). While it is absolutely necessary to recognize the crucial role that postmodernist analyses have played in challenging master narratives and injecting the lived experiences of peoples and cultures into all of our work (Gottesman, 2016; McLaren & Farahmandpur, 2005), a difficulty arises due to postmodernism's general rejection of a material world outside of human perception and subjectivity (Bhaskar, 1989; Perry, 2002). Such a position in reaction to the hegemony of positivist sciences is understandable, but it negates our ability to change material and social conditions, because within the postmodern epistemological-philosophical paradigm we can never establish that those conditions—whether socially just or unjust—actually exist. It all becomes a matter of perception, or in the case of curriculum studies, a matter of language, discourse, and pure theorizing. As such, curricularists may have lost the connection between curriculum studies and the material world (Apple, 2010). On this issue, Beyer and Liston (1996) comment:

> For postmodernists, then, without some sense of words and referents that extend beyond the signifier and signified, their talk amounts to nothing or, if it does indeed amount to something, it undermines their own position. Without the possibility of utterances referring to something outside themselves, postmodernism is locked within a circular narcissism, which undermines not only the claims of modernists but postmodern writing as well. Such circularity is debilitating for those involved in education, who are confronted daily with choices that call for concrete action and that often carry long-lasting consequences. (p. 150)

Thus, while critical scholars associated with the reconceptulization embraced postmodernist subjectivity to lesser and greater degrees (and with lesser and greater effect), a disassociation from material reality is a serious consideration philosophically, epistemologically, and methodologically when postmodernism is brought to bear in any field or discipline (Au & Apple, 2009).

BETWEEN PRAGMATISM AND SUBJECTIVITY

In some ways I, like Wraga and Hlebowitsh (2003), also wish to see a heightened focus on practice in curriculum studies, but on different grounds. Where they simplistically critique reconceptualist scholars for focusing on theory, I see curriculum studies as no different than the rest of social science research generally, which historically has struggled with connecting research with reality (Benton & Craib, 2011; Fine, 2006). Further, Wraga and Hlebowitsh's clarion call for more attention to practice and without "ideological blinders" implies that the study of curriculum should exist in pragmatic isolation from the world so that our study of it can similarly share in what one might see as the positivist guise of objective, ideologically neutral research. However, my desire for an increased focus on practice is grounded in an opposite sensibility; in connecting curriculum to material reality, we acknowledge that it cannot be isolated from the world or separated from context and ideology, and that our study of it should therefore be able to explain how, why, and to what ends those connections exist. Such strong grounding in material reality further requires that we recognize the ways in which those connections manifest through the various lenses of race, class, gender, sexuality, ability, culture, ideology, and so forth that our identities embody as well (Au, 2011a).

If curriculum studies is to be revitalized through an increased focus on practice, then let us focus on practice as it exists in the context of the complex social, political, and cultural relations of the material world. Such a revitalization would necessarily draw upon aspects of subjectivity found in the reconceptualist turn in curriculum studies, as well as the attention to practice for which Wraga and Hlebowitsh call. This revitalization would have to do so on different conceptual grounds that combine the strengths of both, while ameliorating their respective weaknesses of disconnection from material reality (postmodernist/subjectivity) and false pretenses to objectivity and non-ideology (positivist/pragmatism). In what follows, I explain how standpoint theory offers a conceptual, methodological, and epistemological tool.

STANDPOINT THEORY

Standpoint theory originated in the 1970s and 1980s among critical feminist scholars who, drawing on Marxist concepts of proletarian standpoint (Hartsock, 1998b), sought to challenge both masculinist norms and regressive gender politics (Harding, 2004a) found in scientific research. Since then, standpoint theory—along with feminist studies more broadly—has struggled with its own internal politics of difference surrounding issues of race, class, nationality, and sexuality, where feminists of color critiqued earlier manifestations of standpoint theory for upholding the notion of a "universal woman," one that often neglected non-white, non-Western experiences (Foley et al., 2000; Hartsock,

1998b; Sandoval, 2000). In what follows I sketch the outline of standpoint theory in order to argue the political and epistemological explanatory and analytic power that standpoint offers curriculum studies.

Standpoint theory builds from the basic understanding that power and knowledge are inextricably intertwined, that "they co-constitute and co-maintain each other" (Harding, 2004a, p. 67), and that this power relation is socially situated because,

> For any particular interpretive context, new knowledge claims must be consistent with an existing body of knowledge that the group controlling the interpretive context accepts as true. The methods used to validate knowledge claims must also be acceptable to the group controlling the knowledge-validation process. (Hill Collins, 1989, p. 753)

Thus, as an extension of the control over validated knowledge, in terms of methodology and epistemology, standpoint theory also operates under the assumption that ". . . there are some perspectives on society from which . . . the real relations of humans with each other and with the natural world are not visible" (Hartsock, 1998b, p. 107) because of the differential power relations relative to knowledge production and because of the epistemological limits carried with the viewpoint provided by specific social locations.

As it has been articulated by Hartsock (1998b) and Harding (2004a, 2004b), standpoint theory consists of five central themes that guide it epistemologically and methodologically:

- First, standpoint theory asserts that our experiences with material reality—which also constitute our social relations—structure our epistemology of the world in ways that both limit and enable certain ways of understanding (Harding, 2004a; Hartsock, 1998b). That is to say, our social locations both enable us to see and understand the world more clearly with respect to our positionality *and* place limits on our ability to understand the world beyond that same positionality.
- Second, because our experience and material life are embedded in and structured by systems of domination and rule that are organized hierarchically around power relations of race, class, gender, sexuality, nationality, and other forms of socially determined difference, the epistemologies available to groups in power contradict and run counter to the epistemologies of less powerful groups—forming epistemological inversions of each other (Harding, 2004a; Hartsock, 1998b). Put simply, by nature of their different experiences from within their social locations, the ruler's view of the world will in many ways be oppositional to that of the ruled.
- Third, because of differentials in power (and how such power manifests unequally in social, cultural, and political institutions),

the perspectives of those in power are made functional in the lives of everyone regardless of position, because "the ruling group can be expected to structure the material relations in which all people are forced to participate" (Hartsock, 1998b, p. 229), as "all are forced to live in social structures and institutions designed to serve the oppressors' understandings of self and society" (Harding, 2004a, p. 68). Thus, the skewed understanding of the world that is imposed institutionally by those in power illustrates how "epistemology grows in a complex and contradictory way from material life," where a standpoint "explains the 'surface' or appearance, and indicates the logic by means of which the appearance inverts or distorts the deeper reality" (Hartsock, 1998b, p. 107). Put differently, we might say that the unequal distribution of power leads to the unequal distribution of epistemologies, where those with more power can exert stronger influence on our commonsense understandings of the world, even if such commonsense understandings fundamentally operate as distorted conceptions of material reality (Gramsci, 1971).

- Fourth, and as a consequence of the previous, a standpoint is always born of struggle against the commonsense, hegemonic epistemologies of those in power, making it an "achievement" that arises from active, conscious work against the reigning, institutionalized epistemologies, which generally support status quo inequalities. Subsequently a standpoint "must be struggled for against the apparent realities made 'natural' and 'obvious' by dominant institutions" (Harding, 2004a, p. 68), the activity of which "requires both systematic analysis and the education that can only grow from political struggle to change those relations" (Hartsock, 1998b, p. 229). As such, we can never assume that a standpoint is simply given by one's social location—just because one comes from a marginalized social location does not mean that one automatically has taken up a standpoint; people from marginalized or less powerful groups can and do maintain forms of consciousness that are regressive, just as people from dominant groups can also develop forms of consciousness that are progressive. Rather, a standpoint arises from conscious, resistant struggle against the prevailing and hegemonic forms of consciousness that maintain status quo inequalities.
- Fifth, the taking-up of a standpoint by the marginalized and less powerful carries with it the potential for liberation because it "makes visible the inhumanity of relations among human beings" (Hartsock, 1998b, p. 229), emphasizing that,

> An oppressed group must become a group "for itself," not just "in itself" in order for it to see the importance of engaging in political and scientific struggles to see the world from the perspective of its own lives. (Harding, 2004a, pp. 68–69)

Thus, the development of a standpoint necessarily requires the development of "oppositional consciousness" (Sandoval, 2000) as the less powerful create transformative epistemologies as part of their struggle against existing power relations. Indeed, this liberatory potential of standpoint makes it dangerous to the prevailing social order, and therefore gives cause for the more powerful to actively seek to discredit such positions (Hill Collins, 1989).

STANDPOINT, EPISTEMOLOGY, AND "STRONG OBJECTIVITY"

Fundamentally, as outlined above, standpoint theory argues that certain social locations, specifically those of systematically oppressed or marginalized groups, provide the best "starting off thought" for generating ". . . illuminating critical questions that do not arise in thought that begins from the dominant group lives" (Harding, 2004b, p. 128) because ". . . marginalized lives are better places from which to start asking causal and critical questions about the social order" (p. 130). As Hartsock (1998b) explains,

> . . . [T]he criteria for privileging some knowledges over others are ethical and political as well as purely "epistemological." The quotation marks here are to indicate that I see ethical and political concepts such as that of power as involving epistemological claims on the one hand, and ideas of what is to count as knowledge involving profoundly important political and ethical stakes on the other. Marx made an important claim that knowledge that takes its starting point from the lives of those who have suffered from exploitation produces better accounts of the world than that starting from the lives of dominant groups . . . [T]he view from the margins (defined in more heterogeneous terms) is clearer and better. (p. 80)

Thus, social location provides an important epistemological standpoint because not only does "the experience of domination . . . provide the possibility of important new understandings of social life" (Hartsock, 1998b, p. 240), it also provides a sharper view of material and social relations.

From this perspective it follows that, its origins within feminism notwithstanding, standpoint theory is not a singularly feminist project (at least as far as feminism being defined as solely being about "women's issues"). Rather, as Harding (2004b) explains,

> . . . [T]he subject of liberatory feminist knowledge must also be, in an important if controversial sense, the subject of every other liberatory knowledge project. This is true in the collective sense of "subject of knowledge," because lesbian, poor, and racially marginalized women are all women, and therefore feminists will have to grasp how gender, race, and class, and sexuality are used to construct each other. (p. 134)

Hence, standpoint has to contend with issues of power and oppression in a general sense, since, as a paradigmatic orientation, standpoint openly acknowledges that the social location of the oppressed and marginalized (as defined by historical, social, cultural, and institutional contexts) is the best vantage point to start knowledge projects by potentially providing clearer, more truthful lenses for understanding the world.

To be clear, however, in making such arguments, standpoint theory does not argue for total epistemological relativity, where every socially located standpoint simply holds equal value relative to every other socially located standpoint. Rather, as Harding (2004b) asserts, standpoint theory

> . . . argues against the idea that all social situations provide equally useful resources for learning about the world and against the idea that they all set equally strong limits on knowledge. . . . Standpoint theory provides arguments for the claim that some social situations are scientifically better than others as places from which to start off knowledge projects . . . (p. 131)

Thus, rather than a call for epistemological relativism, a standpoint is perhaps better conceived as "a cognitive, psychological, and political tool for more adequate knowledge judged by the nonessentialist, historically contingent, situated standards of strong objectivity" (Haraway, 1991, as cited in Hartsock, 1998b, p. 236). Such a tool allows for "the creation of better (more objective, more liberatory) accounts of the world" (Hartsock 1998b, p. 236)—even if, as Harding (2004b) asserts, "The epistemologically advantaged starting points for research do not guarantee that the researcher can maximize objectivity in her account; these grounds provide only a necessary—not sufficient—starting point for maximizing objectivity" (p. 128).

On a simple reading, it might seem contradictory that an epistemological and methodological orientation such as standpoint, one that essentially emphasizes a specific type of subjectivity related to social location, relies so heavily on concepts of objectivity—either in the form of Hartsock's (1998a) references to "more objective" perspectives on the world or what Harding (2004a) refers to as "strong objectivity." However, there is no contradiction in these scholars' formulations, as they recognize that there is a material world outside of human subjectivity that can in fact be understood, and that such understanding takes place dialectically, through interaction and mutual reaction between humans and their environments (Au, 2011a, 2018). Hence, standpoint argues that we can achieve *more* objective understandings of that objectively existing world by not only recognizing subjectivity in our epistemology, but by also purposefully embracing our subjectivity and actively reflecting on it within our sociopolitical environments (Freire, 1974). Harding (2004b) puts it thusly:

> Strong objectivity requires that the subject of knowledge be placed on the same critical, causal plane as the objects of knowledge. Thus, strong objectivity requires what we can think of as "strong reflexivity." This is because culturewide (or nearly

> culturewide) beliefs function as evidence at every stage of scientific inquiry: in the selection of problems, the formation of hypotheses, the design of research (including the organization of research communities), the collection of data, the interpretation and sorting of data, decisions about when to stop research, the way results of research are reported, and so on. The subject of knowledge—the individual and the historically located social community whose unexamined beliefs its members are likely to hold "unknowingly," so to speak—must be considered as part of the object of knowledge from the perspective of scientific method. (p. 136)

Strong objectivity means that we gain a better, clearer, and more truthful—more strongly objective—understanding of social and material realities from the achievement of a standpoint in our knowledge projects because, as Harding (2004b) puts it, we ". . . can take the subject as well as the object of knowledge to be a necessary object of critical, causal—scientific!—social explanations" (p. 137).

It is critical to stress that strong objectivity be understood within the context of standpoint theory specifically, and as such, its explanatory power does not arise simply from the assertions of Marx, Hartsock, or Harding. Rather, by taking into account the social construction of knowledge and the power relations that are thus expressed epistemologically as a result, standpoint theory is essentially grounded in the social fact that knowledge is a terrain of struggle, and that those with more power socially, materially, and institutionally express their power through the assertion of epistemological norms. Further, standpoint theory recognizes that within these socio-epistemological relationships, because those in power are often served through the obfuscation of reality, the epistemological perspectives of the marginalized are not automatically more truthful—marginalized groups certainly maintain misunderstandings of how the world functions (as we all do). Hence, it is also important to emphasize that standpoint arises from struggle with and against prevailing, commonsense, hegemonic epistemologies. Strong objectivity is thus formed within this context as a struggle to understand material reality in ways that not only take the perspectives of multiple social locations into account, but also recognizes that we must also embrace the power relations embedded in those social locations as a means of getting a fuller and more analytically sharp grasp of the world. Thus, because standpoint theory not only recognizes forms of subjectivity associated with our various contexts, but also recognizes a concrete, material reality as the object of our research, a recognition that also carries within it the need for action (application), it can function as a powerful epistemological and methodological tool for educational research generally, and for curriculum studies specifically because it resolves the subjectivist-pragmatist contradiction in the field.

STANDPOINT IN EDUCATIONAL RESEARCH

Standpoint theory has been used sparingly in educational research. Some of the earliest applications arose within the milieu of the development of feminist pedagogies that challenged heterosexual, patriarchal norms of classroom interactions and sought to emphasize women's narratives and points of view as critical entry points into a deeper and more full understanding of the world (Manicom, 1992; Weiler, 1991). Since then, standpoint theory has been discussed in relation to educational research generally, as well as applied to a smattering of educational research projects. In terms of general discussions focusing on educational research, Greene (1994), for instance, briefly touches upon the concept of standpoint theory in her review of contributions to shifting epistemologies in educational research, and Denzin and Lincoln (2000) and Freeman (2019) see standpoint theory as contributing new perspectives to the body of qualitative educational research. Howe (2009) further highlights standpoint theory as an important challenge to issues associated with objectivist dogma found in positivist paradigms of scientific research, and Glasser & Smith III (2008) note that standpoint theory, as a manifestation of what they refer to as "materialist accounts of gender" (p. 346), is used as one analytic framework for research on how the terms "gender" and "sex" are often conflated in educational scholarship. Foley, Levinson, and Hurtig (2000), despite mistakenly identifying standpoint theory as simply research coming from women's perspectives, ultimately uphold the novel contribution standpoint makes to studies of gender in the field of educational anthropology. Fine (2006) offers strong objectivity as a guiding epistemological frame for critical scholarly research, and Sleeter (2000), in her review of research on teacher education and equity, explicitly equates standpoint theory with what she refers to as "emancipatory research" (p. 235).

While standpoint theory is addressed in synoptic texts on educational research, few specific research projects have made active use of it. For instance, Henry (1996) frames standpoint as "an act of political consciousness" (p. 364) and discusses the role of Black women's oppositional standpoint in her analysis of the ways that Black women teachers negotiate the cultural and pedagogic norms of predominantly white educational institutions. Bloom and Erlandson (2003) draw on a similar framework in their own analysis of Black female school administrators and their struggles for recognition within their school contexts. Yonezawa (2000) also makes use of standpoint theory to understand how parents negotiate and make decisions regarding systems of educational tracking, and Andre-Bechely (2005) applies standpoint theory as one lens for analyzing how parents understand and experience school choice policies differently depending on their social locations. Spatig (2005) makes use of standpoint theory in her feminist critique of developmentalist classroom practices that often advocate hands-off pedagogies that can produce inequalities, and Cooper (2005) uses Black feminist standpoint to analyze how working-class African American women make sense of school voucher programs. Takacs (2002), in discussing how he addresses positionality in his social justice–oriented teacher education courses, specifically refers to his use of strong objectivity in order to have both students and himself see beyond their socially located individual perspectives. Feminist standpoint theory has also appeared in research in physics education (M. Rodriguez et al., 2022; Santana & Singh, 2024), examinations of race in environmental education

(Stapleton, 2020), and research on Black women's interactions with faculty in higher education (Allen et al., 2023).

Connell's (1994) work is one of the few that takes up standpoint theory within curriculum studies specifically. Connell's concept of "curricular justice" suggests that if schools are to work for social justice, then they must examine the world from the "standpoint of the least advantaged" (p. 43), where

> The "standpoint of the least advantaged" means, concretely, that we think through economic issues from the standpoint of the poor, not the rich. We think through gender arrangements from the standpoint of women. We think through race relations and land questions from the standpoint of indigenous people. We think through questions of sexuality from the standpoint of gay people. And so on. (p. 43)

Connell thus advocates that our curriculum take the standpoint of the marginalized or oppressed, a position that she justifies by arguing that "the current hegemonic curriculum embodies the interests of the *most* advantaged. Justice requires a *counter*-hegemonic curriculum . . . designed to embody the interests and perspectives of the least advantaged" (p. 44, original emphasis). Hence, we see Connell taking up the cardinal basis for standpoint—that curricular knowledge is intimately connected to power relations in society, and that such relations are thus transmitted within hegemonic knowledge projects, including in schools.

Of all the educational research and theorizing discussed here, DeLissovoy (2008) offers the most developed treatment of standpoint theory. In his piece, which analyzes conceptions of oppression in educational theory, DeLissovoy accurately traces the lineage of standpoint theory from the Marxist philosopher Lukacs (1971) to Hartsock (1983), whom he says, "transposes the notion of class position in Marxism onto the category of gender in arguing for a feminist political and epistemological standpoint" (DeLissovoy, 2008, p. 84). While highlighting the political-philosophical strength of this epistemological turn, DeLissovoy then goes on to discuss what he sees as the limitations of Hartsock's and other's conceptions of standpoint theory, mainly that if we take each distinct social position as the basis for a standpoint, then "each standpoint ultimately appears inadequate for understanding social life outside of the characteristic experience of that group" (p. 85).

Some educational researchers have also made sharp critiques of the use of standpoint theory. One line of such critiques represents positivist attacks on epistemologies and methodologies that take context and subjectivity into account. For instance, some scholars ultimately seek to deny the contextual basis for all knowledge while simultaneously denying the existence of hierarchies of power that determine social location (see, e.g., Landau, 2008) and hence have incorrectly labeled standpoint theory as a "wholly discredited theory of science" (Pinnick, 2008, p. 1056). Other lines of critique represent misunderstandings and misconstructions of standpoint theory itself. Siegel (2006), for instance, misconstrues epistemological standpoints as perspectives that simply arise from essentialist, universal positionalities associated with identity politics—a position that explicitly contradicts Hartsock's (1998a, 1998b) and Harding's (2004a, 2004b) conception of standpoint, outlined above. In his critique of standpoint theory Siegel (2006) goes on to conflate neutrality with strong objectivity, and then argues for the lack of neutrality in all research. Siegel's critique proves ironic because not only is it factually incorrect since, as I have detailed here, strong objectivity is foundationally based on the idea that there is no neutrality at all, but Siegel then goes on to uphold the very kind of subjectivity that Harding (2004b) advocates for quite clearly in her analysis.

These positivistic and erroneous attacks aside, there are some critical issues to address with how standpoint theory has been used in educational research. Henry (1996), Andre-Bechely (2005), and Foley et al. (2000), for instance, despite their constructive use of the concept, incorrectly frame standpoint theory as simply a feminist project that merely takes women's perspectives into account. Indeed, this applies to DeLissovoy's (2008) explanation of standpoint theory as well, despite his quite powerful analysis. In my read of Hartsock (1983, 1998b, 1998a), I do not see her arguing for a standpoint epistemology that only applies to a singular social group (e.g., women only, as part of a feminist standpoint), as DeLissovoy (2008) specifically outlines in his critique. Rather, as explained in my above detailing of her work (and others'), for Hartsock (1998b) the issue is that of the standpoint of the oppressed, with an explicit recognition of how gender, in combination with other social locations such as race, class, and sexuality, influences how we "know" the world, which in turn influences and informs all research/knowledge projects in some way. As such, educational researchers making use of standpoint theory to look at intersections of gender and race, for instance, could further strengthen their analyses by explicitly acknowledging how class, race, sexuality and other aspects of our identities are an integral part of standpoint theory as well (Harding, 2004b).

However, DeLissovoy (2008) points to perhaps the most significant critique to be made of standpoint theory: It has been under theorized in educational theory generally, and curriculum studies more specifically. This is critical because, if standpoint theory is to be used more widely in education and fields such as curriculum studies, then a more fully elaborated framework is required. In what follows I offer such a framework in hopes that it can exist as a tool for the revitalization of curriculum studies, one that both acknowledges relations of power in school knowledge, but one that also is committed to the reformation of those same relations as they exist concretely in schools and society.

CURRICULAR STANDPOINT FOR CURRICULUM STUDIES

In light of the above discussion, I would argue that it is crucial that standpoint theory be brought more substantively and consciously into curriculum studies as an epistemological, methodological, and conceptual tool for the interrogation of and inquiry into school knowledge, one that recognizes the subjectivity associated with analyses of unequal social and educational relations, as well as one that embraces the centrality of addressing curricular issues in practice. In what follows I articulate a guiding framework for using the key aspects of standpoint theory, outlined above, as a model for what I refer to as curricular standpoint:

- First, curricular knowledge, as an extension and expression of material and social relations, structures our understanding of the world in ways that are both limiting and enabling. In this sense, the curriculum itself communicates epistemologies associated with particular social locations, and in doing so creates potentialities for understanding the world more clearly or in more obscurity relative to such locations.
- Second, because schools and school knowledge exist within institutional and social contexts that are themselves structured by systems of domination and rule organized hierarchically around power relations of race, class, gender, sexuality, nationality, and other forms of socially determined categorical difference, the curricular knowledge asserted by groups in power generally supports status quo, hegemonic social relations and epistemologies. This curricular knowledge thus often contradicts and runs counter to the epistemologies and curricular knowledge advanced by oppressed groups. Put differently, the curriculum of the ruler will in many ways be oppositional to the curriculum of the ruled.
- Third, because of unequal power relations, the curricular perspectives of those in power are made operational in generally hegemonic and commonsense forms in school knowledge for everyone, regardless of social location and regardless of whether or not such perspectives are congruent with (or contradict) the material and social realities of students, teachers, and their communities. Put differently, the unequal distribution of power leads to the unequal distribution of specific curricular knowledge, where those with more power can exert stronger influence on our commonsense understandings of the world vis-à-vis the curriculum, even if such commonsense understandings fundamentally operate as distorted conceptions of material and social reality.
- Fourth, because school knowledge is always embedded within dominant power relations, curricular standpoint requires struggle against those very same power relations. In this sense, curricular standpoint is achieved, not given, because it arises from active, systematic, and conscious reflection on and consideration of the reigning, hegemonic, institutionalized forms of curricular knowledge.
- Fifth, curricular standpoint carries with it the potential for human liberation because it works to reveal unequal social and material relations as part of a process that can (not will) contribute to the taking of action to change those same unequal social and material

relations. Further, curricular standpoint helps in the development of "oppositional consciousness" (Sandoval, 2000), as students, teachers, and researchers potentially develop ways of understanding the world that can trigger their own resistance to both status quo knowledge and relations, which in turn develops their capacity to take transformational action individually, institutionally, and socially. Thus, the potential of human liberation embedded in curricular standpoint move us beyond simple critique, as it also calls upon us to push both epistemological and curricular boundaries of the possible. In this sense, curricular standpoint requires a commitment not only to critique, but also to vision and creativity.

- Sixth, curricular standpoint requires that we seek to develop strong objectivity relative to curricular knowledge, that we be strongly reflexive not only about the standpoint of knowledge itself, but also strongly reflexive about the origins, politics, and process of how knowledge itself makes its way into the curriculum. Indeed, curricular standpoint is itself a product of strong objectivity, as it immediately and explicitly recognizes the politics of school knowledge in such a way that places the curriculum itself (as an object) on the same plane as the subject knowledge contained within the curriculum.

CURRICULAR STANDPOINT IN PRACTICE

In what follows I briefly analyze some curricular materials that embrace standpoint in practice. This undertaking serves two concrete purposes with regard to my discussion here. First, it serves as an example of the importance of linking curriculum studies to what teachers are doing with students in classrooms. Second, by analyzing how these teachers take up standpoint epistemology in their curricular practice, I am also offering an example of how the framework for curricular standpoint developed here can be used for further research in curriculum studies. In a sense, then, in what follows I use curricular standpoint to consider examples of curricular materials that themselves take up standpoint in the manner I advocate for here—offering curriculum standpoint in both form and function.

Although they are not explicitly articulated as such, there already exist a number of lesson plan collections and curricula that take up curricular standpoint (see, e.g., Cuauhtin et al., 2019b; Watson et al., 2018; Zinn Education Project, 2023). Christensen's (2014) "Putting Out the Linguistic Welcome Mat" provides a brief, concrete example of curricular standpoint in practice.

In this piece, Christensen (2014) discusses her curriculum on language and power and includes classroom strategies and resources she uses with her high school language arts students. She explains,

> During 30 years as a language arts classroom teacher, I realized that if I wanted my students to open up in their writing, to take risks and engage in intellectually demanding work, I needed to challenge assumptions about the superiority of Standard English and the inferiority of the home language of many of my black students: African American Vernacular English. . . . When students feel attacked by the red pen or the tongue for the way they write or speak, they either make themselves small—turning in short papers—or don't turn papers in at all. To build an engaging classroom where students from different backgrounds felt safe enough to dare to be big and bold in their writing, I had to build a curricular platform for them to stand on. . . . I finally realized that I needed to create a curriculum on language and power that examined the roots of language supremacy and analyzed how schools perpetuate the myths of the inferiority of some languages. (pp. 138–139)

Using a variety of films, readings, and writing activities, Christensen introduces her students to the origins and grammatical rules of African American Vernacular English (AAVE), and with stunning effect. As she recounts, as her African American students learned that AAVE actually had systemic linguistic roots in West African culture, they actively began to challenge forms of internalized racism they had learned relative to their home languages. Further, Christensen highlights how this curriculum aided students in developing a meta-cognitive understanding of not only the structures of AAVE, but also the relationship between AAVE and Standard English—thus creating the potential for these students to take conscious action relative to their own educational futures through an applied awareness of linguistic tools such as code-switching.

Christensen's (2014) classroom practice clearly takes up curricular standpoint: She explicitly acknowledges the ways in which social relations and systems of domination exist within classroom knowledge and linguistic practice (in this case, AAVE). In an attempt to have her curriculum reflect the social and material realities of her African American students, and in an embrace of the ways in which language intertwines with culture and identity, Christensen's curriculum thus takes up the standpoint of a marginalized form of the English language, while also taking the standpoint of a marginalized racial/cultural group within the United States. In the process she works with students to uncover linguistic relationships that may have been previously obscured from student consciousness. Further, Christensen's curricular standpoint represents a conscious act on the teacher's part, something that, after having reflected on decades of teaching, she had to work to achieve in her practice. Additionally, we see that this curricular standpoint embraces action in that Christensen also sees her curriculum as providing her students with increased abilities to develop their writing skills—a pedagogic move requires action on both the part of the teacher and the students. Finally, although Christensen uses AAVE as her starting point, she is quick to point out that the resources she uses actually speak to a wide range of nonstandard forms of the English language. Thus, the issue for Christensen is the validation of "home language," regardless of the cultural specifics of one's home.

Another good example of curricular standpoint in practice can be found in Gutstein's (2009) "Math, SATs, and Racial Profiling." In this piece, Gutstein describes the work he's done with students using lenses of race and class as a standpoint to connect students with his mathematics content. First, Gutstein discusses his mathematics lesson on racial profiling, where he explains that

> The essence of profiling is proportion and expected value: A higher proportion of African Americans (or Arabs/Arab Americans today) are stopped and searched than would be expected given their percentage in the population—assuming random (i.e., fair) searches or stops. (p. 342)

Using graphing calculators and dice, Gutstein leads students through activities that illustrate the concept of theoretical probability. Students then compare what they've learned about theoretical probability to statistics on police traffic stops, illustrating a clear pattern of racial profiling by police officers in the area.

In the same article, Gutstein (2009) describes similar work with mathematics students regarding issues of economic class and race relative to the college-entrance SAT exam. As part of a unit on data analysis and creating scatter plots (a type of graph that can be used to look at correlations between two variables), Gutstein's students use raw SAT data that has been disaggregated by race and class to look for correlations between the two datasets relative to SAT scores. Students found that SAT scores clearly correlated with family income, and they saw that specific racial groups, such as working-class Mexican Americans (the predominant racial group at Gutstein's school), were clustered close to the bottom. These data raised many questions for the students that revolved around issues of race and class relative to school achievement generally. In response, Gutstein's students wrote critical letters to the Educational Testing Service (the institutional body responsible for creating and administering the SAT) that outlined the correlations they found and that requested changes be made to this gatekeeper college entrance exam.

Much like the above example of Christensen's (2014) language arts curriculum, Gutstein's (2009) mathematics instruction also demonstrates curricular standpoint. Most immediately we see how Gutstein uses the social location both of his students as well as other marginalized communities more generally as a starting point for classroom knowledge projects. In doing so, he further pushes students to confront and reflect upon their social and material reality in a way that not only names important issues they face in their lives but also creates a potential for them to take action—large or small. Again, the curricular standpoint in Gutstein's teaching is also an achievement, because it too required a conscious struggle with the politics of knowledge in what is often incorrectly considered an apolitical subject area—mathematics. Students also took part in the process of achievement on two levels. First, from an academic skills perspective, these students are learning important mathematical concepts and putting them into practice. Second, from an epistemological perspective, these students are also struggling against the same apolitical conception of mathematics knowledge faced by their teacher and are also struggling with the political reality of educational inequality that the curricular standpoint brings to bear. This last point raises one of the most important aspects of Gutstein's curricular standpoint: Mathematics is used here to specifically gain a more strongly objective understanding of how the material and social world functions. Thus, it illustrates a reach for understanding reality more objectively and in ways that run contradictory to hegemonic constructions of both the legal and education systems in the United States as unbiased and individually "fair" institutions. Such understanding is critical because it always carries with it the potential for reconstruction, revision, and transformation (Bernstein, 1996).

TOWARD THE REVITALIZATION OF CURRICULUM STUDIES

In this chapter I've entered the scholarly debate surrounding the present state of the field of curriculum studies, its direction, and its future. I've argued that if the field of curriculum studies is to gain and maintain relevance with regard to education and what happens in schools, then curriculum studies would be well served by interrogating issues that are critically relevant to contemporary educational and social conditions, with particular attention paid to how power and inequality manifest in their myriad forms. The framework for curricular standpoint I've conceptualized and put into brief practice here offers one way (among many possibilities) for the field of curriculum studies to find such critical relevance. As such, I have provided a conceptual tool to justify the privileging of marginalized or oppressed groups in curriculum studies as part of an appeal to understanding material and social reality as it exists in ways that are more truthful and more objective than what hegemonic perspectives provide us. Curricular standpoint thus calls for the revitalization of the field of curriculum studies as a critical, intervening force in the struggle against the problems in our schools that have manifested during the current period of conservative modernization (Apple, 2006).

Part II

RACIAL (IN)JUSTICE AND NEOLIBERAL EDUCATION REFORM

CHAPTER 5

Racial Justice Is Not a Choice

White Supremacy, High-Stakes Testing, and the Punishment of Black and Brown Students

> Education is the great civil rights issue of our time.
>
> —Former U.S. President George W. Bush (2002)
>
> [The educational achievement gap] is the civil rights issue of our time.
>
> —Former U.S. Secretary of Education Rod Paige (2004)
>
> Education is the civil rights issue of our generation.
>
> —Former U.S. Secretary of Education Arne Duncan (2010)
>
> Education is the civil rights issue of our time.
>
> —Former U.S. President Barack Obama (2011)
>
> [Education is] the civil rights issue of our day.
>
> —Former U.S. Secretary of State Condoleeza Rice (2012)
>
> Education is the civil rights issue of our time.
>
> —U.S. President Donald Trump (2017)

Starting with the No Child Left Behind Act of 2001, the mantra has been this: There are race-based gaps in standardized test scores. Closing those gaps should be the goal for achieving racial equality in education. Connected to clear punishments for failure, we can use those tests to achieve this goal.

Since then, politicians from both parties have repeated that educational achievement gaps are the "civil rights issue" of today. This is why a number of mainstream civil rights organizations in May 2015 spoke out against the movement to opt out of high-stakes testing. Their argument: Without the data, we can't hold schools and teachers accountable for racial inequality.

Previously published as "Racial Justice Is Not a Choice: White Supremacy, High-Stakes Testing, and the Punishment of Black and Brown Students," 2019, *Rethinking Schools*, *33*(4). https://www.rethinkingschools.org/articles/racial-justice-is-not-a-choice. Reprinted by permission.

The problem is that high-stakes, standardized testing has not only failed at achieving racial equality, its proliferation from NCLB to the Every Student Succeeds Act has only exacerbated racial inequality and worsened the education for students of color. In a historical moment where we see the rise of Ethnic Studies in schools across the country and a push to make Black students' lives matter in schools, it is critical we understand that high-stakes, standardized tests do not serve students of color and in fact support white supremacy.

THE FAULTY (BIO)LOGICS OF TESTING FOR RACIAL JUSTICE

The logic of high-stakes testing for racial justice is simple: Standardized tests produce data that we can look at in order to identify "achievement gaps" among students. Then, if we don't see the scores of low-performing racial groups increase to close these gaps, teachers, schools, and students will be held "accountable" to punishments like funding cuts, charter school conversions, or withholding diplomas, among other measures, for failure to improve. The idea is that these threats will lead to higher test scores for low-income and kids of color.

There is an important truth underlying the impulse to use high-stakes test scores this way. Given the long history of racism and white supremacy in our public schools in the United States, when communities of color voice their wants to ensure that their children are being educated, it has to be taken seriously. However, despite the racial, cultural, emotional, and historical truth of this impulse, we have to also recognize that high-stakes standardized tests are incapable of achieving equality and also worsen racial inequality.

The arguments for using high-stakes testing for racial equality all assume that our standardized tests provide accurate measurements of teaching and learning such that increases in test scores equal educational improvement. This presumption does not hold true. Test scores correlate most strongly with family income, neighborhood, educational levels of parents, and access to resources—all factors that are measures of poverty that exist *outside* of schools.

This is not to say that schools and teachers are not important in student learning and achievement. However, it is to say that while teachers are central to how our children learn and experience education, the tests offer such narrow measures that they miss most of the processes, experiences, and relationships that define teaching and learning. Further, it is also to say that, as we have seen in so many "miracle" schools, a rise in test scores is rarely connected to genuine improvements in student learning and instead has typically been produced by gaming the system, being selective about who is enrolled in a school, or losing low achievers through attrition or expulsion.

It also important to recognize that high-stakes tests are not race-neutral tools capable of promoting racial equality. At their origins over 100 years ago, standardized tests were used as weapons against communities of color, immigrants, and the poor. Because they were presumed to be objective, test results were used to "prove" that whites, the rich, and the U.S.-born were biologically more intelligent than non-whites, the poor, and immigrants. In turn, the tests provided backing to early concepts of aptitude and I.Q., which were then used to justify the race, economic class, and cultural inequalities of the time.

For instance, in 1916, based on standardized test scores, Stanford professor Lewis Terman (one of the founding fathers of standardized testing in U.S. schools) argued that certain races inherited "deficient" IQs, saying that, "No amount of school instruction will ever make them intelligent voters or capable citizens." He further asserted that "feeblemindedness" was "very, very common among Spanish-Indian and Mexican families of the Southwest and also among negroes [sic]," going on to suggest that, "Children of this group should be segregated in special classes and be given instruction that is practical . . ." Terman reasoned that while these students were unable to "master abstractions," they still could be made into "efficient workers." This testing was then brought en masse into the growing public school system (in large part due to Terman work), and standardized test scores were used to justify educational tracking for kids of color, immigrants, and the poor.

This kind of test-informed inequality stems in part from the design paradigm of our standardized tests themselves: They were (and are) built on the assumption that human intelligence is based on biological aptitude that is "naturally" distributed across populations on a bell curve. This bell curve logic decrees that if a test were given to a large population, some would score high, a lot would be in the middle, and some would do very poorly.

The bell curve underlying the construction of high-stakes, standardized tests means that they will always produce high scorers and low scorers. Put differently, the assumed unequal distribution of intelligence built into the tests makes it impossible for everyone to pass and be deemed successful. This reality paints all discussion of closing the achievement gap in test scores in a new light. It does not mean everyone succeeds on the tests. Rather, "closing the achievement gap" in test scores means proportionate success and failure between groups, such that we have equal numbers of rich and poor students passing and failing, equal numbers of Black, white, Asian, Native, and Latinx passing and failing, etc.—all neatly and equally distributed along the bell curve.

Additionally, the test-and-punish logics of using high-stakes, standardized test to hold schools, teachers, and students "accountable" for race-based score improvement has failed miserably. While it is true that, for instance, according to a National Research Council 2011 report, test scores in math and English/language arts for Black and Latino students have generally risen since the implementation of NCLB, the report also points out that the test scores of white students have risen even more in the same time period. So, after over a decade of the punitive policies of NCLB, the threats against, and disciplining of, teachers, students, and schools have exacerbated racial test score gaps instead of closing them.

HIGH-STAKES TESTING AND THE DISCIPLINING OF BLACK AND BROWN BODIES

The idea of discipline is at the heart of policies and practices aimed at holding students, teachers, and schools "accountable" for raising test scores. There is physical discipline: Students are bound by a set amount of testing time. They must remain silent. Their movements are restricted, and generally they must stay seated. They also are taken out of their regular classrooms and are required to sit in test-specific rooms. They either cannot access resources beyond the assessment or are limited to only using specified resources (e.g., calculators). Testing happens under the disciplinary gaze of an authority (a test proctor) watching for transgressions.

There is also the discipline of enduring the stress and physical limits placed on students for hours at a time, as well as the emotional discipline of handling the stress of the high-stakes of the tests. While this test-imposed violence is bad for all kids, it is especially damaging to young children, who are expected to endure testing experiences that are entirely developmentally inappropriate for them.

High-stakes, standardized tests also discipline curriculum and learning: They determine what knowledge and content is considered legitimate for teaching in the classroom. They also discipline teachers' pedagogy because they compel teachers to teach to the test and place restrictions on depth and breadth of subject matter. Further, the tests discipline educational resources, as money gets used on test-aligned textbooks, teaching materials, technologies, and professional development.

While high-stakes, standardized testing disciplines all students, non-white and low-income students are disciplined with disproportionate intensity because the tests concentrate failure in their schools and communities. This means that low-income and kids of color are tested more; experience the greatest loss of time spent on non-tested or less-tested subjects like art, music, science, and social studies; don't have multicultural, anti-racist curriculum made available to them because those areas are not on the tests; and lose opportunities for culturally relevant instruction because the tests tend to inhibit process-based, student-centered instruction in favor of rote memorization.

Further, because of the increased intensity of testing and more restrictive curriculum and educational environment, high-stakes tests acculturate children of color to a norm of being disciplined by state authorities—they are tested more frequently, have their performance scrutinized more closely by educational officials and policymakers, punished more frequently for test performance, and subjected to more drastic "corrections" in curriculum and pedagogy than their white counterparts. The disciplining of Black and Brown children by high-stakes, standardized testing also manifests in very concrete and material ways; a 2013 study by the Economic Policy Institute found that in one state, having a high-stakes exit exam correlated with a 12.5% increase in the rate of incarceration. Again, given that these tests fail kids of color disproportionately, this study suggests that high-stakes, standardized tests are a conduit for the school-to-prison pipeline (Baker & Lang, 2013).

HIGH-STAKES TESTING AS RETRIBUTIVE JUSTICE

Ultimately, high-stakes, standardized testing, with its focus on surveillance, discipline, and punishment, represents a form of *retributive justice*. Built around the concept of "retribution" for a crime, retributive justice seeks vengeance for a wrongful act, and it is the cornerstone of our entire system of criminal justice in the United States. Howard Zehr (2011), Distinguished Professor of Restorative Justice at Eastern Mennonite University, explains that retributive justice operates along three questions:

- What rule has been broken?
- Who is to blame?
- What punishment do they deserve?

Educational "accountability" based on high-stakes testing is an expression of retributive justice. Our systems of accountability criminalize test failure and, instead of trying to fix the problem, policymakers use the results to punish students, teachers, schools, and communities.

Can we test our way to racial justice? Currently, we cannot. The paradigm of test and punish does not promote justice in any form. Indeed, looking at its impact, high-stakes, standardized tests serve to promote injustice and inflict acute damage on kids of color. However, there are other models beyond retributive justice, such as restorative and transformative justice. If high-stakes testing is retributive, can we conceive of assessments based on these other forms of justice?

RESTORATIVE ASSESSMENT

Restorative justice has become an increasingly popular alternative to models of disciplinary, retributive justice that are all too common in schools. According to Zehr, models of restorative justice ask a different set of questions:

- Who has been hurt and what are their needs?
- Who is obligated to address these needs?
- Who has a "stake" in this situation, and what is the process of involving them in making things right and preventing future occurrences?

Following this, a model of assessment aimed at racial justice would begin by recognizing that students of color have been hurt by institutionalized racism and white supremacy in our schools and that our current assessments have perpetuated this hurt. Further, a restorative assessment model would then need to explicitly name who is obligated to address the institutionalized racism and white supremacy faced by our students in their schools. We would also need to attend to who has voice and power in determining the assessment, as well as their role and responsibility in making things right.

Restorative assessment would also take seriously the idea of healing our kids and communities. Imagine the possibility of an assessment that would be a part of a process of healing the hurt caused by white supremacy and institutionalized racism. Imagine an assessment that was culturally responsive in form and content, one that assessed students for identity development, knowledge of self, cultural knowledge, and confronting internalized oppression/colonization.

Aspects of restorative assessment exist in some places. For instance, much of Linda Christensen's work, which asks students to write powerfully through pain, or to consider race, class, and the power of language in their lives, begins to point the way toward forms of restorative assessment in the classroom. Her lessons often urge students to express their identities through language, in the process humanizing them while opening pathways toward healing. The practices and pedagogy of the banned Mexican American Studies program in Tucson, Arizona also orient us toward restorative assessment, as they engaged their students in deep learning that sought to decolonize curriculum and their cultural selves.

At the elementary level, Milwaukee Public Schools adopted goals and performance indicators explicitly about the need for students to demonstrate anti-racist and anti-biased attitudes vis-à-vis experiences through a multilingual, culturally diverse curriculum. For instance, at La Escuela Fratney, a two-way bilingual elementary school in Milwaukee, students have used gallery walks and student-led parent conferences where they demonstrated knowledge of their own cultures, skills for working in diverse groups, detection of stereotypes, strategies to fights racist experiences, and reading and writing in languages other than English.

These examples also illustrate another important aspect of restorative assessment: It just looks like good, powerful teaching. In this sense, restorative assessment helps us see how teaching that is grounded in students' lives and experiences, teaching that fosters students' understanding of themselves and their communities, is so intimately bound up with how teachers see what students are learning that assessment and instruction can become indistinguishable. Both are happening at once.

Restorative assessment also invites a conversation about the very forms our assessments take. For instance, as opposed to numerical scores generated by the typical high-stakes, standardized test, process-based portfolios and performance assessments allow for more nuanced, human, and complex expressions of student learning, growth, and development that could more accurately embody restoration and healing. It also puts the very idea of A–F and decimal grading systems into question since those singular grades and decimal scores perform the same functions of surveillance and punishment as standardized tests. The types of critical self-reflection and self-evaluation that can be built into strong portfolios and performance assessments, as well as narrative evaluations by teachers, are more restorative since they ask us to assess through conversation, relationships, and centering the power of assessment more within students themselves.

The public New York Performance Standards Consortium schools have produced evidence that this kind of assessment is more effective with students of color in particular. In the consortium, in order to graduate high school, students are required to produce a series of portfolios across multiple subject areas to demonstrate their skills and learning, and then they are also required to defend that portfolio to a panel of teachers, peers, and communities. The consortium schools have significantly lower dropout rates and higher college attainment rates for their low-income students, students of color, and English language learners than other comparable public schools.

TRANSFORMATIVE ASSESSMENT

However, because restorative justice focuses mainly on individual wrongdoing and individual events, many activists see it as just a step toward something bigger: transformative justice—which recognizes the conditions that contributed to and shape wrongdoing. According to Zehr, transformative justice asks a set of distinctly different questions than both retributive and restorative models of justice:

- What social circumstances produced the harmful behavior?
- What structures exist between this structure and others like it?
- What measures could prevent further occurrences?

If we applied these to thinking through what transformative assessment might look like, then it suggests a series of skills and a knowledge base that we want to make sure our students are learning. For instance, we might assess students on their understanding of what historical and socioeconomic circumstances produced the institutionalized racism and white supremacy we see in our schools. Given the continued focus on high-stakes testing in education policy and practice, transformative assessment could also check for student understanding of how testing itself reproduces inequalities and maintains white supremacy.

As is implied by the name, transformative assessment could also assess students on their understanding of, and capacities for, institutional and community transformation. This could include assessing their knowledge of strategies for challenging institutional racism in their schools, districts, and communities.

From an activist and transformational perspective, there are concrete skills, understandings, and forms of resistance that we want to foster and develop in our students as potentially powerful individuals and collectives. If we want to assess those skills, then we are forced to consider forms of assessment that are not retributive and ways that are not connected to our current norms and assumptions about standardized testing and accountability.

For instance, in May 2016, students at Forest Grove High School outside of Portland, Oregon protested a Trump-inspired "build a wall" banner that was hung at their school. Hundreds of Forest Grove High School students walked out and rallied against the act of racism. Soon, as word spread through social media, they were joined by students from six other high schools in the area. In the following days, students from Portland high schools and Portland Community College joined for a rally in the city of Portland itself. It was a powerful moment for student organizing in the Portland area that helped sharpen people's consciousness about anti-immigrant racism in the region.

As just one possibility among many in recent years, the example of Forest Grove High School students shows that there are basic skill sets for organizing that we could see in student learning through transformative assessment. The Forest Grove example also shows that there are forms of consciousness and political orientations that are anti-racist and oppositional to structural authority, helping students understand and act on their collective power in transformative ways. Indeed, activism like that of the Forest Grove students also points to the important relationship between restorative and transformative assessment: Restorative assessment, with its focus on healing, cultural self-knowledge, and decolonization, can help foster the kinds of critical consciousness that can contribute directly to student involvement in mass mobilizations and movements for social justice we might connect with transformative assessment.

Further, student organizing in Forest Grove and elsewhere suggests the possibility that we can create and wield restorative and transformative assessments to foster this kind of activism as a central aspect of public education. Such assessments would have to challenge racism and white supremacy with a focus on cultural and community healing and radical institutional transformation. Such assessments would also have to be constructed to openly challenge hegemonic power and require a complete break from our current system and logics of high-stakes, standardized testing.

RECLAIMING ASSESSMENT

The possibility of restorative and transformative assessment is a call for educators and students to reclaim the very idea of "assessment" from the high-stakes standardized tests and corporate education reformers using them for profits and privatization. It invites us to see the very act of assessment as both a tool of healing and a tool of assessment as a means to fight the white supremacist legacies of public education in this country. Further, this reclaiming of assessment is also critical for activists and educators working to reform the disciplinary practices of schools. The simple fact is that you can't practice restorative and transformative justice in schools that rely on retributive forms of assessment like high-stakes, standardized testing. The healing and hopefulness of one is smothered by the punishment and pain of the other.

Right now, there are real fights in the streets about police killings of Black people, about xenophobia, nationalism, and white supremacy, about native sovereignty and the protection of the environment against the ravages of a fossil fuel economy, about gentrification, livable wages, access to health care, epidemic homelessness, and the lack of affordable housing. Students are struggling with these issues in their lives and are out protesting in the streets. Our students need restorative understandings to help them make sense of their lives and times, and they need to know about transformative strategies and skill sets that they can use in these fights. The possibility of restorative and transformative assessment is a call for educators to create forms of schooling and assessment that are liberatory, partisan, and in the interest of justice.

CHAPTER 6

Dispossession and Defiance

A Race and Class Political Economy of Neoliberal Education Reform

There is a specter haunting public education in the United States—the specter of neoliberalism. Like other "public" services in our country, our system of public education is being transformed in fundamental ways. It is being financialized and turned into a profit-making sector while whatever semblance of democratic, public control and accountability—however imperfect—is steadily eroded in the name of individual "choice" and models of free market competition. This unfurling of neoliberalization in public schools, most often in the name of individual freedom and racial equality, consumes the poor and communities of color, preparing the bulk of our graduates for jobs in the service sector, the unstable hustle of the "gig" economy, and, for Black and Brown kids in particular, transition from hyper disciplinary school systems to the prison system.

This chapter outlines both the structural race and class inequalities perpetuated by today's capitalist, free market–styled education reforms, but also highlights the kinds of grassroots and community resistances that have grown in the struggle for educational justice. I begin this chapter with an overview of neoliberalism and how high-stakes testing and charter schools support the transformation of public education into quasi-markets for capitalist competition and profit. I then explore major problems with charter schools as a tool for equity-based education reform, and I address both the inaccuracies of high-stakes, standardized testing and how such tests only reproduce race and class inequities. I then reframe both high-stakes testing and charter schools as forms of corporate, colonial plundering of communities of color, outlining how they essentially channel economic resources into the coffers of both the testing and charter industries. I conclude this chapter by offering concrete examples of how communities of color have actively organized to resist this corporate plundering.

Previously published as "Dispossession and Defiance: A Race and Class Political Economy of Neoliberal Education Reform," in W. Au, *A Marxist Education: Learning to Change the World*, 2018. Haymarket Books.

NEOLIBERALISM AND THE TRANSFORMATION OF PUBLIC EDUCATION

As Harvey (2007) explains, neoliberalism is "a theory of political economic practices proposing that human well-being can be best advanced by the maximization of entrepreneurial freedoms within an institutional framework characterized by private property rights, individual liberty, unencumbered markets, and free trade" (p. 22). Similarly, Lipman (2011) defines neoliberalism as

> . . . an ensemble of economic and social policies, forms of governance, and discourses of ideologies that promote self-interest, unrestricted flows of capital, deep reductions in the cost of labor, and sharp retrenchment of the public sphere. Neoliberals champion privatization of social good and withdrawal of government from provision for social welfare on the premise that competitive markets are more effective and efficient. (p. 6)

Fundamentally, neoliberalism is the idea that market competition operates to the benefit of everyone, and that any barrier to free market competition needs to be done away with to let the market run free. For neoliberals, regulations associated with environmental protections, minimum wages, unions, worker protections, or taxes are all seen as barriers to the free market, and as such, they should be highly curtailed or abolished completely. In this sense, a fundamental principle of neoliberalism is deregulation. Another principle of neoliberalism that extends directly from deregulation is that the public sector is best served by free market competition as well. This means that according to the neoliberal ideal, anything we might associate with being a "public" service—parks, roads, military operations, public transportation, health care, welfare, state universities, and public schools, among others—would be better and more efficient if they were turned into private, competitive markets. In the neoliberal imaginary, anything public is bad, and anything private is good.

The neoliberal vision of public education is one of a competitive market where students, teachers, schools, and administrators are ranked against one another using high-stakes, standardized test scores as the primary metric for comparison (Au, 2023b). In this vision, teachers' unions are a barrier to the competitive hiring and firing of "good" or "bad" teachers (Compton & Weiner, 2008; B. Jones, 2015)—as determined by student test scores (American Statistical Association, 2014; Amrein-Beardsley, 2014), teacher labor becomes more controlled through test-aligned curriculum (Au, 2011b), and the teaching profession itself is deregulated through quick teacher training programs (e.g., Teach for America), resulting in both the deprofessionalization of teaching and an attack on university-based teacher education programs (Kretchmar et al., 2014; Zeichner & Pena-Sandoval, 2015). Further, within the neoliberal revisioning of public education, and as something akin to small businesses, public schooling is turned into a competition for students through the advent of deregulated charter schools run by for-profit or nonprofit charter management organizations and governed by appointed boards, again to be compared, judged, and potentially closed, also based on test scores (Fabricant & Fine, 2013; Stovall, 2020).

We can also see the neoliberal transformation of public education through the changes in discourse about, and the purposes of, education. For instance, the very language of educational bureaucracies has changed. Borrowing from the corporate sector, high-level district administrators are now referred to as chief executive officers (CEOs), chief financial officers (CFOs), and chief operations officers (COOs), and instead of being concerned with learning, schools are enmeshed in paradigms built around growth targets and benchmarks in test scores. Students and parents are subsequently reframed as consumers/customers, and teachers, schools, and principals are similarly reframed as service providers. This neoliberal shift in language also signals a more profound shift in the very purposes of education: Under neoliberalism, education is increasingly focused on the production of "human capital," "adding value," and meeting the needs of the economy, instead of, for instance, serving the social good or meeting collective needs of communities (Apple, 2001; Lipman, 2011).

Under neoliberalism, responsibilities for governing are also increasingly shifted from democratically elected state governments toward private bodies that are unelected and unaccountable to the voting public. As Lipman (2011) explains, this is a radical shift from *government* to *governance*:

> The "triumph of market ideology" is coupled with an erosion of the idea that informed citizens should make decisions based on the general welfare. The shift from *government* by elected state bodies and a degree of democratic accountability to *governance* by experts and managers and decision making by judicial authority and executive order is central to neoliberal policy making . . . Public-private partnerships, appointed managers, and publicly unaccountable bodies comprised of appointed state and corporate leaders make decisions about urban development, transportation, schools, and other public infrastructure using business rationales. In these arrangements, the state acts as an agent of capital. (p. 13, original emphasis)

In education we see this move toward neoliberal governance in very particular ways. For instance, in several urban school districts there has been a push to discard publicly elected school boards and replace them with autocratic, top-down mayoral control (Kirst, 2002; Stovall, 2020; K. K. Wong & Shen, 2005). We can also see the rise of neoliberal governance through the role that billionaires like Bill Gates and their respective foundations play in setting local and national education policy agendas. Through individual personal donations and via their philanthropies, these elites have leveraged their vast wealth to push their own educational policy agendas through funding a complex network of nonprofit organizations, political advocacy groups, individual candidates running for offices, research centers, endowed university professorships, education reporting, and former employees placed in high-level federal education positions (Au &

Ferrare, 2014; Au & Lubienski, 2016; Barkan, 2011, 2012; Klonsky, 2011; Saltman, 2011; Zeichner & Pena-Sandoval, 2015). They are aided by a neoliberal tax policy that has lowered taxes on the top income earners, transferring wealth from the state—that could have been pumped into cash-strapped public schools—back into the hands of the wealthy. As such, among others, Bill Gates and the Bill and Melinda Gates Foundation were essential in bringing the Common Core State Standards to the United States along with all the itinerant tests, Common Core–aligned textbooks and curriculum, Common Core–aligned standardized tests developed by either the Partnership for Assessment of Readiness for College and Careers (PARCC) or the Smarter Balanced Assessment Consortium (SBAC), and the technological platform required to deliver these tests entirely on computers (Layton, 2014). Gates and other billionaire philanthropists have also pushed charter schools at the local and national levels, among other policy initiatives (Au & Ferrare, 2014).

One of the central problems for this form of neoliberal governance of education is that these billionaires are setting policy agendas for public schools, even though they were never elected. They are powerful purely because of amassed or inherited wealth. What is worse is that they cannot be held accountable for any damage they cause or any of the failures of their policies (Ravitch, 2013). For instance, in 2013, in a talk he gave at Harvard University, Bill Gates commented, "It would be great if our education stuff worked, but that we won't know for probably a decade" (Strauss, 2013). In the meantime, what happens if his policies are failures, as was the case with the Gates-funded small schools movement of the 1990s (Klonsky, 2011)? Who will be held accountable for the potential hurt done to students, schools, and communities left in the wake of these neoliberal education policies being driven by wealthy elites? This points to yet another issue with this kind of neoliberal governance by wealthy elites: They are experimenting on other peoples' children, not their own. The children of Bill and Melinda Gates attended ultra-elite, extremely well-resourced private schools—the kinds of schools that don't bother with high-stakes testing, Common Core standards, or restrictive curriculum reserved for the rest of us, especially the poor (HiPointDem, 2012; KrazyTA, 2014).

Bill Gates is just a convenient example here, and I use him not only because I think he is destroying public education and trampling on whatever limited democracy we have left, but also because I think he embodies a set of class interests and commonsense ideology that is an expression of neoliberal education reform in action. These folks, and others like the Walton and Broad families, simply see the world in terms of markets, profits, and financialization. Again, for the sake of consistency, here is something Bill Gates (2009) said in a speech to the National Conference on State Legislatures as part of the ramp-up to the implementation of the Common Core State Standards:

> When the tests are aligned to the common standards, the curriculum will line up as well—and that will unleash powerful market forces in the service of better teaching.

> For the first time, there will be a large base of customers eager to buy products that can help every kid learn and every teacher get better.

It is a vision of the world, education included, as one giant market, ready for production, purchases, and profiteering.

In this light, the neoliberal transformation of public education is not just about re-creating policy and practice as a financial market, it is also about generating profits from public education resources. As Fabricant and Fine (2013) explain:

> In public education, we have witnessed the ascent of charter schools, virtual learning, market curricula development, and an expansive number of firms engaged in the measurement and assessment of teachers, with a host of entrepreneurs making large and small profits. More specifically, profit making extends from publishers capitalizing on the new standards-based testing curricula, to high-tech companies experimenting and testing their curricula interventions, to real estate operators leasing property to exorbitant fees, to alternative certification programs, and finally for-profit schools. Each of these fragments, pieces of profit making, are part of a new "gold rush" to capitalize . . . public assets being redistributed from neighborhood K-12 public schooling to the marketplace. (p. 25)

Further, as Burch (2021) has found in her research, substantial amounts of the profit-making from public schooling comes through "hidden markets" generated through federal policy—namely in areas like transportation, tutoring, and other services that are contracted out to private firms. Importantly, both high-stakes, standardized testing and charter schools are central to the entire endeavor of the neoliberal transformation of public education.

TESTING, CHARTERS, AND NEOLIBERAL EDUCATION REFORM

High-stakes, standardized tests are just one form of assessment among many possible assessments of learning. They are "high-stakes" if official and unofficial consequences are attached to test results. Such consequences could include not graduating from high school, not receiving funding, not moving from one grade level to the next, not earning college credit, not getting a certificate or diploma, and having a bad public reputation. Tests are "standardized" in that the intent is to give the same test, in the same format, under similar or the same conditions, to a variety of students in different school and classroom contexts. The test questions themselves are also "standardized" because they are (supposedly) constructed to measure whether or not test-takers are meeting standards (specific subject matter standards, the Common Core State Standards, or other sets of goals or objectives), and they are built on the ideal that they measure "normal" levels of performance among student populations (Au, 2023b).

Most of us know standardized testing through our own experiences in schools, where, depending on age, where you lived, and level of education, any one of us might have taken the following tests: CATs (older K–12 test), STAR (the Texas K–12 test), ACT (college entrance), AP (college credit in high school), ITBS (older K–12 test), SAT (college entrance), SBAC (Common Core–aligned K–12 test), PARCC (another Common Core–aligned K–12 test), PRAXIS (teacher education subject matter test), EdTPA (teacher education performance evaluation), LSAT (to get into law school), the state bar exam (to become a licensed lawyer), GRE (general education high school graduation exam), or MAP (K–12 test), among many other possibilities. All of them were timed tests, probably delivered under the watchful eye of an official proctor or teacher or computer program; mainly consisted of a lot of multiple-choice questions, a lot of reading, and some short-answer questions; and your answers and results were determined by either a computer or some unknown, faraway person (or a combination of both). Most importantly, all of them took your effort, time, and testing conditions and boiled them down to a single number or small set of numbers. And this gets at the official point of all standardized testing: to create simplified metrics to easily and efficiently compare students, teachers, schools, states, and countries to one another in order to say, this kid knows more than that kid, that teacher must be better than this other teacher, and this school/state/country is better at educating than this other school/state/country.

Comparison is why high-stakes, standardized testing is so central to the neoliberal transformation of public education: The tests provide the metrics for neoliberals to determine the value of student performance as a product, thereby also creating the conditions for viewing the system of education as a competitive market. Then individual consumers (parents) can use the test scores—almost like stock values—to choose which producer (schools) will make the best product (their "educated" children). Those schools that produce low test scores (a low-quality, low-value product/student) will lose customers and ultimately close, and those schools that produce high test scores (a high-quality product/student) will thrive. Subsequently, in this neoliberal edutopia, the quality of all schooling will improve as the market mechanism works itself out as "bad" schools close and only the "good" schools remain open for business. As an example, here is what George W. Bush's (1999) presidential campaign speech delivered to the conservative think-tank the Manhattan Institute regarding his own business-like vision for public education free market competition:

> Federal funds will no longer flow to failure. Schools that do not teach and will not change must have some final point of accountability. A moment of truth, when their Title I funds are divided up and given to parents, for tutoring or a charter school or some other hopeful option. In the best case, schools that are failing will rise to the challenge and regain the confidence of parents. In the worst case, we will offer scholarships to America's neediest children.

Bush said this decades ago, just as the neoliberal, corporate education reform juggernaut was really being put into motion. In a way he was prescient in that most of these policies all came to fruition in 2002 when No Child Left Behind was signed into law—which leant federal support to both high-stakes testing and charter schools (Au, 2023b), while other Republican presidents have tried to implement a voucher system in the United States that would allow parents to use public monies to enroll their child in highly discriminatory religious private schools (Joseph, 2017).

In this way, charter schools are also strongly linked to high-stakes testing within the project of neoliberal educational reform; the tests establish the metric for the comparison and charter schools establish market-like competition among schools. In theory, charter schools are just that—schools that are granted a charter by some authority to provide education to students using public school dollars. The idea is that the charter schools would be exempt from most of the regulatory requirements and agencies that public schools are connected to (i.e., unions, elected school boards, school districts) in order to be more flexible in terms of curriculum, teaching, structure, and style (Dingerson et al., 2008; Karp, 2013). Then, with this added flexibility and deregulation, charter schools could become hothouses of educational innovation, giving parents and communities more choices for their children's education beyond the regular public system. Or in the language of neoliberalism, charter schools could compete with regular public schools for market share (parent "investment" vis-à-vis student enrollment), under the assumption that the good charters would increase the quality of education and raise student achievement, thereby attracting more students from other charter or public schools (which might eventually close due to loss of market share). Importantly, in this neoliberal vision of the school marketplace, the public tax dollars will follow the children into their school of "choice" (Au, 2012c).

Combined, high-stakes testing and charter schools illustrate two theories of action that underlie neoliberal education reform:

1. The threat of disciplinary action, public scrutiny, and loss of resources attached to standardized tests will cause students, teachers, and schools to try harder, do better, improve teaching and learning, increase test scores, and raise the overall quality of education. Consequently, as a result of such improvement, and as a result of the improved transparency arising from test score data, such testing will also work to close gaps in test scores between the rich and poor, as well as between different racial groups.
2. The deregulation of a specific set of schools—charter schools—will grant more flexibility to those schools, allowing them to be more innovative in program and structure, thereby also allowing them to meet the needs of a variety of students and increasing achievement. Thus, charter schools, operating in competition for students and using

high-stakes test scores as the main metric, will raise the overall quality of education because only good charter schools will survive, while the less effective schools (charter or public) will wither and close as they lose students.

There are, of course, all sorts of problems with this entire model—foremost among them being the idea that opening and closing schools as part of market competition, with total disregard to what school closings do to communities, is somehow healthy and good. Further, this model does not hold up under any kind of empirical scrutiny.

THE TROUBLES WITH CHARTERS

Charter schools, for instance, are not living up to any of their promises. Setting aside the numerous scandals involving embezzlement, cheating, and other illegal practices that have manifested due to deregulation and lack of public oversight (Center for Popular Democracy & Integrity in Education, 2014; Higgins, 2013; Rawls, 2013), charter schools fall short on promises to innovate, increase achievement, and serve all students. Regarding innovation, even staunch supporters of charters, many working in institutes, programs, and research centers paid for by charter and "choice" advocates like the Gates and Broad foundations, are finding in their research that charter schools are not more innovative than regular public schools in form, structure, curriculum personnel, space, bell schedules, grade levels, or use of technology (Lake, 2008; Preston et al., 2012). The findings with regard to charter school performance are similar. A 2012 review of 83 charter school achievement studies spanning 12 years found that charter schools perform similarly to public schools (Miron & Urschel, 2012). The largest studies of charter performance were done by the Center for Research on Educational Outcomes (CREDO). Interestingly, despite CREDO's openly pro-charter school stance, in their 2009 study they found, for instance, that 17% of charters outperformed public schools in mathematics test scores, but also that 46% were indistinguishable, and the remaining 37% performed significantly worse than public schools (CREDO, 2009). Similarly, in their updated, 2013 study, while charter school performance in math improved somewhat—with 29% now outperforming public schools—40% were still indistinguishable, and 31% performed worse than public schools (CREDO, 2013). A 2016 study of Chicago's charter schools found that by nearly every measure they performed worse than Chicago's public schools, with the report's authors explaining:

> This study uses comprehensive data for the 2012–13 and 2013–14 school years to show that, after controlling for the mix of students and challenges faced by individual schools, Chicago's charter schools underperform their traditional counterparts in most measurable ways. Reading and math pass rates, reading and math

> growth rates, graduation rates, and average ACT scores (in one of the two years) are lower in charters all else equal, than in traditional neighborhood schools. The results for the two years also imply that the gap between charters and traditionals widened in the second year for most of the measures. The findings are strengthened by the fact that self-selection by parents and students into the charter system biases the results in favor of charter schools. (Orfield & Luce, 2016, p. 3)

Apparently charter schools are not the magic bullet for student achievement that proponents claim them to be.

Charter schools also fail when it comes to serving all students. As Simon (2013) found in her report for Reuters, charters have several ways of controlling who walks through their doors:

- Applications that are made available just a few hours a year
- Lengthy application forms, often printed only in English, that require student and parent essays, report cards, test scores, disciplinary records, teacher recommendations, and medical records
- Demands that students present Social Security cards and birth certificates for their applications to be considered, even though such documents are not required under federal law
- Mandatory family interviews
- Assessment exams
- Academic prerequisites
- Requirements that applicants document any disabilities or special needs (see also Welner, 2013)

This process is commonly called "creaming," where charter schools attempt to selectively enroll students—one way to try to improve test scores. Whether or not purposefully through selective enrollment, it is clear from multiple studies that charter schools enroll students with disabilities or English language learners at much lower rates than public schools (Frankenberg et al., 2013; Miron et al., 2010; Simon, 2013; Vasquez Heilig et al., 2016). These students are both more expensive to educate (because they require more resources) and tend to perform more poorly on standardized tests.

A brief look at Dr. Steve Perry's Capital Preparatory Magnet School, a much-lauded charter school in Hartford, Connecticut, serves as a prime example. Dr. Perry, the school's principal, has become a darling of neoliberal corporate education reformers because Capital Prep, as it is commonly referred to, annually boasts a 100% college acceptance rate for its graduates. However, we need to look more closely at Dr. Perry's school to understand its apparent success. For instance, when compared to surrounding schools in Hartford, Capital Prep serves far fewer English language learners, far fewer students with disabilities, and far fewer students in extreme poverty—sometimes on the order of 30–50% less comparable in each category (Weber, 2013b). As the blogger Jersey Jazzman explains, "Simply put: Capital Prep does not serve the children of Hartford who are the most difficult and expensive to educate" (Weber, 2013b). Further, Capital Prep loses lots of students between 9th-grade and graduation, where, for instance, the class of 2010 had a 36% attrition rate and the class of 2011 had a 35% attrition rate. And finally, despite having a selective school population, Dr. Perry's Capital Prep actually performs worse on the SAT and only barely does better on state math and reading tests compared to surrounding Hartford schools (Weber, 2013b).

THE TROUBLES WITH TESTING

Of course, just because charter school advocates and neoliberal education reformers use high-stakes, standardized test scores as a metric does not mean that the tests themselves are valid measures of learning or teaching. Policymakers and much of the public generally assume that the scores generated through high-stakes, standardized tests are fairly objective and hence are accurate measures of teaching and student learning. The entire apparatus of neoliberal education reform is built upon this assumption because without it, there would be no way to compare students, teachers, and schools, and hence, no way to create a competitive market or use those test scores to threaten discipline or loss of resources. If we don't presume the accuracy of the test scores, the entire system cannot function. It is the fuel for their machine (Au, 2023b; Au & Hollar, 2016).

The thing is, researchers have regularly and continually found our high-stakes, standardized tests to be wholly inaccurate measures of teaching and learning. For example, there has been a movement to try to use high-stakes tests to evaluate teachers, called value-added measurement (VAM). The idea is that if the teacher is effective, then student test scores will increase, and therefore we can accurately measure how much value the teacher added to the student's learning/test score (Amrein-Beardsley, 2014). Of course, if these tests offered accurate measures of learning, and if learning happened in a simple linear, additive progression, then we might be able to find such causality to be true. However, in one U.S. Department of Education's National Center for Education Statistics report, researchers found a statistical error rate of 35% when using one year's worth of test data to measure a teacher's effectiveness, and an error rate of 25% when using data from 3 years (Schochet & Chiang, 2010). This means that the data produced by tests are so inaccurate that even with 3 years of scores, there is still a one-in-four chance that using those scores to evaluate a teacher's "value-added" will be entirely wrong.

Another study found that students' test scores fluctuated wildly from year to year, where the same teacher was rated as being in the top 20% one year and rated in the bottom 40% the following year (Sass, 2008). Unless this teacher committed self-sabotage in the second year, the only real variable that changed was the students, not the teaching. Another issue that belies the accuracy of high-stakes, standardized testing to measure teaching and learning is the change in test scores based on one-time random, day-of-testing occurrences. One study found that factors like whether or not a child ate breakfast on test day; if a window was open and a distracting dog was barking outside during the test; whether or not a child got into an argument with their parents or classmates on the way to school; what students were in attendance while taking the test; whomever happened to be administering the test; and so forth actually account for 50–80% of any improvement or decline of a student's standardized test score (Kane & Staiger, 2002). If these tests were accurate measures of teaching and learning, then the scores should not be so sensitive to random occurrences and subject to such wild fluctuations.

While there are a whole host of other reasons why high-stakes, standardized tests are not accurate measures of teaching and learning (Amrein-Beardsley, 2014; Au, 2023b; E. L. Baker et al., 2010), there are other important reasons to question the objectivity of the test scores. The lack of objectivity of test scores becomes most clear when it comes to the grading of standardized writing tests. In one account, DiMaggio (2010) worked as a writing test grader for the U.S. testing company Pearson for several years and wrote about what it was like to be a part-time worker on a temporary contract for them:

> In test-scoring centers, dozens of scorers sit in rows, staring at computer screens where students' papers appear (after the papers have undergone some mysterious scanning process). I imagine that most students think their papers are being graded as if they are the most important thing in the world. Yet every day, each scorer is expected to read hundreds of papers. So for all the months of preparation and the dozens of hours of class time spent writing practice essays, a student's writing probably will be processed and scored in about a minute . . .
>
> Scoring is particularly rushed when scorers are paid by piece-rate, as is the case when you are scoring from home, where a growing part of the industry's work is done. At 30 to 70 cents per paper, depending on the test, the incentive, especially for a home worker, is to score as quickly as possible in order to earn any money. . . .

Perhaps even worse, DiMaggio goes on to explain how he and other scorers were told to change their scores to create results consistent with the previous year's tests:

> Usually, within a day or two, when the scores we are giving are inevitably too low (as we attempt to follow the standards laid out in training), we are told to start giving higher scores, or, in the enigmatic language of scoring directors, to "learn to see more papers as a 4." For some mysterious reason, unbeknownst to test scorers, the scores we are giving are supposed to closely match those given in previous years. So if 40 percent of papers received 3s the previous year (on a scale of 1 to 6), then a similar percentage age should receive 3s this year.

These kinds of practices led Farley (2009a; see also 2009b, 2010), a former employee in the U.S. testing industry of 15 years, to reflect:

> . . . [T]he test-scoring industry cheats. . . . It cheats on qualification tests to make sure there is enough personnel to meet deadlines/get tests scored; it cheats on reliability scores to give off the appearance of standardization even when that doesn't exist; it cheats on validity scores and calibration scores and anything else that might be needed. . . . Statistical tomfoolery and corporate chicanery were the hallmark of my test-scoring career, and while I'm not proud of that, it is a fact. Remember, I was never in the testing business for any reason other than to earn a pay check, just like many of the testing companies are in it solely to make a buck. (2009a)

So, if high-stakes, standardized tests are not as objective as we think and are not very good at measuring teaching and learning, what are they good at measuring? Among other things, poverty.

As Berliner (2013) explains, our high-stakes test scores mostly correspond with the kinds of experiences and resources available to children outside of schools:

> Virtually every scholar of teaching and schooling knows that when the variance in student scores on achievement tests is examined along with the many potential factors that may have contributed to those test scores, school effects account for about 20% of the variation in achievement test scores. . . .
>
> On the other hand, out-of-school variables account for about 60% of the variance that can be accounted for in student achievement. In aggregate, such factors as family income; the neighborhood's sense of collective efficacy, violence rate, and average income; medical and dental care available and used; level of food insecurity; number of moves a family makes over the course of a child's school years; . . . provision of high-quality early education in the neighborhood; language spoken at home; and so forth, all substantially affect school achievement.

This is perhaps one of the greatest tricks of the neoliberal education reform project: Their primary tools for reform—charter schools, high-stakes testing to hold teachers and schools accountable, and deregulated teacher education programs, among others—are premised on holding individual teachers and schools wholly accountable for achievement, when we have known from decades of research that non-school factors associated with socioeconomic inequality are overwhelmingly important to school outcomes (including flawed test scores).

We should not be surprised by this, however, because it is entirely consistent with the logic of neoliberalism. In the case of the neoliberal reform of education, instead of addressing the systemic inequalities that produce hunger, housing insecurity, lack of health care, etc.—all things that could improve a child's educational performance in ways more substantial than any single school-focused intervention—the neoliberal's approach to is to hoist all responsibility on the individual who is supposed to hustle, innovate, or gig themselves out of poverty. This is critically important given how rampant poverty is in the United States, and it has been steadily getting worse. According to the Economic Policy Institute, we are currently experiencing levels of income inequality that matches the 1920s, where in 2013 the top 1% of families made 25.3 times that of the other 99% (Sommeiller et al., 2016). In terms of what this means for children in our schools, the National Center for Children in Poverty reports that 43% or 30.6 million children under the age of 18 live in low-income families, and 21% or 14.8 million children live in poor families officially below the federal poverty line—a trend that has been fairly consistent since 2010 (Jiang et al., 2017).

There are three important points about high-stakes testing that are worth adding here. The first is that the above argument—that schools and teachers only account for about 20% of any standardized test score—is often also used by the same neoliberal education reformers to argue that schools and teachers aren't that important, so it doesn't really matter who is teaching students or how much resources a school (or school system) has. Ironically, and contrarily, these reformers also often argued, *at the same exact time*, that teachers are the most important factor in student success in order to justify using test scores for teacher evaluation (Au, 2010b). Regardless, we need to be clear that when it comes to high-stakes, standardized test scores, non-school factors are the most determining factors. However, there are a host of important things that standardized tests do not measure, like cultural awareness, empathy, inter-social relations, artistic and creative abilities, curiosity and sense of wonder, honesty, and resourcefulness (Bracey, 2004; Harris et al., 2011), among others, and schools and teachers are critical to educational experiences and how students learn these things. Teachers and schools are important, just not in the ways measured by the tests.

The second point to make regarding testing is that within a policy ecosystem where testing is not only high-stakes but also profitable for educational corporations, the amount of such testing has proliferated, creating an avalanche of standardized tests for students to take. For instance, according to a study of 66 school districts by the Council of Great City Schools, as of the 2014–2015 school year students took 112.3 tests on average between kindergarten and the 12th grade. The same study found that there were 401 uniquely different tests given across the 66 districts, and that most students took an average of eight standardized tests per year (Hart et al., 2015). Another study of 14 mostly urban districts during the 2013–2014 school year found that students were tested once a month on average, with some tested as frequently as twice a month, and students in grades 3–8 were being tested 10 times a year on average, with some students taking as many as 20 standardized tests a year in those same grades. In the report the researcher, Melissa Lazarin, commented that "There is a culture of testing and test preparation in schools that does not put students first" (Lazarin, 2014, p. 3).

The third point that is important to understand about high-stakes testing is technical, and it has to do with how standardized tests are designed. Fundamentally, all standardized tests are designed to produce what is often referred to as a bell curve of test scores—a line that literally is in the shape of a bell, or perhaps something like a single-humped camel. That is to say, the tests are made such that when a group of students takes the standardized test, some will score high, some will score low, and the bulk will score in the middle. This is what test-makers (also called psychometricians) commonly call a "normal" distribution, and when they design the tests, they intend for it to produce this kind of curve (Au, 2023b). As the blogger Jersey Jazzman (Weber, 2015) so clearly explains:

> [W]e only test students on what we reasonably expect them to be able to do. We don't test fourth graders on trigonometry because we know most of them can't solve those kind of problems and wouldn't be able to even if we drilled them on it repeatedly. Similarly, we don't test high school juniors on adding one-digit numbers because we know that would be too easy. . . . Are there fourth graders that know the difference between a sine and a cosine? Are there juniors who can't add 5 and 4? Of course there are, but we know they are far away from the norm; we don't set our standards based on these outliers. Because we like to see ourselves as normally distributed, we create standards and tests that give us normal distributions. . . . This can't be stressed enough in the testing debates: we design tests not based on objective criteria, but on socially constructed frameworks that assume some of us are above average, some of us are below, and most of us are in the middle.

Now there are two different kinds of common standardized tests. One is called "norm-referenced." Norm-referenced tests are designed to measure students against each other, and these produced bell curves in their initial design. The other type of common standardized test is called a "criterion-referenced" test, and it is designed to test students against a set of criteria. Many of the major K–12 tests given today, especially those that are "standards-based" and connected to state standards or the Common Core standards, are criterion-referenced tests. Theoretically, these tests are designed so that it is possible for everyone to demonstrate that they've met the standards—which means it is theoretically possible for everyone taking these tests to meet proficiency and pass. These tests do not immediately produce a bell curve in the way that norm-referenced test do. However, criterion referenced tests still fall prey to the bell curve of performance: When statisticians interpret, analyze, and report the data from standards-based tests, they "scale" the raw data to produce a bell curve, again based on the assumption that there is a "normal" distribution of scores across the student population (Tan & Michel, 2011; Weber, 2015). So, no matter which kind of standardized test is given, in the end a certain amount of failure is baked into the testing paradigm such that it will produce a bell curve of student test score results.

This technical discussion is important because it draws our attention to a fundamental principle that governs our current standardized tests: They are designed to fail some portion of our student population. This is a critical thing to understand about standardized testing because it means that we cannot test our way to equality, and in fact we can only test our way to inequality. Additionally, the construction of tests to require failure also means that all talk about "closing achievement gaps" in test scores between rich and poor students or between Black/Brown students and white students is generally misleading. Closing the test score achievement gap between rich and poor students, and between Black/Brown students and white students in particular, has become a mantra for education reform spanning all presidential administrations since 2000 and connecting conservative Republicans and liberal Democrats alike (Au, 2023b). It is used to suggest that if we can close these achievement gaps, we will have reached a state of educational equity. However, the reality is that because of the presumed bell curve structured into the outcomes of our standardized tests, "closing the achievement gap" does not mean that everyone succeeds on the tests. Rather, because of the test-designed failure, "closing the achievement gap" means that we reach a point of equal passing and equal failure on the tests—of having proportionate numbers of rich and poor students pass and fail the tests, proportionate numbers of Black/Brown and white students pass and fail the tests, etc. Within the paradigm of the tests, the goal of closing the achievement gap is simply a goal of achieving equally mixed results for everyone.

TESTING, CHARTERS, AND THE COLONIAL PLUNDER OF COMMUNITIES OF COLOR

If high-stakes, standardized tests do not really measure learning or work as a tool to improve educational outcomes, and if charter schools do not really innovate or increase educational achievement, then what do they do? Well, for one, both high-stakes testing and charter schools negatively impact communities of color and contribute directly to the school-to-prison pipeline.

Given that non-school factors associated with socioeconomic status and poverty most strongly correlate with high-stakes, standardized test scores, then we are led to an important conclusion: Because the tests are designed to produce certain amounts of failure, and because the tests essentially function as a measure of poverty, then we have to recognize that as a tool of measurement, high-stakes, standardized testing concentrates failure among poor and working-class children, their schools, and their communities. Further, since Blacks, Latinx, Indigenous/Native Americans, Pacific Islanders, and Southeast Asians are disproportionately impoverished (Au, 2025a; National Poverty Center, 2017), then test-designed failure is most densely concentrated among those students, their schools, and their communities as well. Combined, this means that the effects of testing and other neoliberal education reforms like charter schools and school closings become focused on communities of color, having particularly deleterious effects. For instance, low-income and kids of color are tested more than their more affluent, white counterparts in higher-scoring schools. Low-income and kids of color also experience the greatest loss of time spent on non-tested or less-tested subjects like art, music, science, and social studies, and they don't have access to multicultural, anti-racist curriculum because those subject areas are not on the tests. Further, because the tests inhibit process-based, student-centered instruction in favor of rote memorization, Black and Brown students in particular lose opportunities for culturally relevant instruction (Au, 2009b; Nichols & Berliner, 2007).

Additionally, because of the increased intensity and more restrictive curriculum and educational environments created by the tests, for children of color high-stakes testing serves to acculturate them to a norm of being disciplined by state authorities (Au, 2023b; Vinson & Ross, 2003). The disciplining of Black and Brown children by high-stakes, standardized testing also manifests in very concrete and material ways: A study by the Economic Policy Institute found that in one state, having a high-stakes exit exam correlated with a 12.5% increase in the rate of incarceration (O. Baker & Lang, 2013; see also Fine & Ruglis, 2009). This is particularly concerning given that the implementation of exit exams increased the dropout rates up to 300% in some cases, with the dropouts being disproportionately Black and Latinx (Darling-Hammond, 2007)—suggesting that high-stakes, standardized tests are a conduit for the school-to-prison pipeline.

Charter schools are also becoming notorious for the hyper disciplining of Black and Brown children because they suspend and expel students at higher rates than public schools. A 2016 report by the Center for Civil Rights Solutions found that, nationally, charter schools' student suspension rates were just over 1% higher than public schools. This seems small because it is based on the aggregate whole of charters, and it was found that a fair number of charters were reporting zero suspensions—which is not statistically possible and likely means they were not keeping track of, or reporting, suspensions. However, more specific data in the report were more damning of charter school discipline. In Connecticut, for instance, elementary charter schools suspended and expelled students at a rate of 14%, while the public elementary schools reported a rate of 3%. As another example, in Massachusetts, charter schools are disproportionately represented among the state's highest-suspending schools, with some suspending as much as 35% of their students at least once per year (Losen et al., 2016). Reporting for *The Atlantic*, George Joseph points out that in 2014 in New York City, despite counting for just 7% of the city's student enrollment, New York's charter schools were responsible for almost 42% of all suspensions (Joseph, 2016).

These charter school disciplinary issues have caused Carla Shedd, professor at Columbia University, to observe that "Charter schools are providing a seamless transition for [low-income Black] students in terms of how they are already treated, watched, and surveilled outside" (Joseph, 2016). What's particularly troubling about these charter school suspension and expulsion rates is that numerous studies show that suspensions and expulsions correlate strongly with lower educational achievement, increased dropout rates, and increased likelihood of getting caught up in the juvenile justice system (Balfanz et al., 2015; Noltemeyer et al., 2015; Shollenberger, 2015). Dropping out of schools is particularly a racialized issue, where, for instance, 3 in 10 white male dropouts have served time in the federal penal system compared to the fact that almost 60% of Black male dropouts will be imprisoned at some point in their lives (Ewert et al., 2014). While public schools also have troubles in this area, we have to remember that charter school advocates keep promising that their model is *better*, when the evidence points to the opposite: charters are in fact contributing to the schools-to-prisons pipeline in very racialized ways.

Charter schools also are producing another sharply racialized outcome: intense racial segregation (Frankenberg et al., 2013; Miron et al., 2010). This racial segregation works in two directions. While we tend to think of segregation mainly as the concentration of students of color in a particular school or classroom (which is happening), the other side of racial segregation in charter schools is that white families are using charters to self-segregate away from non-white children and communities. There is a long history of white families making choices to send their children to schools that are either all white, mostly white, or at least "white enough," and this includes charter schools (Bonastia, 2015; Miron et al., 2010; Renzulli & Evans, 2005). A 2005 national study of white flight to charter schools found that ". . . even when whites are the majority in a school district and among their schools, whites who attend schools with nonwhites continue to look for options that are even more white . . ." (Renzulli & Evans, 2005, p. 412), and that these white families were not basing their choices on the academic performance of schools (Renzulli & Evans, 2005). In North Carolina, for instance, researchers found that white parents preferred their children attend schools that had fewer than 20% Black students, and thus chose to pull their children out of schools with "too many" Black students in favor of enrolling them in predominantly white charter schools—resulting in a decline of the white population of North Carolina's public schools and a notable increase in white enrollment in their charter schools (see also Joseph, 2017; Ladd et al., 2017). In 2014, the president of the school board in Hoboken, New Jersey expressed concern that the charter schools there were becoming havens for white flight from public schools, which he said was both bankrupting the public school system and creating a separate school system entirely (Eidelson, 2014).

While high-stakes testing and charters both have racialized outcomes, they also add to the profits of wealthy elites. In 2011, a Rupert Murdoch investing affiliate valued the entire K–12 public education market in the United States at $500 billion (Resmovits, 2011), with other estimates coming in at $788 billion (Fang, 2014). As an example, the Common Core State Standards were a huge financial windfall for testing companies, consultants, textbook corporations, and the educational technology sector. The Fordham Institute estimated that the Common Core cost $12.1 billion from 2012 to 2015 (Murphy et al., 2012), while the conservative Pioneer Institute and American Principles Project estimated a mid-range cost of $15.8 billion over 7 years for the CCSS (Accountability Works, 2012). According to *The New York Times*, in part due to the Common Core, venture capital investment in public education increased 80% from 2005, to a total of $632 million in 2012 (Rich, 2013). Not surprisingly, given that the Gates Foundation invested $200 million in promoting and lobbying for the Common Core (Vicens, 2014), Bill Gates and Microsoft have cashed in on this lucrative market, too; in February 2014, Microsoft announced it was partnering with the Pearson textbook company to install Pearson's Common Core materials onto Microsoft's Surface tablet (Layton, 2014). Amidst these billions of dollars, one thing in particular is important to keep in mind: These are public tax dollars moving into the pockets of private corporations vis-à-vis systems of neoliberal public education reform.

Charter schools, like high-stakes tests, are also proving to be profitable for investors. For instance, hedge fund managers and real estate developers are making money off the charter school sector by taking advantage of a federal program, the New Markets Tax Credit, which rewards investment in low-income communities with a 39% tax credit on loans made to those communities (Rawls, 2013). The promise made to investors and developers is that between the hefty tax credit and the interest rates on the loans they invest in, they can double their investment in as little as 7 years, causing Rawls (2013) to opine:

> Maybe this helps explain why, in 2011, former tennis champion Andre Agassi helped set up a $500 million startup fund for his Canyon-Agassi Charter School Facilities Fund, the first for-profit organization of its kind. . . . The credit may also explain why Facebook CEO Mark Zuckerberg donated $500 million in stocks to a variety of organizations that distribute charter school funding in 2012, or why he opened his own foundation, called Startup: Education, to build new charter schools.

With federal backing, charter schools—whether for-profit or nonprofit—thus become seen as a good investment. As David Brain, head of the Entertainment Properties Trust, told CNBC in 2012 regarding charter school investment:

> Well I think it's a very stable business, very recession-resistant. It's a very high-demand product . . . [I]t's our highest growth and most appealing sector right now of the portfolio . . . And a great opportunity set with 500 schools starting every year. It's a two and a half billion dollar opportunity set in rough measure annually. (Rawls, 2013)

In addition to pure investment, these real estate firms can then turn around and charge charter schools rent on their properties, which in some cases amounts to 20–30% of a charter school's annual budget and can be quite lucrative given the high cost of rent in cities like New York or Chicago (Rawls, 2013; see also Wolff, 2009). In some states, like Arizona (Burris, 2017), charter school law is written such that the physical properties revert back to the charter operator if the charter school closes down—essentially transferring property that was maintained by public monies through rent or mortgage directly to the charter school operators. In other cases, like in Ohio, the state's contract with the charter school operator specified that even though bought with public tax payer dollars, all school property purchased by the charter school (e.g. computers, textbooks, desks) became property of the charter school operator (Pelzer, 2015). Further, in this case, if the State of Ohio wanted to recoup this property—which was already purchased once with public funds—they would have to buy it back from the operating charter, essentially using public monies to pay for it twice. Recent research on charter school expansion has consistently shown that charter school growth has a short-term and long-term negative fiscal impact on public school systems (B. D. Baker, 2016; Lapp et al., 2017), reminding us again that, as with high-stakes testing, between federal programs, state laws, and charter contracts, these are public monies being transferred into the coffers of private industry vis-à-vis the system of public education.

As we can see with the above examples of Common Core testing and charter schools, in the words of Fabricant and Fine (2013), "Entire sectors of the social reproduction side of the welfare state, most critically in health care and education, are being rapidly capitalized as entrepreneurs search for new profitable markets" (p. 25). This process of the neoliberal movement of capital from public projects and institutions into private enterprises is what Harvey (2004) refers to as "accumulation by dispossession" (p. 74), where the public is simultaneously dispossessed of its assets as wealthy elites accumulate those very same assets in a massive transfer of wealth from the poor and working class to the capitalist class.

In these ways, neoliberal, corporate education reform is fundamentally a racist, colonial enterprise. Even as individual kids, classes, and maybe even a school or two may beat the odds in terms of educational achievement, the economic inequalities that correlate with test scores guarantee failure for working-class kids of color in general (Au, 2023b). Rather than address the structural inequalities facing these children and their communities, dismal test results become the basis for concentrating the market-based education reforms like charter schools, school closings, hyper disciplinary programs, Teach for America, and the like, in those communities. In turn, these reforms result in the direct transfer of public wealth from working-class communities of color into the pockets of entrepreneurs, investors, real estate developers, and tech moguls, who profit directly from this relationship.

The colonial reality of these reforms is also present in the fact that the wealthy elites advancing these reforms are not doing so for their own children—they have no interest in sending their children to charter schools or underresourced public schools that feel the weight of high-stakes testing and reforms like the Common Core. Bill Gates's eldest child, for instance, attended an elite, private school in Seattle called Lakeside, which boasts small class sizes, a well-endowed facility, and a rich liberal arts curriculum, and it pays no attention to federal education reforms or most high-stakes tests (HiPointDem, 2012; KrazyTA, 2014; Weber, 2013a). Rather, these predominantly white, wealthy elites are interested in making education policy for other people's children (Au & Ferrare, 2015b). Finally, the colonial nature of neoliberal, corporate education reform is present in the ways that these wealthy elites and their foundations fund, promote, and reward individual people of color (i.e., Michelle Rhee, Kevin Johnson, Steve Perry, Howard Fuller, Geoffrey Canada, Cory Booker, etc.—the list is long) and mainstream organizations speaking on behalf of communities of color (the League of United Latin American Citizens, National Urban League, and the National Council of La Raza, among others) as a means of suggesting that testing, charters, and so forth are really in the best interest of racial justice—ignoring any indicators to the contrary (Au, 2015, 2016a; Au & Ferrare, 2015b; Mayorga et al., 2020).

COMMUNITIES OF COLOR RESIST CORPORATE COLONIZATION

Just looking at the evidence I provided in this chapter, the influence of capitalism on schools in the United States—discussed here as neoliberalism—is in many ways overwhelming. Much as Bowles and Gintis (1976) observed almost 50 years ago, the current, neoliberal model of schooling being advanced by corporate reformers reproduces inequalities that very strongly correlate with the economic inequalities we see produced by capitalism. Further, it is clear these neoliberal education inequalities are simultaneously *raced* and *classed*: They are disproportionately implemented among poor communities and communities of color, meaning they are sucking financial resources out of these communities as well. However, we also need to understand that while the neoliberal educational reforms are hegemonic and they feel universal in their power and reach, human consciousness and action are not so easily controlled or exploited. To that end, communities of color have actively resisted and rebelled against these policies and their deleterious effects.

For instance, there has been a sizable resistance to high-stakes, standardized testing. As just one important example, in January 2013 the teachers at Garfield High School in Seattle, Washington, held a press conference where they informed the world that they would not administer the Measures of Academic Progress (MAP), a district-mandated, high-stakes standardized test. It was a brave act that brought threats from school authorities as well as an outpouring of support locally and nationally. The Garfield Parent Teacher Student Association (PTSA) officially endorsed the boycott, and Garfield student government leaders and leaders of the Black Student Union vocally supported this action. Soon, other schools in the district joined the boycott. Activists in the teachers' union, the Seattle Education Association, lent their support, and the Seattle NAACP also endorsed it (Hagopian, 2014b). National support for the Garfield test boycott also grew. Teachers in Hawai'i, Florida, California, Oregon, and Illinois expressed their solidarity. The national teachers' unions sent letters of support to the Garfield teachers (Hagopian, 2014b), and over 100 scholars from universities around the country signed a petition expressing their solidarity as well (see also Au, 2013; Rethinking Schools, 2013).

The Garfield PTSA circulated a flyer informing parents of their rights to opt out of the MAP test, which resulted in dozens of parents informing the school that they were not allowing their children to take the test. Students also circulated their own flyer telling peers that they did not have to take the MAP test. On the day of the test, many Garfield students refused to leave their seats, essentially performing an impromptu sit-in by refusing to go to the library to be tested. Other students went to the library to take the test but sabotaged the results by rushing through their answers so fast that the computers automatically registered their exams as invalid (Hagopian, 2014b). The combined resistance of teachers, the student body government, the Black Student Union, parents, scholars from around the country, civil rights leaders, and colleagues from around the city defeated the 9th-grade MAP test at Garfield and the district—which was made optional by Seattle Schools the following academic year.

Although the Garfield/Seattle MAP test boycott was a single event, it served as a watershed moment for the national movement against high-stakes, standardized testing. In the years since, we have seen large protests by students in places like Santa Fe, New Mexico and Long Island, New York, and massive opt-out numbers in New York state (200,000 in 2015) and Washington state (over 60,000 in 2015), among others (Foster, 2016; Hagopian, 2015). Further, despite claims that the opt-out movements are mainly for white suburbanites (Pondiscio, 2015), students, parents, and communities of color are leading voices in urban test resistance, as we have seen in Seattle, Chicago, Portland, Philadelphia, and elsewhere (Hagopian & Network for Public Education, 2015; Rethinking Schools, 2014). Other examples of urban communities organizing against such testing include organizing at the Salt of the Earth School to lead an opt-out movement and make a public protest to the NYC schools chancellor, a protest that spread to other schools like the Brooklyn New School (Hagopian, 2014c); parents and teachers at Saucedo Elementary Scholastic Academy in southwest Chicago leading a successful boycott of their state exam, the ISA (Chambers, 2014); and Castle Bridge School in New York City organizing a successful high-stakes test opt-out and boycott movement (Tran, 2014).

Additionally, people of color–led groups like the Journey for Justice Alliance (J4J) have organized powerfully not just against high-stakes testing, but also most other aspects of neoliberal, corporate education reform. J4J is a "national network of intergenerational, grassroots community organizations led primarily by Black and Brown people in 24 U.S. cities" (Journey for Justice Alliance, 2016) whose members lead workshops, organize protests and actions, and speak at conferences around the country. J4J's educational platform calls out educational equity as a central issue for racial inequality in public schools today, and they denounce charter schools, privatization, school closings, racist discipline practices, and the destabilization of urban schools as core aspects of the neoliberal, corporate education policy agenda. They go on to explain that

> J4J believes that we do not have failing schools. We have in fact been failed by a system that has ignored savage inequities in public education, using civil rights rhetoric while violating the human rights of Black and Brown families through privatization schemes like state takeovers, school closings, for-profit charter and alternative schools. (Journey for Justice Alliance, 2016)

Consequently, J4J's seven-point education platform calls for "A Moratorium on School Privatization," "Federal Funding for 10,000 Sustainable Community Schools," an immediate end to zero-tolerance discipline policies, a "National Equity Assessment," a stop to the attacks on Black teachers, an end to "State Takeovers, Appointed School Boards, and Mayoral Control," and an end to the "Over-Reliance on Standardized Tests in Public Schools" (Journey for Justice Alliance, 2016).

Similarly, the #BlackLivesMatter (BLM) education platform also identifies the privatization of public schools as a major problem, including the undue (and undemocratic) influence of billionaire philanthropists like the Bill and Melinda Gates Foundation, racist zero-tolerance discipline policies, cutting of staff positions that directly serve Black students, underresourcing of the classrooms and schools of Black children, and attempts to leave teachers, students, and parents out of decision-making processes. The BLM platform then goes on to suggest an end to school closings, charter schools, "corporate-backed market reformer programs such as Teach For America and the Broad Superintendents Academy," presence of police in schools, and mayoral control, among others—while also calling for substantial increases in school funding, positive discipline practices, and local/democratic control of schools and school boards (Stith et al., 2016).

It is also important to note that even more mainstream organizations representing communities of color have resisted aspects of neoliberal corporate education reform. For instance, despite its support for high-stakes testing (Au, 2015) the National Association for the Advancement of Colored People (NAACP) caused a stir in 2016 when its national board ratified a resolution calling for a moratorium on charter school expansion. After explicitly affirming the NAACP "School Privatization Threat to Public Education" resolution from 2014, the NAACP's 2016 moratorium calls for an end to charter school expansion until

> (1) Charter schools are subject to the same transparency and accountability standards as public schools

(2) Public funds are not diverted to charter schools at the expense of the public school system
(3) Charter schools cease expelling students that public schools have a duty to educate and
(4) Charter schools cease to perpetuate de facto segregation of the highest performing children from those whose aspirations may be high but whose talents are not yet as obvious. (NAACP, 2016)

The NAACP's call for a moratorium was particularly upsetting to corporate education reformers because, like high-stakes testing, charter schools were marketed on the promise that they will improve educational equity and achievement for Black students, among other marginalized populations. The call for a moratorium on charters served as a rebuke of that false promise.

Some teacher union organizing has also embodied ways that communities of color have resisted neoliberal, corporate education reforms. Most notably, behind the leadership of Karen Lewis, the Chicago Teachers' Union responded to the intense privatization of Chicago's schools by organizing with parents there under the banner of fighting for a quality education. This campaign included critiques of privatization efforts vis-à-vis charter schools, school closings, and high-stakes testing, among others (B. Jones, 2015; McAlevey, 2019). Similarly, in Milwaukee, Wisconsin, under the leadership of Bob Peterson, the Milwaukee Teachers' Education Association built relationships with immigrant rights groups and the local NAACP to fight for public school funding and to resist school closings. In St. Paul, Minnesota, the teachers' union there invited the community to participate in the shaping of the union's contract demands. This work all foreshadowed the 2013 convening of the Alliance to Reclaim Our Schools, which brought together the major teachers' unions with groups like J4J, the Alliance for Educational Justice, the Gamaliel Network, and the Center for Popular Democracy, among others (Fine & Fabricant, 2014). This model has spread to other cities as well, where, for instance, in the 2015 contract negotiations, the Seattle Education Association included demands for racial equity teams across the district (Whelan, 2015).

Concretely, the failure of these neoliberal education reforms and the popular pushback from students, parents, and communities has forced the past U.S. presidents, such as President Obama, to say publicly that there was too much testing, and it forced the U.S. Congress to recognize right of parents to opt out of testing in their 2016 reauthorization of the Elementary and Secondary Education Act (Au & Hollar, 2016; Hagopian, 2015). Further, as *Education Week* reported in summer 2017, according to a poll completed by the conservative, free market–supporting think tank Education Next (housed at the Hoover Institute), national support for charter schools plummeted from 51% in 2016 to 39% in 2017. The poll also showed that support for charters was down among both Democrats and Republicans, as well as among Blacks and Latine peoples. In their reporting, *Education Week* suggested that the NAACP charter school moratorium, the anti-charter platform of #BlackLivesMatter, and the unpopularity of then-president Trump's focus on charters and "choice" might explain the recent shift (Prothero, 2017). While we do not know the exact cause of the shift in people's attitude toward charter schools, the resistance to charters and other neoliberal, corporate education reforms by teachers, students, parents, and community activists illustrate that schools and education are not entirely dominated by the interests of wealthy elites.

CHAPTER 7

Meritocracy 2.0

High-Stakes, Standardized Testing as a Racial Project of Neoliberal Multiculturalism

INTRODUCTION

Over the last several decades, the United States has experienced a conservative modernization (Apple, 2006) that in part has manifested in a broad project of reshaping public education along the lines of free-market capitalism. This project has been advanced through a bevy of policy initiatives: an increase in school choice and school voucher programs (Apple & Pedroni, 2005; Ravitch, 2010), the deregulation of teacher education (Kretchmar et al., 2014; Zeichner & Pena-Sandoval, 2015), a decrease in democratic oversight of public schools (Au & Ferrare, 2014; Ravitch, 2013; Scott & Jabbar, 2014; D. Stovall, 2020), and the contracting of public school services out to private industry (Burch, 2006, 2021), among other market-oriented, neoliberal policies and structures (Fabricant & Fine, 2013; Saltman, 2012). Within this milieu of free-market, neoliberal education policies, high-stakes, standardized testing has emerged as perhaps the most crucial piece underlying these reform efforts. The high-stakes, standardized tests provide the data upon which student, teacher, and school value are measured, establish the basis for viewing education as a market where consumers can make choices about where to send their children to school (Au, 2023b), afford a framework for the construction of an achievement gap that organizes racial discourse and contributes to the racial imaginary (Leonardo, 2011), and offer a basic paradigm for public education to be reformed through profit-making interventions (Apple, 2006; Fabricant & Fine, 2013).

Further, it is critical to understand that, in direct discursive response to the legacies of entrenched racism of public institutions in the United States generally and in U.S. schools specifically (Ladson-Billings, 2006; Love, 2023), current neoliberal-imbued education reform efforts are often constructed around

Previously published as "Meritocracy 2.0: High-Stakes, Standardized Testing as a Racial Project of Neoliberal Multiculturalism," 2016, *Educational Policy*, *30*(1), 39–62. Reprinted by permission.

narratives of racial equality (see Scott, 2013), including the use of high-stakes, standardized testing (Heubert, 2001; Madaus & Clarke, 2001). In this chapter I frame high-stakes, standardized testing as a racial project, and consider the ways it has consistently reproduced racial inequality in the United States. I further argue that, given their presumed objectivity, such standardized testing fundamentally masks the structural nature of racial inequality within an ideology of individual meritocracy, an ideology that advances a racialized neoliberal project that reconstitutes "anti-racism" as being against the very act of naming race itself. That is to say, as I argue here, the neoliberal project has reconstructed "anti-racist" as being against any identification around race (and any itinerant signification) in favor of a post-racial identification constructed around freely acting and competing individuals. This interplay of neoliberalism, the reconstitution of "anti-racism" in ways that deny the structural and material realities of racism, and high-stakes testing coalesce in what I name here as "Meritocracy 2.0."

I begin here with a discussion of the conceptual frames that guide the present analysis, specifically neoliberalism, racial projects, and neoliberal multiculturalism. I then go on to consider standardized testing as a racial project in the United States historically, specifically addressing the ways that the ideology of meritocracy operates as the root justification for structural educational inequality. Subsequently I take up an analysis of high-stakes, standardized testing as a racial project in modern-day education policy, attending specifically to the ways that it empirically increases racism in education while ideologically denying structural inequalities, through neoliberal forms of meritocracy and anti-racism. I conclude this chapter with a discussion of the implications of my analysis for civil rights discourses surrounding the use of high-stakes testing to achieve racial equality in the United States, arguing that high-stakes testing cannot dismantle racial inequality because it fundamentally and materially advances the project of increasing racialized injustice.

CONCEPTUAL FRAMEWORK

My analysis in this chapter broadly falls under the banner of critical policy analysis (S. Taylor, 1997) in the spirit of critical educational theory and practice (Apple & Au, 2009), because I focus on the interplay between structures of power and ideology and how they manifest within the advancement of particular education policies. More specifically, I draw on a handful of concepts that provide the framework for understanding the relationship between high-stakes, standardized testing and racial inequality. The first concept is that of neoliberalism. While there are competing definitions and conceptions of neoliberalism, for the purposes of my analysis I draw on the work of Harvey (2007), who explains that neoliberalism is a combination of political and economic theories and practices built upon the assumption that "human well-being can be best advanced by the maximization of entrepreneurial freedoms within an institutional framework characterized by private property rights, individual liberty, unencumbered markets, and free trade" (p. 22). As such, neoliberalism seeks to attack the public sphere because the neoliberal human ideal resides in the deregulated private sphere, under the assumption that individual capitalist competition is both more efficient and more effective than anything done more collectively through the public (Lipman, 2011). Within education policy and the structure of schooling, neoliberalism can take many forms, most of which revolve around the creation of quasi-markets built on notions of school choice, the deregulation of the teaching profession, a shift away from democratic governance, competition for resources and production of educational outputs (e.g., high test scores), and providing profit-making corporations with access to resources devoted to public education (Apple, 2006; Au & Ferrare, 2015a; Fabricant & Fine, 2013; Lipman, 2011). High-stakes testing generally appeals to the neoliberal educational project because the data produced by the tests can then be used as the metrics for competition in the educational marketplace (Apple, 2006). Within these marketplace logics, "good" teachers and schools produce high test scores in students and "bad" teachers and schools produce low test scores in students; parents can use the data to then make choices about where to send their children (a.k.a. where the investment of their public monies should go), "bad" teachers can receive low evaluations and be fired, "bad" schools with low test scores will lose market share and be closed, and "good" schools with high test scores will remain open and be successful. Simply put, the tests allow education to be reconstructed around a simple model of commodity production and consumption (Au, 2023b).

However, my intent here is not to just think through high-stakes, standardized testing as a tool of market-oriented reforms. Rather, it is critical that we understand that capitalism and the neoliberal project has always been signified, operationalized, and instantiated through the racialization of economic class (R. D. G. Kelley, 2017; Leonardo, 2012), and that standardized testing has played a direct role in constructing this race-class nexus within education. As such, for my analysis here I also draw on what Melamed (2011) refers to as *neoliberal multiculturalism*, which she explains

> has disguised the reality that neoliberalism remains a form of racial capitalism. . . . Race has continued to permeate capitalism's economic and social processes, organizing the hyper extraction of surplus value from racialized bodies and naturalizing a system of capital accumulation. . . . Yet multiculturalism has portrayed neoliberal policy as the key to a postracist world of freedom and opportunity. (p. 42)

Within the framing of neoliberal multiculturalism, the empirical question becomes whether or not high-stakes, standardized testing, as the fulcrum upon which free-market education policy mechanisms pivot, ameliorates or exacerbates educational inequality experienced by children of color in the United States. Thus, it also becomes important to understand education policy generally, and high-stakes, standardized testing specifically, as structures and tools that further a particular "racial project" (Omi & Winant, 2015, p. 125) of neoliberal multiculturalism, because such testing structures our meaning-making of racialized inequality in education in particular ways. As a racial project, high-stakes, standardized testing constructs which children (and communities) are identified as "failures" by the tests, how such "failure" is used to justify neoliberal conceptions of individualist educational attainment and the denial of structural inequalities (Meritocracy 2.0), and, subsequently, what policies and practices are to be enacted upon those children and communities identified by the tests as "failures." Further, to understand high-stakes, standardized testing as a racial project of neoliberal multiculturalism means that we also must consider the constructions of racialized inequality embedded in the material histories of such testing as well.

Finally, in addition to understanding high-stakes, standardized testing within the framework of neoliberal multiculturalism (Melamed, 2011) and as a racial project (Omi & Winant, 2015), I return to Melamed (2011) because such testing is thus also as an expression of "official anti-racism" by the state apparatus. As she explains,

> Tropes such as *race reform*, *racial progress*, *racial integration*, *ending racism*, *bringing in excluded voices*, and *living in a postracial society* have become the touchstones for racial projects that recalibrate state apparatuses, expand the reach of normative power, and implant norms during the performative constitution of human subjectivities. By controlling what counts as a race matter, an antiracist goal, or a truism about racial difference, official antiracisms have structured legitimate knowledges in the domain of law, public policy, economy, and culture. (p. 11, original emphasis)

As I will argue later, high-stakes, standardized testing is used by the state not only to racialize our understanding of structural inequalities, but also to control "what counts as a race matter," thereby shifting racial discourse in educational policy.

In what follows I outline the history of standardized testing (the progenitor of high-stakes, standardized testing) as a racial project. I then address how this testing was used to justify an ideology of meritocracy, built upon the presumed objective measurement of human intelligence. From there I move on to consider modern-day high-stakes, standardized testing as a racial project of neoliberal multiculturalism, including how civil rights discourse is attached to the tests, despite the empirical evidence of the deleterious effects of such testing on children of color specifically. I conclude by discussing the intractable contradiction posed by attempting to use high-stakes, standardized tests as a tool for ending racial inequality in education.

A HISTORY OF STANDARDIZED TESTING AS A RACIAL PROJECT

Standardized testing has always been a racial project in the United States. The idea of intelligence testing was originally imported from France, where in 1904 French psychologist Alfred Binet first developed the IQ test to assess if young children had mild developmental disabilities. The IQ, or "intelligence quotient," of a child was determined by dividing mental age (according to the test score) by the chronological age. However, cognitive psychologists in the United States such as Henry Goddard, Lewis Terman, and Robert Yerkes misappropriated Binet's idea, distorted the original use of the tests, injected their own underlying presumptions about humans and human ability, and fit their findings into the race and class politics of the United States at the turn of the 20th century (Gould, 1996). With the explicit support of educational philanthropists like Carnegie, these psychologists contributed greatly to the idea that IQ was hereditary and fixed, thus establishing the justification for the use of standardized testing to sorting and ranking of human populations by race, ethnicity, gender, and class according to supposedly inborn, biologically innate intelligence (Au, 2023b; Gould, 1996; Karier, 1972).

In 1917 Yerkes, working with Goddard and Terman, developed the Alpha and Beta Army tests and administered them to 1.75 million Army recruits during World War I in order to sort incoming soldiers and to determine their "mental fitness." Based on the results of what he deemed to be an objective assessment, Yerkes concluded that the intelligence of European immigrants could largely be judged by their country of origin, with the lighter-skinned northern and western Europeans being more intelligent than the darker peoples of eastern and southern Europe. Similarly, Yerkes found that those of higher income were more intelligent than those of lower income as well (Giordano, 2005; Gould, 1996). As Karier (1972) explains, the results of such testing were strongly connected to the existing social order:

> Designing the Stanford-Binet intelligence test, Terman developed questions which were based on presumed progressive difficulty in performing tasks which he believed were necessary for achievement in ascending the hierarchical occupational structure. He then proceeded to find that according to the results of his tests the intelligence of different occupational classes fit his ascending hierarchy. It was little wonder that IQ reflected social class bias. It was, in fact, based on the social class order. (pp. 163–164).

Even at this time standardized testing was a racial project. Not surprisingly, among his other findings, Yerkes also concluded that African Americans were the least intelligent of all peoples (Giordano, 2005; Gould, 1996), and with the explicit support from these psychologists, eugenicists of the time advanced the idea that race mixing was spreading the supposedly inferior intelligence genes of African Americans, other non-white peoples, and immigrants (Selden, 1999). Thus, over 100 years ago and at their very origins, standardized tests were being used to structure racial inequalities through providing "scientific" proof to notions of the inherent inferiority of Black people, specific ethnicities, and the poor, among other groups.

With the promise of the efficient sorting of students, standardized IQ testing soon found its way into education. As Tyack (1974) explains,

> Intelligence testing and other forms of measurement provided the technology for classifying children. Nature-nurture controversies might pepper the scientific periodicals and magazines of the intelligentsia, but schoolmen found IQ tests an invaluable means of channeling children; by the very act of channeling pupils, they helped to make IQ prophecies self-fulfilling. (p. 180)

Indeed, in 1919, Terman, then a Stanford University professor of psychology, and under the sponsorship of the National Academy of Sciences, was central in adapting the Alpha and Beta army tests into the National Intelligence Tests for use with schoolchildren. By 1920, over 400,000 copies of these tests had been sold nationwide, and by late 1925 Terman reported sales of this test at nearly 1.5 million copies of the Stanford Achievement Test, which he developed. A survey of 215 cities with populations over 10,000 in 1925 found that 64% of these cities used intelligence tests to classify and sort elementary students, 56% used tests to sort junior high school students, and 41% did the same for high school students (Chapman, 1988). By 1932, 112 of 150 large city school systems in the United States were using intelligence testing to place students into ability groups, and universities had also begun to use these tests to justify admissions as well (Haney, 1984).

The responses of communities of color to standardized IQ testing in the early-to-mid 1900s can also help us understand early standardized testing as a racial project. For instance, prominent African American educators were acutely aware of the ways in which IQ testing was being used to further racial inequality and support the racist eugenics movement. Horace Mann Bond,—the Director of the School of Education at Langston University in Oklahoma, was one of the earliest African American educators to publicly challenge the findings of prominent psychologists involved in the IQ testing and eugenics movements. In 1924 Bond critiqued IQ testing and eugenics in *Crisis,* the magazine of the National Association for the Advancement of Colored People. Additionally, writing in 1940, W. E. B. Du Bois recalled,

> It was not until I was long out of school and indeed after the [first] World War that there came the hurried use of the new technique of psychological tests, which were quickly adjusted so as to put black folk absolutely beyond the possibility of civilization. (as quoted in Guthrie, 1998, p. 55)

As Stoskopf (1999) explains, the lower scores of African Americans were regularly used to track Black students into vocational education or for white teachers to explain away any difficulties they might be having with Black students in their classrooms.

MERITOCRACY, OBJECTIVITY, AND STANDARDIZED TESTING AS A RACIAL PROJECT

As the above quotation from Du Bois illustrates, one of the things that Black educational leaders challenged was the fundamental bias underlying standardized IQ testing—a challenge worth making based on the racialized and class-based test scores. However, despite these challenges, with the support of leading psychologists and popular opinion, such standardized testing was seen as providing an objective measure of intelligence and ability. In turn, this presumptive objectivity provided the foundation for the idea that standardized testing offered a fair and accurate measurement of individual effort, paving the way for psychologists, philanthropists, and educators to sort students using test scores and ultimately serving ideologically to deny structural inequalities (Au, 2023b). The logic of test-based structural denial works thusly: If standardized tests provide for the fair and objective measurement of individuals, then standardized testing holds the promise that every test-taker is objectively offered a fair and equal chance at educational, social, and economic achievement. Problems like racism and class privilege are thus supposedly neutralized through testing. As Sacks (1999) notes, these logics were advanced in the early years of standardized testing, where such tests were seen as a means for challenging class privileges. This is the root of the idea that standardized testing, both historically and today, can be a means of challenging inequality, and it is the way that standardized testing helps uphold the ideology of meritocracy in the United States.

The ideology of meritocracy asserts that, regardless of social position, economic class, gender, race, or culture (or any other form of socially or institutionally defined difference), everyone has an equal chance at becoming "successful" based purely on individual merit and hard work. Consequently, the ideology of meritocracy also asserts that failure is due to an individual person's (or individual group's) lack of effort and hard work (Lemann, 1999; Sacks, 1999). As a racial project, if standardized tests provide an objective measure, then low test scores and the educational failure of working-class children of color is due to their own deficiencies (personal, cultural, racial, or otherwise), lack of hard work, or a lack of "grit" (Horn, 2012; Love, 2019; Thomas, 2014). This construction of standardized testing as an objective measure of merit was, as Karier (1972) explains, built by those in power who believed in the superiority of their own talents:

> Most testers refused to admit the possibility that they were, perhaps, servants of privilege, power and status, and preferred instead to believe and "hope" that what they were measuring was, in fact, true "merit." This was also an act of faith, a faith based on the belief that somehow the "prestige hierarchy of occupations" and the people in it who provided the objective standard upon which the tests were based, were there not because of privilege, wealth, power status and violence, but because of superior talent and virtue. This was a fundamental axiom in the liberal's faith in meritocracy which emerged in twentieth century American education. (p. 169)

In this way, and continuing to think through standardized testing as a racial project, we are reminded of the material construction of these tests. They were (and are) created, administered, interpreted, analyzed, reported on, and made sense of by actual people—people with social, cultural, racial, and economic locations; vested interests; questioned or unquestioned assumptions; biases; histories; etc. To understand standardized testing as a racial project (both the fundament of testing historically and its modern progeny in high-stakes, standardized testing), then we have to understand the ways that testing was used to shape "what race *means* in a particular discursive or ideological practice and the ways in which both social structures and everyday experiences are racially *organized*, based on that meaning" (Omi & Winant, 2015, p. 125, original emphasis). As such, with the empirical evidence provided by presumptively "objective" standardized tests, whites and wealthy elites could mask their own structural advantages, deny the existence of systemic racism, justify racial hierarchies, and structure specific racial groups as less intelligent and inferior (Au, 2023b), all under the guise of "naturally" occurring aptitude among individuals (Bisseret, 1979) competing within a meritocratic framework.

It is important to take a moment and note that test-based, racialized notions of IQ are not simply archaic ideas thrown to the dustbins of history. In the modern era, for instance, using standardized test scores for their data, Herrnstein and Murray (1996) claimed that there was an intelligence hierarchy of races, where African Americans were the least intelligent of all races, followed by Latinos, whites, and Asian Americans, who, according to the authors, were supposedly the most intelligent. As another example, Rushton and Jensen (2005) asserted that genetically based racial differences in IQ are real (Jensen is professor emeritus of educational psychology at University of California, Berkeley), and others such as Barrow and Rouse (2006), a senior economist at the Federal Reserve Bank of Chicago and a professor of economics and public affairs at Princeton, respectively, explicitly rely on the work of Herrnstein and Murray (1996) as a baseline for their analysis of the relationship between race, education, and pay. Indeed, "race science" based on antiquated and white supremacist racial logics has been found to be on the rise generally in the United States (Evans, 2018). As such, race-based and biological notions of IQ are not artifacts of the early 20th century but are instead still living among us.

MERITOCRACY 2.0 AND HIGH-STAKES TESTING AS A MODERN-DAY RACIAL PROJECT

Now, over 100 years removed from the early years of standardized testing and in the midst of the ubiquity of high-stakes, standardized testing in schools, we see the same mix of the presumed objectivity of standardized test measurement, the ideology of meritocracy, and the notion that testing can be used to ameliorate racial inequalities. However, one key difference is that this modern-day mix is swathed in neoliberalism, and in the current context it is critical to understand how the ideology of meritocracy fits the neoliberal project in such a complementary manner. As discussed previously, neoliberalism is in part based on a core concept of individual free choice and competition within a deregulated market (Harvey, 2007; Lipman, 2011). Thus, the neoliberal individual is in essence an individual free from the constraints of social, economic, historical, institutional, and cultural structures. Likewise, the neoliberal individual can freely compete as an individual against other freely competing individuals, and the hardest-working, savviest, most virtuous individual will succeed. For the neoliberal individual, racism and other forms of systematic power outside of the market are considered obsolete and nonexistent, and all that matters for success is individual drive, determination, sacrifice, and hard work. Fundamentally, this is the ideology of meritocracy of old, but reborn within the framework of global free market capitalism as Meritocracy 2.0.

The neoliberal frame also shifts the racial project of standardized testing in critical ways because it recasts high-stakes, standardized testing using neoliberal multiculturalism as a form of official, neoliberal anti-racism (Melamed, 2011). In this neoliberal recasting, high-stakes, standardized testing plays a dual role. On the one hand, testing and test data are constructed as the basis for competition in the education market under the neoliberal multicultural assumption that the test-based market mechanism can and will promote racial equality. On the other hand, taking the form of official, neoliberal anti-racism, high-stakes, standardized tests establish the right of individuals of all races to gain access to education through the supposedly their fair, objective, test-based measurement as (de-raced) individuals—since within the framework Meritocracy 2.0 race or racism does not really exist within the parameters of test performance. Thus, while disregarding the existence of structural racism and how it impacts all aspects of educational performance, as well as disregarding any bias in the testing instrument itself, raising the test scores of children of color and closing test score achievement gaps between different racial and economic groups become the paramount expression of official, neoliberal anti-racism in corporate education reform.

The neoliberal multicultural project as expressed through neoliberal anti-racism is perhaps most clearly articulated through U.S. federal education policy in recent decades. High-stakes, standardized testing rose to prominence in education reform in the United States through the 1990s and culminated in federal education policy in the 2002 reauthorization of the Elementary and Secondary Education Act, redubbed the No Child Left Behind Act (NCLB). NCLB amounted to a federal mandate to require standardized testing in every U.S. state, with the threat that if test scores were not raised across various subgroups related to race, economic class, students with disabilities, and English language learners, among others, schools and districts would face a variety of possible punishments, including loss of control of federal education monies, the complete reconstitution of a school's staff, takeover by a charter management organization, or school closures (Au, 2023b; Karp, 2003). Further, NCLB officially ushered in the era of neoliberal, market-driven education reform in the United States because it used the scores generated by the high-stakes, standardized tests as the baseline metric and data for choices, punishments, and survival within the educational market, and it encoded competition, deregulation, the privatization of formerly public services, and concepts of choice into federal education policy in the form of charter schools and private contracting, among other reforms (Apple, 2006).

NCLB, as part of the neoliberal multicultural project, was itself built on a cornerstone of official, neoliberal anti-racism. Indeed, as the name explicitly decrees, no child will be left behind. As federal policy, NCLB was thus constructed around using arguments that high-stakes, standardized testing is a tool for achieving racial equality. For instance, in 2002, using a refrain that has become all too common, then President George W. Bush asserted that "education is the great civil rights issue of our time" (CNN, 2002), as part of his argument in support of his education reform agenda. Two years later, in a speech delivered at Harvard, Bush's then Secretary of Education, Rod Paige, suggested that closing race-based achievement gaps in test scores was "the civil rights issue of our time" (Feinberg, 2004). During a question-and-answer period after the same speech, Paige answered a question critical of testing in a way that illustrates the assumptions underlying his support of high-stakes, standardized tests. He stated, "We should enable success, but I don't object to making decisions based on how a student performs on a valid, reliable, objective assessment tool" (Feinberg, 2004). This wielding of civil rights discourse to name educational inequality and support the continued use of high-stakes standardized testing as a tool in the fight against racial inequality continued into the administration of President Barack Obama, where, for instance, reflecting the neoliberal turn in Black politics (Spence, 2013), President Obama said that education is the "civil rights issue of our time" (H. Cooper, 2011), and his Secretary of Education, Arne Duncan, also asserted that "Education is the civil rights issue of our generation" (Duncan, 2011). Meanwhile, the Obama administration's signature education policy program, the Race To The Top initiative (U.S. Department of Education, 2009), not only further advanced the neoliberal, corporate education reforms seeded in NCLB, it also pushed for even more strident use of high-stakes, standardized testing in student, teacher, and school evaluation (Au, 2016b; Karp, 2012).

As the above examples illustrate, educational policymakers, as well as many others in the United States, have established a tradition of wrapping education reforms around civil rights discourse, fundamentally linking the use of high-stakes, standardized testing to concepts of racial justice in education and beyond (E. Brown, 2015; Darling-Hammond, 2004; Heubert, 2001). In this way, the advancement of testing in the name of civil rights and in the deployment of state-sanctioned policy highlights how high-stakes testing is used as an expression of official anti-racism within neoliberal multiculturalism (Melamed, 2011). Here we have heads of state, drawing on legacies of racial justice and equality, expressly recalibrating the state apparatus of federal education policy around an agenda of official anti-racism, attempting to control the idea that high-stakes testing "counts" as a race matter, and attempting to structure these racialized linkages as legitimate, commonsense knowledge within the domain of education policy and practice. Consequently, the use of high-stakes, standardized testing becomes linked with discourses of anti-racist political activism, where testing for racial equality can now be equated with marches, sit-ins, and other forms of protest. This idea, that modern-day high-stakes, standardized testing is being used to promote racial justice, is empirically testable, insomuch that we can turn to empirical research to interrogate the fundamental claim advanced by advocates for using testing to achieve racial justice in education. Namely, we can pose the question: Has the use of high-stakes, standardized testing produced more equitable outcomes (e.g., closed race-based achievement gaps) and improved the quality of education of children of color?

Answering the first part of the above question is fairly straightforward. Analyses of National Assessment of Educational Progress (NAEP) test scores, as well as other cross-state test-score analyses, show that not only have test score gaps between white students and students of color (particularly Blacks and Latinos) not closed, they have increased since the implementation of NCLB and the federal mandate requiring the use of high-stakes, standardized testing (J. Lee, 2006; National Research Council, 2011; Ravitch, 2013). As for the relationship between high-stakes testing and the quality of education for children of color, empirical research can answer that as well. Nationally speaking, multiple individual studies (see, e.g., Center on Education Policy, 2007; Renter et al., 2006; Rosenbusch, 2005) as well as analyses synthesizing large bodies of research on testing (Au, 2007) have established that high-stakes testing environments compel teachers and schools to focus increasingly on tested subjects like mathematics and literacy to the increasing exclusion of less tested subjects like social studies and sciences, and sometimes to the total exclusion of art, music, and physical education. Further, these studies have confirmed that teachers, in direct response to the pressures exerted by high-stakes, standardized tests, have increasingly resorted to less engaging, more teacher-centered, rote lecture in order to cover tested materials—where in some cases teachers are required to follow the district-mandated instructional scripts that dictate exactly what they are allowed to say to students (Au, 2011b). Further still, because high-stakes, standardized testing, as a racial project, functions to concentrate failure in low-income communities of color, this phenomenon of test-related curricular and pedagogic squeeze happens at significantly higher rates for these populations (Nichols et al., 2005; Nichols & Berliner, 2007; von Zastrow, 2004). Consequently, as a result of high-stakes testing, low-income children of color are subjected to a qualitatively different educational experience than that of their white, more affluent counterparts—who have a much higher likelihood of accessing a more engaging, content-rich education.

The test-induced curricular and pedagogic squeeze also illustrates how modern-day high-stakes, standardized testing operates as a racial project of neoliberal multiculturalism. In this case we have high-stakes testing being used as a tool to support market mechanisms within education and advocated for in the name of racial justice. However, it is crucial to note that even the above-mentioned curricular and pedagogic squeeze is racialized; in the same way that specific curriculum and teaching strategies are being diminished, high-stakes testing has also forced multicultural curriculum and culturally relevant pedagogies that can speak more directly to children of color and their communities out of the curriculum and out of the classroom (Au, 2009b; Darder & Torres, 2004; McNeil, 2000). Thus, consistent with Meritocracy 2.0 and neoliberal anti-racism, and as evidence of what Bonilla-Silva (2013) refers to as color-blind racism, we see a process where in the name of racial equality in education, race and culture in teaching and learning become anathema to the officially sanctioned, raceless, "correct" knowledge and pedagogy as defined by the tests. In this sense, and as part of the neoliberal multicultural project, to be "anti-racist" is defined as being against the act of naming race—since race has nothing to do with test-validated knowledge and learning—and being against the admission that systemic racism even exists—since the "objectivity" of the test excludes that possibility.

HIGH-STAKES TESTING AND THE DISCIPLINING OF BLACK AND BROWN BODIES

Another way that modern-day high-stakes, standardized testing operates as a racial project of neoliberal multiculturalism is through the ways that these tests are used to discipline Black and Brown students specifically and disproportionately. Significant test score achievement gaps between rich and poor students and between racial groups are persistent (Ladson-Billings, 2006; Love, 2023; National Research Council, 2011), meaning that failure, as defined by test scores, is concentrated in low-income children of color. This is why, as discussed earlier, children of color have experienced sharper curricular and pedagogic squeeze, resulting in a qualitatively different education than that experienced by their white, affluent counterparts (Au, 2023b; Nichols et al., 2005; Nichols & Berliner, 2007). An outcome of this process is that low-income students of color (as well as their teachers and their schools) are rendered visible as failures through high-stakes, standardized testing. This kind of visibility allows disciplinary power to be enacted on low-income children of color by arranging them as racialized objects of failure (Melamed, 2011). As Foucault (1995) explains, such visibility

> . . . assures the hold of power that is exercised over them. It is the fact of being constantly seen, of being able always to be seen, that maintains the disciplined individual

> in his subjection. And the examination is the technique by which power, instead of emitting the signs of its potency, instead of imposing its mark on its subjects, holds them in a mechanism of objectification. In this space of domination, disciplinary power manifests its potency, essentially, by arranging objects. (p. 187)

As such, systems of high-stakes, standardized testing place low-income students of color within an ever-increasing web of surveillance (Hanson, 2000), where the high stakes attached to the tests function to discipline and punish not just the system of public education itself (Vinson & Ross, 2003), but also Black and Brown children. Put in more grounded terms, systems of high-stakes, standardized testing and the policies built around them establish a system of surveillance and an environment of teaching and learning under constant threat. For children of color, then, high-stakes testing serves to acculturate them to a norm of being disciplined by state authorities.

The relationship between high-stakes standardization and the disciplining of Black and Brown bodies becomes even more concrete when we look at evidence surrounding high school exit exams and the school-to-prison pipeline. We know that, just like all other high-stakes, standardized tests, high school exit exams have a disproportionately negative impact on non-white children (Zabala, 2007), where Black and Latino students fail such exams at higher rates than their white peers and are far more likely to drop out of high school as a result. For instance, when Massachusetts implemented a high-stakes test-based accountability system in the 1990s, it witnessed a 300% increase in dropouts, and with the implementation of a graduate exit exam, it saw a 4% decline in graduating students. Predictably, the exit exam failures and dropouts were disproportionately African American and Latino (Darling-Hammond, 2007). Further, there is a direct relationship between exit exams, dropping out of high school, and increased incarceration rates; a study commissioned by the National Bureau of Economic Research found that standards-based high school exit exams correlated with an increase the rate of incarceration by 12.5% (O. Baker & Lang, 2013). Hence, high-stakes, standardized testing, as a racial project of neoliberal multiculturalism, empirically works to surveil, discipline, and punish Black and Brown children, all in the name of racial justice and neoliberal anti-racism.

CONCLUSION

In this chapter I have argued that standardized testing has functioned as a racial project historically, and that its progeny, modern-day high-stakes, standardized testing, now functions as a racial project of neoliberal multiculturalism. In doing so I have discussed how standardized IQ testing was stitched together with the presumed objectivity of the tests to mask structural racism in schools and society through the ideology of meritocracy. I have also argued that these very same strands exist today, albeit transformed under neoliberalism in what I called Meritocracy 2.0. To make these arguments, I used the concepts of neoliberal multiculturalism, official anti-racism (Melamed, 2011), and racial projects (Omi & Winant, 2015) to explain how high-stakes, standardized testing, as an assessment tool, can be wrapped around concepts of racial equality vis-à-vis forms of neoliberal anti-racism—which we see operationalized through the use of civil rights discourse to promote testing. I then drew upon empirical research on high-stakes, standardized testing to highlight how such testing has negatively impacted the education of children of color in terms of curriculum and pedagogy, as well as research on high school exit exams and dropouts to point out how high-stakes tests materially contribute to not only the disciplining of Black and Brown students specifically, but also directly to the school-to-prison pipeline.

The central point of my argument here has been to assert that any and all claims to the use of high-stakes, standardized testing to promote racial equity and justice are ideologically driven and demonstrably false in the face of the materially racist effects of testing on children of color. While this argument is not particularly new (see, e.g., Karier, 1972), nor is it one that can be relegated solely to the United States (see, e.g., Gillborn, 2013, for similar policy moves in England), the struggles over the relationship between high-stakes testing and racial inequality in the United States are currently at a critical juncture. For example, the sharp increase in high-stakes, standardized testing has provoked a significant, popular backlash among students, parents, and teachers such that a movement to "opt-out" and refuse to take the tests has developed in its wake (Au & Hollar, 2016; Foster, 2016; Hagopian, 2014a). The opt-out movement is particularly threatening to current neoliberal education reform efforts because it removes the tests and the data they produce from the equation altogether, thus challenging the fundamental metric upon which neoliberal education reforms depend entirely. In response, a group of 12 mainstream civil rights organizations issued a press release decrying the opt-out movement, claiming that test score data were critical to pushing for racial justice and fighting racial inequality in education (E. Brown, 2015). Consequently, education activists (Hagopian & Network for Public Education, 2015) and other, more progressive civil rights organizations (J. Brown, 2015) pushed back, citing evidence of the ways that high-stakes testing was harmful to children of color specifically, and public education generally (Au, 2018, 2023b). As this example illustrates, not only are the discourses of civil rights, high-stakes testing, and racial equality still circulating, but the issue is still very real, alive, and important in educational policy in the United States because neoliberal education reformers are essentially marketizing civil rights and racial equality to advance their policy agendas (Scott, 2013). Taken as a whole, the evidence and arguments I have offered here illustrate the way that high-stakes, standardized testing is implicated in the very process of racialization itself, where

> *Racialization converts the effects of differential value-making processes into categories of difference that make it possible to order, analyze, describe, and evaluate what*

> *emerges out of force relations as the permissible content of other domains of U.S. modernity (e.g., law, politics, and economy).* (Melamed, 2011, p. 11, emphasis in original)

In terms of racialization, we see that high-stakes, standardized testing has a direct role in both the differential value-making process and the conversion of that process into categories of difference, which are then in turn utilized in our racialized sense-making in education and other institutions and domains.

Any recommendations that might flow from the above analysis depend entirely on one's goals. The process of racialization exists, and it is expressed through high-stakes, standardized testing (among other educational policy tools). As such, if the goal is to subvert the entire process of both the neoliberal reform agenda and the role that testing plays in racialization, then one possible recommendation would be to follow the lead of educational activists, students, and teachers in Seattle, New York, and elsewhere, and push for a broader-based and widespread opt-out movement (Au & Hollar, 2016; Foster, 2016; Hagopian, 2014a). As noted above, opting out renders the test data meaningless and subsequently throws the entire logics and function of the system into question. Opting out also highlights and sharpens the tension surrounding the use of high-stakes, standardized testing as a tool for racial equality, thus also highlighting the contradictions implicit in the neoliberal multicultural education reform project specifically.

In light of the above analysis, another possible recommendation would be to make use of forms of assessment that correlate more strongly with teaching and learning, as opposed to using the current high-stakes, standardized testing, which correlates most strongly with economic class and other forms of structural inequality (Berliner, 2013).

Other forms of assessment, such as multiple-subject portfolio defenses, have been used with great success within the New York Performance Standards Consortium—which have shown to have more equitable outcomes relative to the graduation and college attainment for children of color, working-class kids, and students whose first language is not English (Foote, 2007; Meier & Knoester, 2017). These types of assessments do not address the structural issues extant to public schooling, but the data seem to indicate that they produce less discriminatory outcomes, perhaps because they are flexible enough to accommodate the variation of students' needs. Of course, a major limitation of these two recommendations, and a major shortcoming of focusing purely on public education and schooling in general, is that they neglect the structural inequalities that are so prevalent outside schools. Indeed, taking the issue of racialized inequality in schools seriously absolutely requires that we take the issue of racialized structural inequality outside of schools just as seriously (Dumas, 2008; Dumas & Anyon, 2006).

In the end, high-stakes, standardized testing as a racial project of neoliberal multiculturalism, the wielding of civil rights discourse to support testing, and the market logics of neoliberal anti-racism are all belied by the material realities of the tests themselves. These tests are far from objective measurements of teaching and learning (Au, 2023b), they are not improving the education of children of color, and research has consistently confirmed that test scores are determined more by structural conditions affecting students than any kind of individual, meritocratic effort. Ultimately this is why relying on high-stakes, standardized testing to achieve racial justice in education is fundamentally about ideology and not meeting the material and cultural needs of children and communities. By focusing on testing as the lever for equitable education and social reform, policymakers, politicians, pundits, business leaders, and pro-testing nonprofits are essentially pretending that a faulty thermometer can cure the root causes of a fever—because as I have argued here, historically and contemporarily, high-stakes, standardized testing is an artifice and carrier of racial inequality, not a destroyer of it.

Part III

ASIAN AMERICAN RACIALIZATION AND EDUCATION

"Superachievers" vs. "Super Predators"

How the Racist Love of the Model Minority Is Weaponized Against Black and Asian American Students

In 1987, *Time Magazine* published an article titled "The New Whiz Kids," which labeled Asian American students as "superachievers." In 1996, then-First Lady Hillary Rodham Clinton infamously referred to Black teenagers as "super predators" who lacked empathy and conscience. Made nearly a decade apart, these two statements highlight how the racialization of Black and Asian American students have been tightly linked historically through the Model Minority stereotype—a stereotype rooted in white supremacy and anti-Blackness that has hurt both Black and Asian American students.

There was nothing new about *Time Magazine*'s article; it was merely a recycling of the well-worn stereotype of the Asian American Model Minority, which originated in January 1966, when the *New York Times* published "Success Story: Japanese-American Style," by William Petersen.

Centering around the idea that Japanese Americans have overcome racism better than other groups, Petersen crowed, "By any criterion of good citizenship that we choose, the Japanese Americans are better than any other group in our society, including native-born whites." He went on to claim that, like European immigrants, Japanese Americans have also taken "advantage of the public schools, the free labor market and America's political democracy" and "climbed out of the slums, took better-paying occupations and acquired social respect and dignity." By comparison, Petersen contended, this has not been true for groups he labeled as "problem minorities," specifically: "negroes, Indians, and Mexicans."

According to Petersen, education was "key" to Japanese American success. After interviewing Japanese American college students at UC Berkeley, he found

---

Previously published as "'Superachievers' vs. 'Super Predators': How the Racist Love of the Model Minority Is Weaponized Against Black and Asian American Students," 2025, *Rethinking Schools*, *39*(2). https://rethinkingschools.org/articles/superachievers-vs-super-predators-how-the-racist-love-of-the-model-minority-is-weaponized-against-black-and-asian-american-students/. Reprinted by permission.

them to be clean, neat, studious, and, importantly, law-abiding and respectful—unlike the "bohemian slob" students he saw protesting on campus at the time. Petersen also argued that Japanese culture pushes Japanese Americans to work hard and have an "achievement orientation," something which he asserted is lacking in "lower class Americans, whether negro or white."

In December of that same year, *U.S. News & World Report* published its own Model Minority article titled "Success Story of One Minority Group in U.S." This piece focused on Chinese Americans, calling them "a model of self-respect and achievement in today's America."

The article repeatedly asserted that Chinese Americans are self-sufficient and used this to continually assert the racist idea that Black people were too dependent on state support and were draining resources. At one point the article fallaciously argues that "At a time it is being proposed that hundreds of billions be spent to uplift Negros and other minorities, the nation's 300,000 Chinese Americans are moving ahead on their own—with no help from anyone else." The article then went on to say that Chinese Americans have been successful because they are willing to work at any job, "don't sit around moaning" about their situation, are good citizens with strong families, and are obedient and hardworking in their jobs and at school—all the while implicitly suggesting Black people were the opposite.

The article ends by quoting a social worker who asserts that "it must be recognized that the Chinese and other Orientals in California were faced with even more prejudice than faces the Negro today. . . . The Orientals came back, and today they have established themselves as strong contributors to the health of the whole community."

These articles established the architecture of the Model Minority stereotype: Despite having experienced significant racism historically, due to hard work, cultural values, obedience, respecting authority, family structure, achievement orientation, valuing education, and self-reliance, Asian Americans have still been successful.

Further, by both tacit and explicit implication, so-called "problem minorities"—especially Black Americans—just need to stop complaining, take note of Asian American success, and simply realize that racism is not really a problem. Thus, the Model Minority stereotype was born in 1966 of racism, white supremacy, and anti-Blackness.

Of course, the appearance of the Model Minority stereotype at this time was not coincidental. The Watts Rebellion had occurred in 1965, and the Voting Rights Act of 1965 had passed as well. The *Moynihan Report*—which advanced racist arguments that Black families were weak and that a culture of poverty was the reason for their social and economic status—was published in the same year.

In this context, the stereotype of the respectful, clean, and non-rebellious Asian American Model Minority also served as a racial counterpoint to the increasingly organized and militant Black and Brown Liberation movements of the time. Consequently, the Model Minority stereotype also serves as an argument about respectability politics and the "right" way to achieve racial justice through quiet, hard work, rather than loud, disruptive, or "scary" protests.

From *Fortune* magazine declaring Asian Americans to be "America's Super Minority" in the 1980s, to the racist, eugenicist *The Bell Curve* arguing that Asians had the highest IQs of all races in the 1990s, to *The Wall Street Journal*, *The New York Times*, *Bloomberg*, *The Economist*, and *CNBC* all publishing articles promoting the Asian American Model Minority in 2015, media, politicians, and pundits have ensured the stereotype's durability for nearly 60 years.

Educational achievement has also been central to the Model Minority narrative, where across the decades Asian American students have been called "academic marvels" by *U.S. News and World Report*, the "reigning academic stars of academia" with "dazzling academic success," and "stellar" by *The New York Times*. As author Stacey J. Lee notes in her 2009 book, *Unraveling the "Model Minority" Stereotype*, these portrayals of Asian American student success are consistently attributed to high expectations of parents, two-parent homes, Confucian values, being studious, being quiet, being obedient, working hard, and valuing education.

Like the more general stereotype, the Asian American Model Minority student also gets used against Black students. Rather than looking at racism and economic stratification as sources of educational disparities, the stereotype instead reinforces racist tropes of Black students being unintelligent, lazy, "bad," and uncaring educational failures who lack discipline and drive, and who have low educational expectations compared to their Model Minority peers.

THE RACIST LOVE OF THE MODEL MINORITY

Ultimately, despite its portrayal as a "positive" stereotype, the Model Minority is based on a racist, white supremacist love—a kind of love that both upholds Asian Americans to be used against other racial groups while also subjecting them to ongoing anti-Asian hatred and violence. Reflecting on the rise in attacks on Asian Americans in the early 2020s, in her book *Racist Love*, Leslie Bow (2022) discusses how this love

> . . . transforms into racist hate with dizzying speed. . . . [R]acial feeling easily flip-flops its mode of existence. . . . For Asian Americans, hard-won taboos against hate speech evaporated overnight. . . . The contemporary moment of undisguised anti-Asian bias pulls me full circle: from philic to phobic, from compliment to slur. . . . [I]n the shift to racial hatred, what remains operative is racial feeling on a continuum, adoration and animosity as flip sides of the same coin. (p. 195)

To Bow's point, over the last 6 decades, the "positivity" of the Model Minority stereotype has never protected Asian Americans from the violence of white supremacy. From the early 1980s murder of Vincent Chin in Detroit by two recently laid-off white male auto workers, to a white gunman killing 5 and wounding 32 Asian American school children in the late 1980s, to the white supremacist "dot busters" in New Jersey who violently targeted South Asian Americans in the 1990s, to the 2012 killing of six South Asian Americans at a Sikh temple in Wisconsin, to the thousands of reported incidents of anti-Asian hate that took place between March 2020 to March 2021 amidst the onset of the COVID-19 pandemic, to the 2021 shooting of six Asian American women by a white male gunman in Georgia—the stereotype of the good, hardworking, and law-abiding Model Minority has never stopped Asian Americans from being seen as a threat to American whiteness. Indeed, one could easily argue that the racial exceptionalism underlying the stereotype of Model Minority success has likely only increased anti-Asian violence.

The Asian American Model Minority student has similarly been viewed as a threat to the education of white students. During the 1980s, newspaper articles regularly described Asian American students as "surging" like a "tidal wave" into elite universities, and graffiti saying "Stop the Asian Hordes" appeared at UC Berkeley. White university students also joked that UCLA (the University of California, Los Angeles) stood for "University of Caucasians Living Among Asians," that MIT (the Massachusetts Institute of Technology) was really an acronym for "Made in Taiwan," and that UCI (the University of California, Irvine) really meant "University of Chinese Immigrants."

In March 2011, a white UCLA student went viral on social media after posting a video titled "Asians in the Library," where she complained about "hordes of Asian people" and racistly mimicked Asian languages—all of which supports Nolan Cabrera's 2014 research, which found that even though Asian Americans are the only racial group in the United States to attend universities proportionate to the overall population, white college students still view Asian American students with resentment and feel they are over represented in higher education. What some might find surprising is that, because of the stereotype, many Asian Americans have also come to resent themselves.

INTERNALIZING RACIST LOVE

The reality is that many Asian Americans have internalized the Model Minority stereotype as a kind of racial identity. As Erin Ninh (2021), author of *Passing for Perfect*, explains:

> . . . [T]he model minority is coded into one's programming—racialization becoming feeling and belief—its litmus test is whether an Asian American *feels pride or shame* by those standards. If you have enjoyed what Tiger parenting memes say about you (laughed ruefully, maybe, but knowingly): Congratulations, you have tested positive. With your click, like and share, you affirm an identity set apart from other racial groups: a feeling that *our bar is higher*. (p. 6)

The internalization of the Model Minority stereotype means that if we are not successful, society does not see us as "real" Asian Americans, nor do we see ourselves as "real" either. This reality moves Ninh to ask a particularly painful question: "[I]f Asian Americans are recognized as persons *by their communities and their country* only by the success frame, then whose public identity is a failure allowed to use? Whose racial reputation and likeness if not their own?" (p. 13).

Consequently, there is a lot of evidence that the Model Minority stereotype contributes to the poor mental health of Asian Americans, especially students. For instance, one study of Asian Americans aged 18–30 found that pressures associated with the Model Minority and racial discrimination in school resulted in increased stress, what some have specifically referred to as "model minority stress."

Additionally, the Model Minority stereotype is predicated on a kind of Asian American, able-bodied perfection, such that we do not risk asking for help—since needing help means we are imperfect and potentially misaligned with social, community, and even our own expectations of ourselves *as Asian Americans*. As such, research also finds Asian Americans resist reporting bullying and harassment and are also unlikely to seek mental health supports, and that many doctors incorrectly presume that Asian Americans face fewer mental health issues than other racial groups. Many Asian Americans have their psychological conditions under diagnosed and misdiagnosed because of this.

Hence, as one Asian American psychologist explains in an article for *Axios*, "We self-harm. We quietly continue to do our homework, even though we're super depressed or anxious. We act out inside the house, but it never shows outside the house. . . . So this system of schools has . . . always been like, 'Oh, you're good, you're fine'" (Chen & Doherty, 2023). These issues all contribute to the fact that suicide is the second leading cause of death for Asian Americans ages 15–34, with the highest concentration between ages 20–24. For Asian Americans, the Model Minority stereotype is literally killing us.

Clearly, the Asian American Model Minority stereotype comes at a cost: It supports anti-Black racism and deficit views of Black people, subjects Asian Americans to white supremacist fears and violence, and damages the Asian American psyche. But what if all that stereotypic Asian American achievement—that magical sauce for Model Minority success—is not magical at all, but instead simply confirms what we already know about income and education disparities in the United States?

CONFIRMING THE OBVIOUS

If you took most educational data at face value, you might conclude that the Asian Americans really are a Model Minority. According to the National Center for Education Statistics, in 2022 Asian American students were tops among all racial groups in total NAEP and SAT scores, and data from 2021 show a 4-year college enrollment rate for Asian Americans of nearly 76%, compared to a rate between

40% and 43% for Black and Latine students. Additionally, census data from 2022 show that 61% of Asian Americans have college degrees, a rate that significantly outpaces Latine peoples (20.8%), Black Americans (28.1%), and whites (41.9%).

However, what is lost in these data is that Asian American achievement simply proves what has been obvious across decades of educational research: Parental education and economic class have almost an ironclad correlation with academic achievement.

After decades of Asian immigration to the United States being illegal, the federal government passed the Immigration and Nationality Act of 1965, giving preference to Asian immigrants who already held higher education degrees and who had professional skills. This had a profound effect on the educational outcomes of Asian Americans. For instance, between 1966 and 1977, over 80% of the immigrants from India were professional and technical workers, including 40,000 engineers, 25,000 doctors, and 20,000 scientists with PhDs. As another example, between 1966 and 1985, 25,000 well-educated nurses immigrated to the United States from the Philippines. Importantly, the Pew Research Center estimates that over 98% of Asian Americans either immigrated after 1965 or are descendants of post-1965 immigrants.

Currently, U.S. immigration policy gives preference to the immediate family of permanent U.S. residents and gives second preference to educated professionals. Wealthy immigrants can also gain entrance to this country by investing in U.S. businesses in the amounts of either $900,000 or $1.8 million. Again, these rules influence the Asian American population. Data from 2017–2019 show that over 60% (over 490,000) of the immigrants to the United States were from Asia, mostly on the H-1B visa used heavily by the technology, banking, and entertainment sectors.

There is also a selection process in many Asian home countries that limits who immigrates to the United States. As Prachi Gupta (2023) explains in *They Called Us Exceptional,* in India, "middle-and upper-class Indians from dominant castes typically access the best schools and jobs that feed into opportunities in America, which favor immigrants who bring specialized skills in tech and science" (p. 7). The result is a highly selective Indian American community where 68% of Indian immigrants to the United States already have a college degree. This rate is 3.5 times that of the general U.S. population, and more importantly, it is nine times that of the general population in India itself (Sanjoy, 2016).

Research consistently shows that achievement markers like college attainment and SAT scores correlate very strongly with family income and education levels of parents. Given that so much of the Asian American population is sharply skewed toward a select group of immigrants, the majority of whom likely came to the United States with college degrees and professional jobs already in hand, it is no wonder large numbers of Asian American students are getting high test scores and attending college.

Southeast Asian Americans also confirm the tight relationship between levels of family income and education with academic achievement. Since 1975, refugees from Cambodia, Laos, and Vietnam, including the Khmer and Hmong/Hmoob peoples, have been resettled in the United States after fleeing persecution due to U.S. imperialist military incursions in their home countries. While initial decades of resettlement resulted in over 1.1 million refugees being relocated to the United States, more recent Southeast Asian immigrants have arrived through visas for family members or employment such that there are over 2.5 million Southeast Asian American in the United States.

Contrary to the Asian American Model Minority stereotype, nearly 44% of Southeast Asian Americans are officially low-income, with 460,000 of those officially living in poverty. Notably, Hmong/Hmoob Americans experience a 58% low-income rate, with 26% officially living in poverty—rates nearly double that of white Americans and on par with Black Americans. College attainment rates for Southeast Asian Americans are also significantly lower than other Asian American groups: For Vietnamese Americans it is 29%, Burmese Americans 21%, Hmong and Laotian Americans 18%, and Cambodian Americans 16%. Data from California (where the highest concentrations of Southeast Asian Americans live) also indicate that almost 30% of Southeast Asian Americans there have not earned a high school diploma.

Whether at the top or the bottom of income and education levels in the country, Asian American academic achievement simply confirms the obvious fact that our system of education reproduces social and economic inequities that privilege families with higher levels of education and financial resources.

MODEL MINORITY DIVESTMENT

In 1903, in *The Souls of Black Folk*, W. E. B. Du Bois posed this question to African Americans: "How does it feel to be a problem?" Nearly 100 years later, in *The Karma of Brown Folk*, Vijay Prashad (2000) suggests that the question for the Asian American Model Minority is instead, "How does it feel to be a solution?" (p. viii).

And that is just it. Framed as a Model Minority, Asian Americans are presented as a solution to racism: Just keep your head down, work hard, stay quiet, be self-sufficient, respect authority. It is the mythology of Horatio Alger's rags-to-riches, pull-yourself-up-by-your-bootstraps American meritocracy, only this time in yellow face.

When it comes to the Asian American Model Minority stereotype, we are left with a choice: Maintain this investment in the Model Minority and, by extension, maintain the investment in white supremacy, racial capitalism, settler colonialism, and anti-Blackness that comes with it, or divest from the stereotype entirely—including ditching the internalized identity for Asian Americans themselves—because it does not serve anyone's humanity.

Such divestment would require developing more critical understandings of Asian Americans by all racial groups, as well as developing critical, radical understandings of the deep connections between Asian Americans and non-Asian Americans—what Pulitzer Prize–winning author Viet Thanh Nguyen (2024) refers to as "expansive solidarity."

Part of this process could include uncovering, radically reconstructing, and relearning Asian American histories that includes progressive, radical, and even revolutionary activism that operates in direct contradiction to the Model Minority stereotype. This could include learning about historical heroes like Yuri Kochiyama and Grace Lee Boggs, radical Asian American activists who worked closely with Black community organizers on issues of justice and solidarity. More recent examples could include activists like Connie Wun, Tamara Nopper, and Dylan Rodriguez, all of whom have been making deep and serious connections between Asian American communities and the abolitionist movement. Similarly, groups like Tsuru for Solidarity, Red Canary Song, the Asian Prisoner Support Committee, AAPI Women Lead, and Butterfly have also been working in a wide range of abolitionist projects.

We should also be supporting K–12 Asian American Studies curriculum, especially by those doing it from a more liberated Ethnic Studies approach. For instance, we can see this work being brought to schools, communities, and teachers through Sohyun An and Noreen Naseem Rodriguez's (2022) "Stop AAPI Hate Asian American Studies Curriculum Framework," which asks students to critically consider "Imperialism, War, & Migration," "Citizenship & Racialization," "Resistance and Solidarity," and "Reclamation & Joy." An and Rodriguez have continued this work with their colleague, Esther Kim, through their excellent book *Teaching Asian America in Elementary Classrooms* (Rodriguez et al., 2024), which provides a strong conceptual framing along with concrete examples for helping students develop critical consciousness surrounding Asian American histories and communities.

These examples demonstrate the potential of Asian American activists in concert with K–12 Asian American Studies to show how Asian Americans are deeply connected to all racial groups who have struggled against settler colonialism, anti-Black racism, and white supremacy. Indeed, recognizing these connections harkens back to the very origins of the racial category of "Asian American" itself, which largely grew out of the Black and Brown power movements of the late 1960s.

Ultimately, there is nothing positive about the Model Minority stereotype. The racist love of the Asian American student superachiever simply helps justify the white supremacist framing of Black youth as super predators. In the process it flattens the humanity of Asian Americans, disregards the material role that conditions of immigration play in educational achievement, causes mental trauma among Asian Americans, and gets used to argue that racism does not exist—all the while promoting white supremacist beliefs about Black and Brown peoples. The Model Minority needs to be abandoned as a racist stereotype and replaced with an identity that is anti-racist and based on expansive solidarity with other peoples.

CHAPTER 9

"Isn't That What the Case Is About, the Discrimination Against Asian Americans?"

Conservatives Use Racial Wedge to Attack Affirmative Action

On June 29th, 2023, the U.S. Supreme Court voted 6–3 to effectively end affirmative action considerations of race in university admissions. Many of us have dreaded this expected outcome, but it was consistent with the slew of other conservative decisions the Court has made this year and last, including striking down *Roe v. Wade* and upholding the right for private service providers to discriminate against LGBTQ folks.

The struggle around affirmative action has been heated, and for good reason: Like so many issues related to education, affirmative action requires that we wrangle with the ironclad trio of racism, meritocracy, and high-stakes testing. Unfortunately, a relatively small group of conservative Asian Americans have been given an outsized voice in a fight launched by white conservatives.

And this fight has important implications for K–12 schools.

WHY AFFIRMATIVE ACTION?

Affirmative action programs originated in 1961 with the Kennedy administration's attempts to challenge discrimination in workplace hiring and treatment. In university admissions, affirmative action was meant as a recognition that historical and institutional racism in education and our communities have created unfair systemic advantages for whites and the rich. We know from decades of educational research that this is true. Students whose parents went to college and come from affluent backgrounds have obvious advantages when it comes

---

Previously published as "'Isn't That What the Case Is About, the Discrimination Against Asian Americans?': Conservatives Use Racial Wedge to Attack Affirmative Action," 2023, *Rethinking Schools*, *38*(1), 14–19. Reprinted by permission.

to high school graduation, standardized test scores, and college attainment (Au, 2023b).

When we overlay this fact with histories of racial segregation, racist lending practices, redlining, racial disparities in wages and generational wealth, racist university admissions practices, and racial disparities in education funding, our country's history of white supremacy comes alive in the modern-day differences in educational experiences available to Black and Brown and poor children. For example, almost half of a typical school's budget comes from local property taxes. Because of this, richer, whiter neighborhoods—themselves often the result of historically racist real estate and employment practices—ultimately have better resourced schools than poorer, typically less-white neighborhoods.

As Justice Ketanji Brown Jackson (2023) remarked in her dissent to the ruling, "Our country has never been colorblind. Given the lengthy history of state-sponsored race-based preferences in America, to say that anyone is now victimized if a college considers whether that legacy of discrimination has unequally advantaged its applicants fails to acknowledge the well-documented 'intergenerational transmission of inequality' that still plagues our citizenry."

Prior to the latest Supreme Court case, affirmative action in university admissions was already banned in nine states, with real impact. For instance, according to a 2020 study, within 2 years of when California banned affirmative action in 1996, Black and Latinx enrollment at UCLA and UC Berkeley fell by an estimated 40%, with most of those students going to other universities (Bowman, 2023).

Contrary to what some believe, the affirmative action that did still exist was not based on quotas for admitting certain numbers of protected classes of students. Rather, given a pool of qualified applicants, most university programs looked at race as one factor for admission among potentially dozens of others (one of the defendants, the University of North Carolina, used 40).

Although affirmative action was never going to fix systemic racial and economic inequities, it was at least one policy aimed at trying to ameliorate our history of institutionalized racism and white supremacy. This is exactly why it has come under constant attack by conservatives seeking to propagate the myth of individual equality in America.

AFFIRMATIVE ACTION UNDER ATTACK

Conservative whites have sought to end affirmative action in university admissions for decades. In the 1978 case *University of California v. Bakke*, Allan Bakke, a white applicant turned down by several medical schools, claimed he did not get into programs because other, less qualified non-whites were admitted. In the *Bakke* decision, the Supreme Court upheld that race could be considered as one among a number of factors for admission. Nonetheless, the *Bakke* decision was considered a blow to affirmative action because racial quota systems were deemed illegal, and activists felt it was the first step toward ending affirmative action altogether (Au, 2025).

In 1997, Barbara Grutter, a white woman, sued the University of Michigan Law School, claiming that the school's race-conscious admissions was not constitutional, and that same year, Jennifer Gratz, also a white woman, sued the University of Michigan when she was not admitted for undergraduate studies. The conservative Center for Individual Rights supported both cases. The Supreme Court upheld the Michigan Law School policy but struck down the undergraduate policy (Au, 2025).

In 2008, Edward Blum recruited Abigail Fisher, a white woman, to sue the University of Texas at Austin for its race-conscious admissions policy. This resulted in two separate rulings. In the 2013 *Fisher I* ruling, the U.S. Supreme Court sent the case back to the Fifth Circuit to be reviewed. The Fifth Circuit found that the university's policy met the legal requirements outlined in *Grutter*. Fisher appealed, and in the 2016 *Fisher II* ruling, the U.S. Supreme Court affirmed the constitutionality of the University of Texas at Austin's admissions policy (Au, 2025).

Edward Blum is an important character here. A white, conservative, failed congressional candidate from Texas, he was behind several court cases regarding redistricting and voting, including *Shelby v. Holder*, which gutted protections in the Voting Rights Act that supported more voters of color. According to *Slate*, between 2015 and 2020, Blum's two nonprofits received $11.2 million (while he drew $900,000 in salary) from the ultra-conservative Searle Freedom Trust, the Scaife Foundation, Bradley Foundation, and Donors Trust—itself funded by the Koch and DeVos families (Au, 2025).

In 2014, as *Fisher II* was still in process, Blum founded the Students for Fair Admissions (SFFA) organization. That same year, SFFA sued the University of North Carolina at Chapel Hill and Harvard University for discriminatory admissions policies. Using anonymous Asian Americans as plaintiffs, the Harvard suit charged that the university was functionally using racial quotas to deny Asian Americans admission, and that admissions should be based solely on standardized test scores and similar metrics (Au, 2025).

THE ASIAN AMERICAN RACIAL WEDGE

After the *Fisher II* ruling, Blum said, "I needed Asian plaintiffs," and he has been purposeful in using Asian Americans to propel his well-funded anti–affirmative action campaign ever since. As he formed SFFA, Blum sought out Asian Americans through community events and websites to further challenge affirmative action. Blum's organizations accessed networks of conservative Asian American activists, themselves funded by right-wing think tanks like Pacific Legal Foundation, and tapped Chinese immigrant leaders to help organize demonstrations against affirmative action (Au, 2025).

Blum's thinking was not new. As legal scholar Claire Jean Kim (2018) argues, Asian Americans have long been used as racial "spoilers" in affirmative action arguments. In the 1978 *Bakke* ruling, for instance, Supreme Court Justice Powell used Asian American achievement as a foil to arguments that systematic "social discrimination" exists, even as he made arguments in favor of using race as one factor in college admission on the grounds that diversity was an important goal. Similarly, in his dissent of the *Fisher II* ruling in 2016 Justice Alito argued that Asian Americans should qualify for affirmative action admissions programs given the amount of discrimination they have overcome.

Given popular media coverage and Blum's tactics, you would think that the SFFA case was really *Asian Americans v. Affirmative Action*. At one point during the trial, Justice Roberts interrupted a Harvard lawyer to ask, "Isn't that what the case is about, the discrimination against Asian Americans?"

In reality, a small but vocal minority of anti-diversity Asian Americans has been given an oversized platform in this debate, while the true relationship between Asian Americans and affirmative action has been lost.

ASIAN AMERICANS AND AFFIRMATIVE ACTION

Historically, Asian American activists led calls for affirmative action programs and admissions processes that are equitable for communities of color. Well before the recent spate of high-profile cases, Asian Americans had fought for affirmative action and fair university admissions. Author Jeff Chang (2023) explains: "As early as the 1950s, after the mass incarceration of Japanese Americans, Asian Americans called for affirmative action programs for racially excluded minorities. From the 1960s through the 1980s, Asian Americans helped force higher education open for excluded communities of color and benefited from affirmative action programs."

For instance, in 1986, when some affirmative action programs excluded Asian Americans, UC Berkeley professor Ling-Chi Wang noticed that Asian American enrollment at Berkeley had leveled out, and through his investigation he discovered that Asian students were being denied enrollment through unofficial decision-making admission processes—referred to as "negative action" in admissions (J. Kang, 1996).

Jeff Chang (2023), a student organizer at Berkeley at the time, explains: "We were able to get the University of California to actually admit that they had discriminated against Asian Americans by dis-advantaging them in what were supposed to be head-to-head, merit-based types of competitions between Asian and white students." Others in the Asian American community saw similar trends at elite universities like Yale, Harvard, Stanford, Brown, and UCLA, and, as part of a broader movement for college access for all non-white racial groups, they pressured these universities (sometimes successfully) to become more transparent in their admissions processes.

This legacy of Asian American support for college access has not disappeared. According to the *2020 Asian American Voter Survey*, (APIA Vote et al., 2020) 70% of Asian Americans support affirmative action when it is understood as a program to help "minority" groups get access to higher education, while 16% are opposed (with the remaining being indifferent or not knowing what affirmative action was). *AAPI Data 2021* shows that Chinese American attitudes toward affirmative action have shifted, with 41% supporting affirmative action in 2016, increasing to 56% supporting it in 2021 (Lee et al., 2021).

CONSERVATIVES FLIP THE SCRIPT

Regardless of Asian American historical and contemporary support for affirmative action, conservatives seized on the Asian American struggles for justice in admissions in the 1980s and inverted it for their anti–affirmative action campaign. White conservatives like Congressman Dana Rohrabacher and columnist George Will co-opted and reframed the "negative action" against Asian Americans to be the same as "affirmative action" since, according to their logic, preferential racial quotas that favored specific groups over individual merit were inevitable once race was a consideration in college admissions. Since then, white conservatives began to claim Asian American protests against discrimination in admissions as part of their campaign against affirmative action (J. Chang, 2023).

With the recent successful SFFA challenge to affirmative action, we see a small but vocal number of conservative Asian Americans—many of whom are Chinese American—with support from conservative whites like Blum, being used to advance a white supremacist cause of ending admissions practices that attempt to remediate institutionalized racism. Scholars Oiyan Poon and Megan Segoshi (2018) have written about how conservative Asian Americans have been used (and used themselves) as "racial mascots" in the anti–affirmative action campaigns.

CONSERVATIVE ASIAN AMERICANS AND THE LOGIC OF MERITOCRACY

Given the history of Asian American discrimination in university admissions in the 1980s, as well as the spike in anti-Asian violence in recent years, it is easy to understand the fear and insecurities driving Asian Americans opposing affirmative action. One of their core beliefs is that a discriminatory "Asian penalty" keeps them out of universities. In turn, this thinking leads them to believe that seats in universities that should go to Asian Americans are wrongfully filled by "less qualified" Black and Latinx students, admitted through affirmative action programs (Au, 2025).

Within this logic, using holistic admissions criteria appears to create an unjust double standard for college admissions that manifests as anti-Asian bias: Asian Americans succeed in the white people's game of American success and now you penalize us for it? Scholar Natasha Warikoo (2022) recalled that during a panel on education, one Asian American woman in the audience explained, "You know, just as we figure out your system of meritocracy, it feels like you're pulling the rug from underneath us" (as quoted in, Yam, 2022).

For conservative white and conservative Asian Americans alike, the solution to the "problem" of affirmative action is clear: high-stakes, standardized tests as a true and objective measure of merit for university admission. This is illustrated by Yukong Zhao, president of the conservative Asian American Coalition for Education, who, in his arguments agains affirmative action, argued that "abolishing standardized testing is a dangerous assault on American meritocracy by radical progressives. Without a fair and transparent process offered by standardized tests, our colleges cannot select and educate the best and brightest to make critical contributions to our economic prosperity, technological leadership and national security" (Asian American Coalition for Education, 2021)

TESTING, ASIAN AMERICANS, AND HOLISTIC ADMISSIONS

As I've written in *Rethinking Schools* and elsewhere, high-stakes, standardized tests are not objective measures of student merit. Instead, they perpetuate inequities associated with white supremacy and capitalism. They sort students into a hierarchical "bell curve" of inequality. Decades of research show that tests reproduce the same race and class inequities. Statistically, test scores correlate most strongly with socioeconomic class. There is nothing objective about standardized test scores. They are inaccurate, do not measure "merit," and should not be used for university admissions (Au, 2023b).

Misuse and misunderstanding of tests aside, research shows that not only is the idea that Asian Americans are being denied admissions to universities a myth, but also that limiting college admissions to only test scores will not significantly increase the number of admitted Asian American students.

In their study of Asian American college admissions using almost 20 years of data, researchers Carnevale and Quinn (2021) found no strong evidence that universities create caps on Asian American enrollment—even if the proportion of Asian Americans with high test scores attending universities has remained remarkably consistent and that, yes, Asian American acceptance rates at the most selective colleges are lower than other groups (to explain the latter, the researchers found that Asian American students apply to highly selective colleges at much higher rates than other groups—making their rate of rejection higher by comparison).

Carnevale and Quinn also found that if college admissions were based purely on test scores, the percentage of Asian American students accepted into elite universities would rise by only 2 percentage points. One reason is that, according to the study, 40% of Asian American student test scores are considered "below average" (contrary to stereotype, not all Asians are good at tests). This would result in one in five Asian American students not being admitted for not meeting the threshold, and perhaps ironically, denying admittance to those Asian American students who might have benefited from affirmative action programs.

It is also critical to understand that although Asian Americans might be overrepresented in elite college admissions, they are represented proportionally in higher education generally. In 2019, Asian Americans made up roughly 5.9% of the U.S. population, and during the 2018–2019 school year Asian American undergraduates made up 6.6% of the total undergraduate college population. Granted, other non-white racial groups are extremely underrepresented in higher education, and some Asian American subgroups share in that extreme underrepresentation. However, contrary to popular notions of too many Asian American students admitted into universities, Asian Americans are perhaps the only racial group to be proportionately represented in higher education (especially given that whites are overrepresented) (Au, 2025).

DEFEND RACE EQUITY IN HIGHER EDUCATION

We should not support Harvard's admissions practices, even if they were one of the defendants in this historic anti–affirmative action lawsuit. Harvard is an elite—and elitist—university with a history of highly discriminatory admissions. In 2019, NBC News reported that 43% of the white student population admitted to Harvard are non-competitive admits as recruited athletes, children of staff, children of donors, or "legacy" children or grandchildren of Harvard alumni (Silva, 2019). A 2022 *New Yorker* article highlighted how 66% of Harvard students hail from the richest 20% of income earners (J. C. Kang, 2022). Harvard doesn't want to democratize access to their institution because if they let everyone walk their hallowed halls, they would no longer be "elite."

Similarly, we should not defend affirmative action as the cure to ending institutionalized racism in education. Affirmative action was never going to fix the problem, but it has been important to defend it as one potential gain in the struggle for racial equity in education, especially when it—along with critical race theory, anti-racism, LGBTQ students and communities, and educational justice generally—are all attacked by right-wing forces.

IMPLICATIONS FOR K–12 EDUCATION

In K–12, one of the sharpest fights revolves around testing, diversity, and admissions into elite high schools in cities like New York and San Francisco. Even though in 2007 the Supreme Court already ruled that race could not be considered for equity purposes in K–12 public school admissions (*Parents Involved in Community Schools v. Seattle Public School District No. 1*), the ending of affirmative action in higher education and arguments to focus on test scores bolsters conservative arguments against diversifying elite K–12 schools.

K–12 teachers could teach about the affirmative action ruling in several ways. For instance, there are a lot of misconceptions about affirmative action and about the Supreme Court cases. Teaching the reality and history of affirmative action could dispel myths and misunderstandings propagated through media.

Some arguments against affirmative action rely on the notion that high-stakes, standardized tests provide accurate and objective measures of student learning, hard work, and merit. Teachers can teach about the racist history of standardized testing and its origins in eugenics and white supremacy, as well as the inaccuracies of the tests and questions about what they really measure.

The stereotype of the model minority also lays at the heart of how Asian Americans have been used to attack affirmative action. Teachers could dispel the model minority stereotype by teaching about the immense ethnic, class, political, educational, and historical diversity that exists under the umbrella category of Asian American. Teaching about the roots of the model minority stereotype and how it was built as a form of anti-Blackness would be critical, too. Additionally, to combat how the model minority stereotype and struggles over affirmative action have divided communities of color, teachers could teach about instances of Asian Americans organizing in solidarity with other racial groups through organizations like the Third World Liberation Front, movements to found Ethnic Studies, protests over Vincent Chin's murder, Asian American support for Black Lives Matter, and more recent multiracial protests against anti-Asian violence, among other possibilities (Au, 2025).

Ultimately, whether it is about affirmative action or Asian Americans, conservatives and white supremacists rely on campaigns of misinformation, racist dog-whistle politics, and a racial divide-and-conquer strategy to keep us splintered and, ultimately, less effective. As always, the answer is to educate and organize.

CHAPTER 10

Asian American Racialization, Racial Capitalism, and the Threat of the Educational Model Minority

There is an established literature about the racialization of Asian Americans[1] in education and its dominant form, the Model Minority (see, e.g., S. J. Lee, 2009; V. Yi et al., 2020). Much of this literature has challenged stereotypes as well as advanced our understandings of Asian American educational life and the positioning of Asian Americans relative to other racial groups. However, I have found our educational theorization has been inadequate for us to fully account for why the racialization of Asian Americans allows Asian Americans to be positioned and used as Model Minorities. In this chapter, I seek to address this conceptual shortcoming by arguing for an Asian American racialization that takes seriously the political economy of racial capitalism (A. L. Brown & DeLissovoy, 2011; H. Chang, 1985; R. D. G. Kelley, 2017; Leonardo, 2012). To do so, I first discuss the racial category of Asian American, and then take up the myth of the Model Minority as an illustrative case of this Asian American racialization in education. I go on to connect the Model Minority to the tropes of Yellow Peril and Orientalism, arguing that our shortcomings of understanding Asian American racialization generally, and in education specifically, require us to develop a different theory of Asian American racialization that is not wholly confined within the boundaries of the United States. Following the racial political economy of Day (2016), I then discuss a conceptualization of Asian American racialization as that of abstract and efficient alien labor, and point to the ways this explains how Asian Americans have been used within racial dynamics in the United States. I conclude with a discussion of the implications this reconceptualization of Asian American racialization has for the construction of the Model Minority in education.

Previously published as "Asian American Racialization, Racial Capitalism, and the Threat of the Educational Model Minority," 2022, *Review of Education, Pedagogy, and Cultural Studies*, *44*(3), 185–209. https://doi.org/10.1080/10714413.2022.2084326.

THE CATEGORY OF "ASIAN AMERICAN"

Relative to other racial categories, "Asian American" is a recently constructed identity, one that consolidated amid U.S. wars in Korea and Vietnam, the burgeoning Civil Rights Movement in the United States, anti-colonial liberation movements around the world, and shifts in U.S. immigration policies that allowed for a new wave of Asian immigrants post-1965. The term originated among community activist and college students in the late 1960s as part of radical movements for racial justice in the United States that included the Black Liberation movement and the movement for Ethnic Studies (B. Chang, 2017; Ishizuka, 2016). Before then, however, Asian Americans were either referred to as "Orientals" or they were called by their specific, individual national origins (Hong, 2020). In these ways, "Asian American" has always been an identity based on a kind of coalition politics, stitching together significant and far-ranging heterogeneity in politically powerful ways.

In 2019 there were over 23 million people of Asian or mixed Asian descent in the United States (or 5.9% of the total U.S. population) spread across 21 different officially named ethnic and national groups (American Community Survey, 2020). Listed alphabetically using the government's terms, these include Asian Indian, Bangladeshi, Bhutanese, Burmese, Cambodian, Chinese, Filipino, Hmong, Indonesian, Japanese, Korean, Laotian, Malaysian, Mongolian, Nepalese, Okinawan, Pakistani, Sri Lankan, Taiwanese, Thai, Vietnamese, "Other Asian, specified" and "Other Asian, not specified." A Pew Research Center analysis found that 34% of Asian Americans self-identified as speaking only English at home (the number rises to 65% for those who are U.S.-born) (Budiman & Ruiz, 2021), and the largest language groups are Chinese (17%), Hindi (13%), Tagalog (9%), and Vietnamese (7%) (American Community Survey, 2020). Other major Asian language groups include Bengali, Formosan, Gujarati, Hmong, Ilocano, Indonesian, Japanese, Laotian, Malayalam, Mon-Khmer or Cambodian, Punjabi, Tamil, Telugu, and Urdu, among others (B. Chang, 2017).

Even though the data illustrate significant heterogeneity within the racial category of Asian American, there are deeper levels of diversity within these groupings. For instance, the ethnic, national, and linguistic category of "Chinese" conceals as much as it reveals. The Han ethnic group officially makes up over 90% of the of Chinese population in China itself. While Mandarin is the official language of the country, there are at least 1,500 "dialects"—supposed offshoots of Mandarin—that in reality are mutually unintelligible languages that have less in common with each other than European languages have with each other (French, 2005). This linguistic (and ultimately cultural) diversity does not even include the other 55 non-Han ethnic Chinese minorities like the Uyghurs and Tibetans (Montefiore, 2013). Taiwan is also technically and officially designated as being part of "China," but it has its own island indigenous peoples (Nesterova, 2019), and the island has experienced different waves of migration from "mainland" China under distinct circumstances that add complexity to that identity (B. Chang, 2017).

Similar histories and complexities exist for most Asian nations. India has a mix of castes, religions, ethnicities, nation-states, languages, and indigenous peoples (Oommen, 2004). Japan has indigenous populations of the Ainu people, and it has control of the island of Okinawa—itself a former sovereign kingdom of indigenous island peoples that now struggles against military occupation, environmental degradation, and the colonizing powers of both the United States and Japan (Hibbett, 2019; Murphy-Shigematsu, 2004). The Philippines fundamentally consists of indigenous peoples with multiple languages who were colonized by both Spain and the United States (Herrera, 2015). Indeed, it is important to remember that most Asian Americans have either descended or immigrated directly from countries that, like the Philippines, have struggled with the legacies of colonization and imperialism: the Dutch and Portuguese colonized Indonesia; the British colonized the Malayan peninsula and parts of China, and India; France colonized Vietnam, Cambodia, and Laos; and Japan occupied all or parts of many East and Southeast Asian nations during World War II (Yang, 2015). As such, in addition to histories of communities with linguistic, ethnic, religious, class, caste, and indigenous diversity, most Asian Americans have lineages that, somewhere in their past, connect with terrible legacies of colonization and imperialism from foreign powers, colonization of indigenous peoples internally, and imperialist wars.

The varying conditions of Asian immigration also matter greatly. For the majority of the current Asian American population, immigration to the United States has largely been structured by the Immigration and Nationality Act of 1965, which gave preference to those who already held educational degrees and who had professional skills. The Pew Center estimates that over 98% of Asian Americans either immigrated or are descendants of immigrants after 1965. Current immigration policy gives first preference to immigrants who have immediate family who are permanent residents in the United States and second preference to educated professionals. Wealthy immigrants also have the option of investing in U.S. businesses (in the amounts of either $900,000 or $1.8 million) in order to immigrate. On average, spread across both permanent and temporary work visas, over 60% (over 490,000) of the immigrants to the United States per year from 2017 to 2019 have been from Asia. Many of these visas include the H-1B visa, which is the visa heavily used by the technology sector, as well as by investors, bankers, and the entertainment industry (Watsky et al., 2020). These policies and practices have contributed directly to the fact that in 2019, 58.2% of Asian Americans held a bachelor's degree (United States Census Bureau, 2020).

However, in sharp contrast to these more highly educated and wealthier immigrants, refugees from Southeast Asia and their familial networks also make up a sizable and important portion of the Asian American population, and the data about their experiences tell a much different story. The peoples of Cambodia,

Laos, and Vietnam, including the Khmer and Hmong, have been resettled in the United States, fleeing persecution in their home countries after the U.S. military incursion in Southeast Asia ended. This refugee resettlement began in 1975 and has resulted in over 1.1 million refugees being relocated to the United States across 3 decades. More recent Southeast Asian immigrants have arrived almost solely through visas for family or employment, and currently there are over 2.5 million total Southeast Asian Americans, comprising 14% of the broader Asian American community (SEARAC & AAJC Los Angeles, 2020).

Nationally, almost 1.1 million Southeast Asian Americans are officially designated "low income," with 460,000 of those living in poverty. Hmong Americans are one of the poorest groups in the country, with 58% low income and 26% officially living in poverty. For comparison, these rates are essentially double that of white Americans, and they are on par with that of Black Americans. We know that income correlates strongly with educational attainment, and this remains consistent with Southeast Asian Americans. For instance, 2011–2015 data from California (where the highest concentrations of Southeast Asian Americans live) show that almost 30% of Southeast Asian Americans have not earned a high school diploma, with Cambodian Americans having the highest rate of 34%. While the total percentage of Asian Americans who hold a bachelor's degree is over 50%, only 25% of Southeast Asian Americans hold the same degree. Laotian Americans have the lowest rate of higher-education degree attainment (14%), followed closely by Hmong Americans and Cambodian Americans, both at 17% (SEARAC & AAJC Los Angeles, 2020).

The conditions faced by Southeast Asian American refugee immigrants versus that of more privileged and elite Asian American immigrants illustrate a broader trend: As of 2018, Asian Americans had the greatest in-group income inequality in the United States (Kochhar & Cilluffo, 2018). There are almost 1.7 million undocumented Asian immigrants, and many have limited English skills. These highly vulnerable populations face housing insecurity and are often relegated to low-wage jobs. Such conditions contribute greatly to 25% of the Asians in New York City and just over 26% of those in Boston living in poverty (Yee, 2021). These kinds of economic class divisions are consistent with those that have existed between different Asian American groups and within individual groups historically (Kwong, 1996; Lan, 2011; S. J. Lee, 2009; Lew, 2006).

The heterogeneity within the racial category of Asian American highlights an important contradiction within the category itself. There is power to be found in the stitching together of a community based on a kind of coalitional politics. If we can say that the Asian American exists as a unitary category, then we can feel the strength in those numbers. However, the broadness of the category does us a disservice because it also masks significant cultural, political, and material fractures within our community as well. The construction of Asian Americans as the Model Minority is built on a similar contradiction, simultaneously upholding the idea of Asian Americans as a monolithically successful group while hiding the diversity of material realities we face.

THE ASIAN AMERICAN EDUCATIONAL MODEL MINORITY

The Model Minority has been the defining form of racialization for Asian Americans in education. It is the idea that Asian Americans, as a racial group, have been able to overcome any obstacles to succeed educationally, professionally, and racially—making them a "model" racial group to which all other racial groups should aspire (Poon et al., 2016; V. Yi et al., 2020). The term "model minority" first appeared in popular media in 1966, where in January of that year, *The New York Times* published an article titled "Success Story: Japanese-American Style" (Petersen, 1966). That story was followed that December with a *U.S. News and World Report* article, "Success Story of One Minority in the US" (U.S. News & World Report, 1966). In the 1980s, popular media expanded this view to include Southeast Asian Americans among the examples of Asian American "Whiz Kids" reaching academic success (S. J. Lee, 2009; Osajima, 1988). In the 1990s, Korean Americans were upheld as hardworking immigrants with strong families, and in 2006, a prominent columnist for *The New York Times* lauded Asian American students for being so successful (S. J. Lee, 2009). In 2012, a *Mercury News* headline read, "Asian Workers Dominate Silicon Valley Tech Jobs," and a 2017 *New Yorker* column ended by arguing that Asian Americans were one of the most "prosperous, well-educated, and successful ethnic groups in America" (Sullivan, 2017) because their hard work, education, and family structure enabled them to overcome a history of discrimination. In 2021, Iowa Senator Chuck Grassley addressed a Korean American nominee for a judicial post by remarking, "If I've learned anything from Korean people, it's a hard work ethic. And how you can make a lot out of nothing. . . . So I congratulate you and your people" (Pfannenstiel, 2021).

The Model Minority was a crafted narrative of successful Asian American assimilation doubling as an argument either that racism did not exist in the United States or that racism could be overcome through hard work and the right cultural values. In turn, this narrative racialized Asian Americans in the form of an attack on other racial groups for their supposed inability to overcome structural racism and even as an attack against Asian Americans themselves as they struggled to meet the norms established through this identity formation (S. J. Lee, 2009; Suzuki, 1977). In education specifically, propagators of the myth of the Model Minority typically treat Asian American students as a monolithic, homogenous group, pointing to their scores on standardized tests, high school graduation rates, college attainment rates, acceptance rates into elite universities, and levels of college degrees as proof of the myth (S. J. Lee, 2009; Poon et al., 2016; V. Yi et al., 2020).

Some of the most robust responses to the myth of the Model Minority in education have critically analyzed it through tracing its history, use, and impact within the context of Asian American racialization in the United States, particularly through critical lenses of intersectionality and transnationalism (B. Chang, 2017; Coloma, 2006; Iftikar & Museus, 2018; V. Yi et al., 2020). Much of this work empirically examines the material conditions and experiences of Asian Americans, paying particular attention to the heterogeneity within the category itself. For instance, S. J. Lee (2005, 2006, 2009), Lew (2006), Louie (2001), Pang et al. (2003), Buenavista et al. (2009), Wing (2007), and Ng et al. (2007), among others, have done important research into the ways that socioeconomic class, gender, ethnic subgroup, cultural capital, and generation of immigration have produced varying educational outcomes and relationships to schooling—including significantly lower educational performance for working-class students and students from specific Asian American subgroups. Additionally, many scholars point to the significant impact of the Immigration and Nationality Act of 1965, which gave preference to those Asian immigrants who already held educational degrees and who had professional training and skills, which is important in explaining the high number of East and South Asian Americans with bachelor's degrees and other markers of educational attainment, but also important in explaining the educational attainment of their children (S. J. Lee, 2009; Watsky et al., 2020). In turn, these analyses have been used to both highlight the material diversity of Asian American educational experiences and deconstruct the ways that a homogenous understanding of the category of "Asian American" invisibilizes the difficult realities faced by many Asian Americans (Budiman & Ruiz, 2021; B. Chang, 2017).

However, it is also important to understand that the stereotype of the Model Minority also racializes Asian Americans as a threat, where the very same stereotypes that are used to uphold them are also used against them. As Okihiro (2014) explains:

> The Asian work ethic, family values, self-help, culture and religiosity, and intermarriage—all elements of the model minority—can also be read as components of the yellow peril. Asian workers can be "diligent" and "slavish," "frugal" and "cheap," "upwardly mobile" and "aggressive," while Asian families and communities can be "mutual aid" and "self-serving" institutions, "inclusive" and "exclusive" groupings, "multicultural enclaves" and "balkanized ghettoes." . . . "Models" can be "perils," and "perils," "models" despite their apparent incongruity. (pp. 141–142)

History underscores Okihiro's point, because the depiction of Asian Americans as a successful Model Minority also made Asians a threat to white America and white entitlement to resources. For instance, in the early 1980s, white fears about the rise of the Japanese automobile industry contributed to a bout of anti-Japanese racism, including the murder of Vincent Chin (a Chinese American) by two white auto workers in Detroit. In the late 1980s, a white gunman opened fire on a California elementary school, killing 5 and wounding 32 schoolchildren, all of whom were of Cambodian or Vietnamese descent (J. Chang, 2021). In the 1980s and 1990s, Asian American students were framed in popular media as "surging" like a "tidal wave" into top universities (Osajima, 2005, p. 221), and graffiti like "Stop the Asian Hordes" appeared at UC Berkeley. White university students also expressed resentment at the increased presence of Asian national and Asian American students at this time, joking that MIT (the Massachusetts Institute for Technology) was short for "Made in Taiwan" and that UCLA (the University of California, Los Angeles) stood for "University of Caucasians Living Among Asians" (Osajima, 2005).

Amid exaggerated reports of Chinese espionage in the United States in the 1990s, Chinese American scientist Wen Ho Lee was targeted as a potential spy, fired from his job, and jailed by the U.S. government despite a lack of evidence and the fact that he had been a well-educated, longtime, trusted employee of a U.S. Defense lab (Wang, 2007). In the aftermath of the September 11, 2001 bombing of the World Trade Center, many racist and nationalist Americans ignorantly associated Sikh turbans and dark skin with terrorism—resulting in a rash of attacks against the South Asian American community at the time and contributing to a gun massacre of six by a white supremacist at a Sikh temple in Wisconsin in 2012 (J. Chang, 2021; United Sikhs, 2019). More recently, in the context of China's ascent as a global economic power, an increase in anti-Chinese rhetoric by then-President Donald Trump, and amid the COVID-19 global pandemic, which most likely began in China (Devlin et al., 2021; Salcedo, 2021), the United States experienced a massive spike in anti-Asian hate crimes during 2020–2021, the majority of which have targeted Asian women in particular (Jeung et al., 2021; Yellow Horse et al., 2022).

Research also shows us that the Model Minority has similarly operated as a threat within education. For instance, the construction of the Asian American Model Minority student has been used against non-white students. The stereotypical Asian American Model Minority student is supposed to be obedient, quiet, studious, and "good"; put in extra hours of work; value education; get high test scores and grade point averages; and attend elite universities (S. J. Lee, 2009; Okihiro, 2014). This "model" then gets used, for instance, against African American students who are subject to stereotypical anti-Black constructions of being lazy, uncaring, unintelligent, educational failures with disciplinary problems (Dumas, 2015, 2016). As an empirical embodiment of this relational use of the Model Minority threat, research has found that for some Asian American college students, stronger internalization of the Model Minority stereotype predicted stronger feelings of anti-Blackness and stronger opposition to affirmative action programs (J. Yi & Todd, 2021).

Additionally, as opposed to being a "positive" stereotype that helps Asian American students, the myth of the Model Minority is in fact a racist stereotype that is used threateningly against Asian American students themselves (B. Chang, 2017; Iftikar & Museus, 2018; V. Yi et al., 2020). For instance, we know that several Asian American subgroups (e.g., Filipinx Americans and Southeast Asian Americans) are invisibilized by the Model Minority stereotype, leading to their educational needs being overlooked or ignored (Buenavista et al., 2009; S. J. Lee, 2005, 2006). Additionally, Asian American students who do not fit the Model Minority stereotype often silence themselves (S. J. Lee, 2009), face feelings of inadequacy and self-hate (E. McGee, 2018; V. Yi et al., 2020), and experience strong feelings of either being an impostor (Cokley et al., 2013) or an inauthentic Asian (Luthar et al., 2021). Asian Americans also suffer internalized racism due to the Model Minority and other stereotypes (Hwang, 2021) and demonstrate higher levels of psychological distress and an unwillingness to seek help from others (Gupta et al., 2011; P. Y. Kim & Lee, 2014). Importantly, the Model Minority stereotype also operates as a form of political threat against Asian Americans, because it effectively casts the legacies of radical resistance and activism that exist in our communities as "not really" Asian American since those legacies don't match the constructed model (Ishizuka, 2016; Liu et al., 2008; Maeda, 2009).

The constructed Asian American Model Minority student has also been used against white students. As noted above, there is a history of white students complaining about too many Asian American students at universities (Dong, 1995; Osajima, 1988), and more recent research confirms that white students still feel that Asian Americans are overrepresented in higher education (Cabrera, 2014). Other research has found that the Model Minority stereotype increased the likelihood of Asian American college students being viewed by white peers with resentment, envy, and as a threat (Ho & Jackson, 2001), and that white college students disdain Asian students for what they perceive as working too hard (Lin et al., 2005). One study of high school students in California also points to whiteness being associated with "lower-achievement, laziness, and academic mediocrity," while Asianness is "linked with high achievement, hard work, and academic success" (Jimenez & Horowitz, 2013, p. 864). The perceived threat that "successful" Asian American students pose to white students highlights how, ultimately, the myth of the Model Minority partially upends a hegemonic racial-educational order that is supposed to privilege whites above all others (Allred, 2007). In doing so, the threat of the Model Minority—historically and in education—is in many ways a manifestation of the expression of all anti-Asian racism in the United States since the 1800s: Yellow Peril.

Yellow Peril is the idea that Asian immigrants globally, and in this case Asian Americans domestically, represent a foreign threat to take over the United States and displace white "Americans" in areas of employment, education, and access to other valued resources, as well as a threat to displace Western civilization with the barbarism of the "Orient" (Day, 2016; Okihiro, 2014). Ultimately, Yellow Peril is based in Orientalism (Said, 1978), a European imperialist binary typology that designates the West as the Occident and the East as the Orient. Within this paradigm, the Occidental represents civilization, cleanliness, goodness, justice, progress, Christianity, and cultural superiority. Conversely, the Oriental is considered to be the opposite: backward, heathen, barbaric, uncivilized, inferior, dirty, scary, and, importantly, *alien* (Day, 2016; E. Lee, 2015). To the Occidental, the Oriental represents a constant threat of degenerate hordes threatening to overwhelm the "civilized" West (Said, 1978). The "Oriental" is gendered, too, because Orientalism frames Asian women as sexually exotic and particularly lascivious and excludes Asian men from the social construction of Western masculinity (Day, 2016; R. E. Lee, 1999). Even though Said's (1978) original analysis mainly focused on the European construction of Western and Southern Asia, the concept of the Oriental evolved into an expression of Western views of all of Asia and Asians (Iftikar & Museus, 2018; Ngai, 2000). Additionally, early Chinese immigration to North America set the stage for an "American Orientalism" that "homogenized Asia as one indistinguishable entity, positioned and defined the West and the East in diametrically opposite terms, and used those distinctions to claim American and Anglo American superiority" (R. E. Lee, 1999, p. 239).

In many ways, this requiring Asian labor on the one hand, and then finding that labor as threatening on the other, has always been the racial contract (Mills, 2014) for Asian Americans. Early waves of Chinese, Japanese, Filipino, Korean, and South Asian immigrants were, each in their turn, used as cheap labor by white industrialists to work the railroads, mines, farms, canneries, and sawmills, to name a few. Then, again each in their turn, these communities were systematically targeted as threats to white America because of their labor, through racist arguments that "Orientals" were morally and culturally depraved, dirty, conniving, uncivilized, and ultimately unassimilable to whiteness. Historically this resulted in a series of laws excluding Asians from immigration and land ownership, violent white mob attacks on each of these Asian immigrant groups, the burning of Chinatowns and the lynching of Chinese workers, and the incarceration of Japanese Americans and transfer of most of their farms to white agribusiness during World War II (E. Lee, 2015; Lye, 2005). In contemporary times, we've witnessed similar impulses with the above-mentioned periods of anti-Asian attacks. From the early Chinese "coolies" working on the railroads to the "high tech coolies" (Wang, 2007) we see now, Asian Americans have been valued for their productive labor (hard labor historically and intellectual labor now) and then treated as an Oriental, Yellow Peril threat for that same productive labor—resulting in anti-Asian propaganda, restrictive laws, incarceration, and/or violence. However, we still have not fully theorized what it is about Asian American racialization that has historically positioned these communities in such a threatening way. To do so requires that we revisit theories of Asian American racialization (Au, 2025a).

TOWARD A TRANSNATIONAL ASIAN AMERICAN RACIALIZATION

Historically, Asian American racialization has generally been theorized as being constructed within the paradigm of Black/white power relations in the United States, essentially arguing that Asian American positionality is contingent upon a foundation of anti-Black racism (Bonilla-Silva, 2002; Day, 2016; C. J. Kim, 1999; Lye, 2008). One important example that has been used widely is that of C. J. Kim (1999). In C. J. Kim's triangulation, Asian Americans are minoritized as non-white but placed in a position of privilege relative to Black Americans such that "White supremacy has pushed [Asian Americans] down, and anti-Blackness has provided the floor beneath which they cannot fall" (C. J. Kim, 2018, p. 10). Bonilla-Silva (2002) similarly maps Asian Americans onto a Black/white field, where he suggests that some Asian American subgroups can be classified as "Whites," some as "Honorary Whites," and others as "Collective Blacks" (p. 4). Likewise, Ong (1996) discusses how within the context of a Black/white racial discourse, some Asian American subgroups, like successful Chinese Americans, have been ideologically "whitened" while others, like working-class Cambodians, have been ideologically "Blackened."

To be clear, there is truth and power in these conceptions, since we know that anti-Black racism has been central to racial formation generally in the United States (Delgado & Stefancic, 2012; Ladson-Billings & Tate, 1995). We also know that the racial formation of Asian Americans has taken place in the context of anti-Black racism, as evidenced in the ways that the Model Minority stereotype has been wielded against Black people (Chow, 2017) and as evidenced in anti-Black racism among some Asian Americans (J. Yi & Todd, 2021). However, even as the above statements hold true, what I am arguing here is that there are aspects of Asian American racialization that exceed the explanatory power provided by a framework of racialization defined *only* by a Black/white field based purely on anti-Black racism in the United States (Day, 2015, 2016; Lye, 2008; Ng et al., 2007).

The central problem with this "Asian American analogical dependency" (Lye, 2008, p. 1735) on anti-Blackness is that it describes "Asian ostracism as deriving from a white-supremacist ideology that has already been put in place by the contradictions of a slave republic" (p. 1733). Further, as Day (2016) explains, such an approach "constrains our ability to elaborate the specificity of Asian racialization that isn't merely a by-product of a foundational antiblackness" (p. 23).[2] That is to say, if Asian American racialization is solely built on a foundation of anti-Black racism, then it not only limits how we can understand it on its own terms (Ng et al., 2007), it also leaves significant gaps in explaining aspects of that same racialization.

One critical gap is that anti-Asian racism in the United States cannot be explained entirely through a lens of foundational anti-Blackness. Rather, as discussed above, anti-Asian racism in this country is built on an ideological legacy that includes Orientalist racialization of Asian Americans as both alien and a threat (a threat, I have argued here, that exists within the Model Minority stereotype and Yellow Peril). Asian American racialization thus in part arises from the European imperialist project of Orientalism—a project that, while linked to the enslavement of African peoples through white supremacy and systems of empire, originated outside of the Americas. In this sense, while anti-Asian racism in the United States is in part born of domestic racial formations clearly connected to anti-Blackness, it is also carries with it a fundamental, underlying conception of Asian Americans that is also transnational in origin. We therefore cannot fully explain or understand anti-Asian racism if our analysis is kept strictly within the theoretical confines of the continental United States. As Day (2016) explains:

> . . . [T]he racialization of Asian Americans and Asian Canadians has unfolded as a parallel evolution of yellow peril to model minority. . . . This mirrored arc of Asian racialization, therefore, cannot be entirely attributable to an inherited legacy or second-order version of antiblack racism given the absence of a similar regime of plantation-based slavery in Canada . . . To put it another way, a transnational framework contradicts an understanding of anti-Asian racism as solely derivative of a prototypical racialization of blackness. (p. 23)

It is important to recognize that in the field of education, Coloma (2006) does call for a turn toward transnationalism in Asian American racialization, and that Iftikar and Museus (2018) also argue for a transnational Asian American racialization and do not reduce anti-Asian racism to anti-Black racism. However, despite these important advances, we still lack a more robust theory of the racialization of Asian Americans in education that attends to the role of Asian immigrant labor as part of global racial capitalism. Day's (2016) theorization helps us do just that.

ASIAN, ALIEN, AND ABSTRACT LABOR

Day (2016) suggests a theorization of Asian racialization that is "translational but distinctively national" (p. 17) and directly linked to racial capitalism by proposing a different racial triangular framework for North America: Native, settler, and alien labor. This framing is critical because it enables us to understand what it is about the racialization of Asian Americans, as a Model Minority (and as Yellow Peril), that has positioned them to be used as a threat. The first two points of this triangular framework, Native and settler, are overall relatively consistent with other work in the area of settler-colonial studies, which generally seek to account for the colonization of North America by white Europeans, the historical and ongoing processes of dispossession of Indigenous peoples, struggles in the establishment and maintenance of indigenous sovereignty, and the maintenance of a settler-colonial state (Coulthard, 2014; Tuck & Yang, 2012).

However, Day's (2015, 2016, 2021) work also departs from previous theorizing of racialization in important ways. For instance, Day's designation argues against categorizing Asian immigrants as settlers. Instead, Day (2016) suggests that, "[s]imilar to African Americans, Asians represented an alien labor force that mixed with Indigenous land to transform it into white property and capital" (p. 31). This is not to imply that Asian immigrants are absolved of potential complicity with the settler colonialism, for as Saranillio (2013) explains,

> While migration in and of itself does not equate to colonialism, migration to a settler colonial space, where Native lands and resources are under political, ecological, and spiritual contestation, means the political agency of immigrant communities can bolster a colonial system initiated by White settlers. (p. 286)

It is also important to note that Day (2016) recognizes that Hawaii is a specific case where several waves of Asian immigrant labor, combined with land ownership, has evolved into Asian Americans there assuming status as settlers (see also Okamura & Fujikane, 2013; Saranillio, 2013). However, distinguishing the positionality of alien labor in North America as distinct from the settler recognizes that Asian immigrant labor exists as "willing or unwitting participants in a settler colonial structure that is driven to eliminate Indigenous people" (Day, 2015, p. 21), while also recognizing that "their racialized vulnerability and disposability supports a settler colonial project" (p. 21).

To be clear, in grouping Black and Asian Americans together as alien labor, Day (2015, 2016, 2021) does not suggest that the racialization of Asian and Black Americans is equivalent or even similar. Day (2015) is expressly cognizant that this triangulation represents a significant departure from the Afro-pessimist arguments about the absolute primacy of anti-Blackness in all forms of racialization in the United States, as well as arguments about enslaved Africans *only* existing as property and not also as labor (Bilge, 2020; Winnubst, 2020). Rather, Day (2016) argues that "the divergent historical and economic contexts of Asian and African labor highlight the heterogeneity contained within an alien position" (p. 31). In an extensive treatment of this issue, Day goes on to discuss how Asian and Black alien labor in North America were treated in different ways specific to racial, economic, cultural, and historical contexts. Specifically, Day notes that Asian labor came to North America just as the economy built around chattel slavery began to decline in the 1830s. The flexibility provided by an immigrant workforce, as opposed to an enslaved one, "inoculated Asians from assuming the status of unfree labor" (p. 31). Indeed, as Jung (2008) observes, early Chinese labor was "viewed as a natural advancement from chattel slavery . . ." (p. 6).

Day (2016) goes on to explain that historically "a logic of exclusion is the *prerequisite* for the recruitment of alien labor" (p. 34, original emphasis), but that exclusion has taken different forms for Asian and Black labor in North America. Whereas chattel slavery relied on segregation and Jim Crow laws (forms of exclusion internal to the United States), Asian exclusion mainly took the form of border control and immigration policy (e.g., the Chinese Exclusion Act of 1882), in what Day refers to as a "form of Jim Crow in a transnational context" (p. 32). Day further argues that because African Americans were not immigrants who could be subject to deportation, but also could not be biologically assimilated by white settlers, they were treated as an "*undisposable* alien labor population" (p. 33, original emphasis) that could only be dealt with either by internal exclusion, "domestic social control" (p. 33), or death. Conversely, for Asian immigrants, "the settler state produces a less fixed and more volatile racialization" (p. 33) that not only allowed for them to be controlled through immigration and exclusion at the border but also "inhibited Asian exposure to more sustained domestic logics of racial exclusion and elimination" (p. 33) faced by Blacks.

Day's (2016) overall point is, then, at least threefold. One is to emphasize the heterogeneity of racialization within the category of alien labor in a way to account for the specifically different treatments of Black and Asian labor in the United States. By extension, another is to suggest that this heterogeneity is necessary to understand that the racialization of Asian alien labor cannot be fully grasped solely through a lens of "prototypical antiblackness" (p. 31) because that racialization has been both national and transnational in nature. Third is to explain that "the vicissitudes of Asian racialization are primarily shaped by the evolving economic landscape of settler colonialism within a global economy" (p. 31). This, in turn, orients us toward what Day argues is the fundamental framing for Asian racialization in North America: an association with abstract labor.

Abstract labor is a form of labor coined by Marx (1967) in *Capital*. Ever the dialectician, Marx argued that every commodity contains two types of labor within it—concrete and abstract—and that these two types of labor manifest in commodities in different, but related, ways. For Marx, concrete labor is connected to the production of use value within a commodity (how "useful" something is), and this in turn is connected to the qualitative value of a commodity (something being of high- or low-quality construction). Abstract labor, on the other hand, is connected to the quantitative value in a commodity (how much something is "worth"), which can be measured in money. Understanding commodities as the expression of a dialectical unity between concrete and abstract labor is important in a Marxist analysis because it allows us to demystify the relations of capitalist production present in any commodity. Rather than separating the "concreteness of labor, commodities, and nature, on the one hand, and the abstractness of money and finance, on the other" (Day, 2016, p. 14), a unified view helps us see that overall value is not just generated by mysterious forces of the market or controlled by faraway financiers and investors, but instead is generated by workers and materials through a combination of the quality of what they produce and how long they take to produce it.

In a Marxian view, then, efficiency—less time spent on production—becomes a key aspect for generating value, because the more efficient a worker is in production, the more value can be gained from the commodity. Day (2016, 2021) thus argues that abstract labor and efficiency are the key to understanding the racialization of Asians as alien labor in North America, where Asians have been associated with "the abstract dimensions of capitalism through *labor time*" (Day, 2016, p. 16) either as cheap or efficient labor. Day (2021) also clarifies how this association of Asianness with abstract labor helps us reframe the racialization of Asian American threat into one based on a form of productive efficiency that disrupts the relations of capitalist production, explaining:

> . . . [I]n North America, Asians have personified a destructive value regime rooted in the excessive efficiency of their labor, whether in conflicts between capital and labor against the backdrop of Reconstruction, or in fears over Japanese agricultural monopolies during the early-twentieth century, or in the evisceration of the US auto industry by Japanese competition in the 1980s. . . . Moreover, the passage of neoliberal immigration reforms in 1965 that favored Asian immigrants from investor and managerial classes, alongside the rise of Asian economies, has further reinforced the identification of Asians with the speculative dynamism of finance capitalism.

Thus, the "menacing foreignness" (Day, 2021) lurking behind both the Model Minority and Yellow Peril tropes creates a form of dehumanization such that Asian Americans can be ". . . reduced to an economic functionality based on labor efficiency, identified not with the qualitative substance of their bodies but with the quantitative rate of their labor" (Day, 2021). In this way we see that, ultimately, ". . . 'yellow peril' and the 'model minority' stereotype function as complementary aspects of the same form of racialization, in which economic efficiency is the basis for exclusion *or* assimilation" (Day, 2016, p. 7; see also, Lye, 2005). The racialization of Asian Americans as efficient through their association with abstract labor thus is the basis for their positioning as an ever-present, racial threat expressed through the construction of the Model Minority.

REFRAMING THE MODEL MINORITY IN EDUCATION

Following Day (2016, 2021), the form of racialization of Asian Americans that I have argued for here—as efficient workers associated with abstract labor—allows us to understand the Asian American Model Minority in education and its use as a threat against all racialized groups in a new way. Whereas Black students and other non-Asian American students of color have been constructed as *culturally deficient* to explain their disparate educational outcomes (Blanton, 2003; Ladson-Billings, 2017; S. J. Lee, 2009), we can now see that the Asian American Model Minority student has been constructed as *culturally efficient* to explain their educational success. That is to say that, within the myth, the Asian American Model Minority achieves in education because they are supposedly more efficient with their educational labor than other groups, and that this efficiency is explained by stereotypes about Asian culture. The possibility of this construction is created through the association of Asian Americans with abstract, efficient labor because the Asian American subject is functionally being abstracted from the concrete conditions faced by Asian American students and their communities. Higher test scores, graduation rates, and college attainment for Asian American students are thus articulated through a form of racialization that masks the heterogeneous material conditions that produced those educational outcomes for specific groups in favor of a myth that the homogenous Asian American Model Minority simply works harder, can achieve more with less than whites, and can even achieve more than other peoples of color despite also experiencing a history of racism and discrimination in the United States. The myth of Asian American *cultural efficiency* is thus used oppositionally as proof of the *cultural deficiency* of others, because it appears to partially disrupt the white supremacist racial order of educational labor.

Understanding the Asian American Model Minority racialized as abstract, efficient labor also helps illuminate an intersection of race and neoliberalism in education. Importantly, some scholars have already connected the Model Minority stereotype directly to neoliberalism. S. J. Lee (2009), for instance, noted that

> The continuing dominance of the model minority stereotype reflects the fact that the stereotype continues to support the rhetoric of the achievement ideology. Asian Americans as model minorities are the ideal neoliberal subject—motivated, self-sufficient, and successful. The model minority success of Asian Americans is interpreted as evidence that markets are neutral and color-blind. (p. 11)

Similarly, Jun (2011) argues that through the Model Minority, Asian Americans have come to embody the neoliberal theories of human capital, individual entrepreneurship, and self-regulation in the post-1965 era of Asian immigration to the United States. The theorizing of Asian American racialization presented here buttresses these arguments, since it identifies that labor efficiency is central to how Asian American Model Minority success is constructed as individual merit based on hard work, rendering potential structural barriers as negligible or nonexistent.

Bringing this line of analysis to bear in education is important because if, as S. J. Lee (2009) suggests above, the Asian American Model Minority represents the "ideal neoliberal subject" (p. 11), then we can now also see that the Asian American Model Minority student comes to represent the ideal neoliberal *educational* subject. In this construction, Asian American student success is explained by their supposed ability to work harder and faster and triumph over their peers in the free market competition of individual achievement, all due to the excessive efficiency of their educational labor. The Asian American Model Minority student racialized as educationally efficient labor thus becomes the physical and cultural embodiment of meritocracy—the myth that all it takes to succeed in the United States is hard work (Lemann, 1999). This, in turn, also explains the positionality of some conservative Asian Americans, who in coalition with conservative whites have attacked affirmative action programs as discriminatory. We can interpret conservative Asian American outrage at perceived discrimination as a combination of their own internalized belief in the racist Model Minority stereotype (Poon et al., 2019; J. Yi & Todd, 2021) and feelings that they or their children are not being rightly rewarded for what they perceive as the efficiency of their own educational labor. Relatedly, Asian American students in higher education who feel self-hate and isolation if they do not live up to the Model Minority stereotype (Gupta et al., 2011; P. Y. Kim & Lee, 2014) can be explained as them feeling like they are not efficient enough to fit into their own racialization as Asian Americans.

The association with efficient productivity and abstract labor ultimately dehumanizes Asian Americans, and this dehumanization points to how the Asian American Model Minority in education (and society) is dependent on the fungibility of Asian American labor. *Fungibility* is a legal and economic term that refers to the interchangeability and substitution of one thing for another, and it signals the way that economic systems require abstraction and homogenization in order to establish markets where one thing can be exchanged for another (Ong, 2016; Winnubst, 2020). Looked at dialectically, fungibility implies both a usefulness or value of something and a disposability or a willingness to exchange that same thing. In this light, we might understand the history of Asian Americans being both valued and despised as an embodiment of the fungibility of Asian American labor; each specific Asian immigrant group was used for their labor, and when that labor was construed as a threat, one group was exchanged for another. In this way, Asian American fungibility is also at the heart of anti-Asian violence because Orientalist Yellow Peril relies on the Western construction of an abstracted, homogenous Asian "Oriental" such that any Asian American subgroup can be cast as a target of violence, incarceration, or exclusion depending on historical, political, cultural, or economic conditions. Indeed, the myth of the Asian American Model Minority in education and society is built upon an abstracted homogeneity that renders Asian Americans fungible such that the educational and economic success of one subgroup can be substituted in exchanges as being true for all groups.[3] This abstraction and fungibility of Asian American educational labor thus illuminates how the myth of the Model Minority invisibilizes the varied educational experiences and educational outcomes of specific Asian American subgroups and how the myth has been leveraged in a threatening manner against all racial groups (Au, 2025a).

CONCLUSION

I began this chapter with a discussion of the definition of the racial category of Asian American, and then moved on to the framing of Asian Americans as a Model Minority generally and within education specifically. I then argued that the Model Minority was rooted in Yellow Peril and Orientalism, but that in order to fully understand the Model Minority, we also need to retheorize Asian American racialization itself to account for our positionality within the context of U.S. racial formation and relative to transnational racial political economy as well. To do so, I drew heavily upon Day's (2015, 2016, 2021) insightful analyses of both racial triangulation and the association of Asian North Americans with abstract labor and productive efficiency as central to Asian American racial formation. This in turn enabled me to explore the basis of the threat that underlies the myth of the Model Minority in education, as well as constructions of Asian Americans as both culturally efficient and fungible.

My hope is that this work has contributed to a deeper understanding of Asian American racialization and the Model Minority in education by taking seriously the importance of racial political economy in that process (A. L. Brown & DeLissovoy, 2011; R. D. G. Kelley, 2017; Leonardo, 2012), because understanding the myth of Asian American students as Model Minorities as simply a cultural, political, historical, and sociological phenomenon (as has been mostly the case) is not enough. Rather, as I have contended here, we need to understand the racialization of Asian American students also in terms of global capitalist political economy, since that has been a defining force in how Asian Americans have been more broadly positioned and used as alien labor. Indeed, if there is one way that this chapter has hopefully deepened our analysis of Asian American education, it is through the reframing of the Model Minority as fundamentally an expression of white supremacist, anti-Asian racism rooted in the transnational, imperialist ideology of Orientalism, and manifested within the specificity of racialized, settler-colonial capitalism of the United States. In terms of Asian American students specifically, my analysis here further suggests that it is critical that we understand them both within the context of the United States, but also as part of transnational communities that have been racialized as alien labor. This would mean that we see Asian American student subjectivity as being produced both within the context of U.S. race relations *and* by the global political, economic, and cultural forces that contributed to the construction of "Asia." Not only do we need to eviscerate the myth of the Model Minority on similar grounds, but we also need to attend to the identities and experiences of Asian American students and communities in ways that recognize the complex dynamics and tensions produced through this racialization (Au, 2025a). Finally, I also hope my use of Day (2015, 2016, 2021) as a key theoretical foundation within the context of Asian American education helps extend and deepen similar lines of analysis about racialization more broadly within capitalist and settler colonial contexts in education.

NOTES

1. In this chapter, I am strictly referring to "Asian Americans" and not "Asian-Pacific Americans." I do so because while I recognize the political legacy of the formation of the Asian-Pacific American category, this chapter focuses on Asian American racialization, which in my view is entirely distinct from the racialization of the Indigenous peoples of the Pacific Islands. Further, there is also a history of Pacific Islander peoples being marginalized, neglected, or ignored under the banner of "Asian-Pacific American," and I do not wish to perpetuate this phenomenon.

2. See Lye (2008) for other critiques of this issue that I did not include here.

3. This analysis also suggests that the relatively common occurrence of racial microaggressions where Asian American employees, colleagues, and peers are mistaken for each other (Chen, 2021; Gorman, 2021) is actually a manifestation of this racial fungibility at the individual level.

References

ABC. (2018, February 22). *Timeline: The Black Lives Matter movement.* ABC News. https://www.abc.net.au/news/2016–07-14/black-lives-matter-timeline/7585856

ABC10 News. (2017, February 16). *Florida teacher reassigned after criticizing "Day Without Immigrants" movement.* http://www.10news.com/news/national/naples-teacher-reassigned-after-immigration-post_

Accountability Works. (2012). *National cost of aligning states and localities to the Common Core Standards.* Pioneer Institute American Principles Project Pacific Research Institute. www.pioneerinstitute.org

Agarwal, K. (2019, January 11). Texas revises history education, again. *Perspectives on History.* https://www.historians.org/publications-and-directories/perspectives-on-history/january-2019/texas-revises-history-education-again-how-a-good-faith-process-became-political

Allen, M., Smith, A., & Dika, S. (2023). Black feminism and Black women's interaction with faculty in higher education. *Oxford Research Encyclopedia of Education.* https://oxfordre.com/education/view/10.1093/acrefore/9780190264093.001.0001/acrefore-9780190264093-e-1723

Allred, N. C. (2007). Asian Americans and affirmative action: From yellow peril to model minority and back again. *Asian American Law Journal*, *14*(1), 57–48.

American Community Survey. (2020). *Asian alone or in any combination by selected groups.* U.S. Census Bureau. https://data.census.gov/cedsci/table?q=asian&tid=ACSDT1Y2019.B02018

American Statistical Association. (2014). *ASA statement on using value-added models for educational assessment.* American Statistical Association. https://www.amstat.org/asa/files/pdfs/POL-ASAVAM-Statement.pdf

Amrein-Beardsley, A. (2014). *Rethinking value-added models in education: Critical perspectives on tests and assessment-based accountability.* Routledge.

An, S., & Rodriguez, N. N. (2022). *Stop AAPI Hate Asian American Studies K-12 framework.* Asian American Research Initiative, San Francisco State University, Stop AAPI Hate. https://asianamericanresearchinitiative.org/wp-content/uploads/2022/06/aari-resources-asian-american-studies-k-12-framework-v2.pdf

Anderson, T., Jimenez, I., & Rogers, C. (2020, February 6). *Clarifying the movement history of the Black Lives Matter Week of Action, or #BlackLivesMatterAtSchool.* Medium. https://medium.com/national-blm-week-of-action-in-schools/clarifying-the-movement-history-of-the-black-lives-matter-week-of-action-or-6f917d7b75de

Andre-Bechely, L. (2005). Public school choice at the intersection of voluntary integration and not-so-good neighborhood schools: Lessons from parents' experiences. *Educational Administration Quarterly*, *41*(2), 267–305.

Anyon, J. (1980). Social class and the hidden curriculum of work. *Journal of Education, 162*(1), 67–92.

APIA Vote, AAPI Data, & Asian Americans Advancing Justice. (2020). *2020 Asian American voter survey*. APIA Data. https://aapidata.com/surveys/2020-asian-american-voter-survey-aavs

Apple, M. W. (1971). The hidden curriculum and the nature of conflict. *Interchange, 2*(4), 27–40.

Apple, M. W. (1973). Curriculum design and cultural order. In N. Smimahara (Ed.), *Educational reconstruction: Promise and challenge* (pp. 157–183). Charles E. Merrill Publishing Company.

Apple, M. W. (1986). *Teachers and texts: A political economy of class and gender relations in education*. Routledge & Kegan Paul.

Apple, M. W. (1995). *Education and power* (2nd ed.). Routledge.

Apple, M. W. (2001). Comparing neo-liberal projects and inequality in education. *Comparative Education, 37*(4), 409–423.

Apple, M. W. (2006). *Educating the "right" way: Markets, standards, God, and inequality* (2nd ed.). RoutledgeFalmer.

Apple, M. W. (2010). Fly and the fly bottle: On Dwayne Huebner, the uses of language, and the nature of the curriculum field. *Curriculum Inquiry, 40*(1), 95–103. https://doi.org/10.1111/j.1467-873X.2009.00469.x

Apple, M. W. (2013). *Can education change society?* Routledge.

Apple, M. W. (2014). *Official knowledge: Democratic education in a conservative age* (3rd ed.). Routledge.

Apple, M. W., & Au, W. (2009). Politics, theory and reality in critical pedagogy. In A. Kazamias & R. Cowen (Eds.), *International handbook of comparative education* (pp. 991–1007). Springer Netherlands.

Apple, M. W., & Pedroni, T. C. (2005). Conservative alliance building and African American support of vouchers: The end of Brown's promise or a new beginning? *Teachers College Record, 107*(9), 2068–2105.

Archibald, A. (2016, October 19). *Seattle teachers undaunted by threats, renew Black Lives Matter efforts*. Real Change News. https://www.realchangenews.org/2016/10/19/seattle-teachers-undaunted-threats-renew-black-lives-matter-efforts

Asian American Coalition for Education. (2021). *Our impact*. https://asianamericanforeducation.org/en/impact/our-impact/

Au, W. (2000). Teaching about the WTO. *Rethinking Schools, 14*(3), 4–5.

Au, W. (2007). High-stakes testing and curricular control: A qualitative metasynthesis. *Educational Researcher, 36*(5), 258–267.

Au, W. (2009a). Decolonizing the classroom: Lessons in multicultural education. *Rethinking Schools, 23*(2), 27–30.

Au, W. (2009b). High-stakes testing and discursive control: The triple bind for non-standard student identities. *Multicultural Perspectives, 11*(2), 65–71.a

Au, W. (2009c). The "building tasks" of critical history: Structuring social studies for social justice. *Social Studies Research and Practice, 4*(2). https://doi.org/10.1108/SSRP-02-2009-B0002

Au, W. (2010a). Critical reflection in the classroom: Consciousness, praxis, and relative autonomy in social studies education. In A. P. DeLeon & E. W. Ross (Eds.), *Critical theories, radical pedagogies, and social education: New perspectives for social studies education* (pp. 163–181). Sense Publishers.

Au, W. (2010b). Neither fair nor accurate: Research based reasons why high-stakes tests should not be used to evaluate teachers. *Rethinking Schools*, *25*(2), 34–38.

Au, W. (2011a). *Critical curriculum studies: Education, consciousness, and the politics of knowing*. Routledge.

Au, W. (2011b). Teaching under the new Taylorism: High-stakes testing and the standardization of the 21st century curriculum. *Journal of Curriculum Studies*, *43*(1), 25–45. https://doi.org/10.1080/00220272.2010.521261

Au, W. (2012a). The false promise of charter schools. *The Seattle Times*. http://seattletimes.com/html/opinion/2017379325_guest31au.html

Au, W. (2012b). The long march toward revitalization: Developing standpoint in curriculum studies. *Teachers College Record*, *114*(5), 1–30. https://doi.org/10.1177/016146811211400508

Au, W. (2012c, February 29). *Learning to read: Charter schools, public education, and the politics of educational research*. Washington State PTA Public Charter School Forum, Seattle, WA.

Au, W. (2013). Proud to be a Garfield bulldog. *Rethinking Schools Blog*. http://rethinkingschoolsblog.wordpress.com/2013/01/12/proud-to-be-a-garfield-bulldog/

Au, W. (2015, May 9). Just whose rights do these civil rights groups think they are protecting? *The Answer Sheet*. http://www.washingtonpost.com/blogs/answer-sheet/wp/2015/05/09/just-whose-rights-do-these-civil-rights-groups-think-they-are-protecting/

Au, W. (2016a). Meritocracy 2.0: High-stakes, standardized testing as a racial project of neoliberal multiculturalism. *Educational Policy*, *30*(1), 39–62. https://doi.org/10.1177/0895904815614916

Au, W. (2016b). Techies, the Tea Party, and the Common Core: The rise of the new upper-middle class and tensions in the rightist politics of federal education reform. *The Educational Forum*, *80*(2), 208–224. https://doi.org/10.1080/00131725.2016.1135378

Au, W. (2016c, May 6). Letter to the editor: "Half-truths, spin, and obfuscation about Summit Sierra Charter." *The International Examiner*. http://www.iexaminer.org/2016/05/letter-to-the-editor-half-truths-spin-and-obfuscation-about-summit-sierra-charter/

Au, W. (2017). When multicultural education is not enough. *Multicultural Perspectives*, *19*(3), 1–4. https://doi.org/10.1080/15210960.2017.1331741

Au, W. (2018). *A Marxist education: Learning to change the world*. Haymarket Books.

Au, W. (2019). Racial justice is not a choice: White supremacy, high-stakes testing, and the punishment of Black and brown students. *Rethinking Schools*, *33*(4). https://www.rethinkingschools.org/articles/racial-justice-is-not-a-choice

Au, W. (2020, November 25). *California vetoed ethnic studies requires for public high school students, but the movement grows*. The Conversation. https://theconversation.com/california-vetoed-ethnic-studies-requirements-for-public-high-school-students-but-the-movement-grows-148486

Au, W. (2021). A pedagogy of insurgency: Teaching and organizing for radical racial justice in our schools. *Educational* Studies, *57*(2), 109–123. https://doi.org/10.1080/00131946.2021.1878181

Au, W. (2022). Asian American racialization, racial capitalism, and the threat of the model minority. *Review of Education, Pedagogy, and Cultural Studies*, *44*(3), 185–209. https://doi.org/10.1080/10714413.2022.2084326

Au, W. (2023a). "Isn't that what the case is about, the discrimination against Asian Americans?": Conservatives use racial wedge to attack affirmative action. *Rethinking Schools*, *38*(1), 14–19.

Au, W. (2023b). *Unequal by design: High-stakes testing and the standardization of inequality* (2nd ed.). Routledge.

Au, W. (2024a). Introduction. In W. Au (Ed.), *Rethinking multicultural education: Teaching for racial and cultural justice* (3rd ed., pp. 9–11). Rethinking Schools, Ltd.

Au, W. (2024b). It is all indoctrination: Power and the impossibility of apolitical social studies curriculum. In E. W. Ross (Ed.), *The social studies curriculum: Purposes, problems, and possibilities* (5th ed., pp. 31–48). SUNY Press.

Au, W. (2025a). *Asian American racialization and the politics of U.S. education.* Routledge.

Au, W. (2025b). "Superachievers" vs. "super predators": How the racist love of the model minority is weaponized against Black and Asian American students. *Rethinking Schools*, *39*(2). https://rethinkingschools.org/articles/superachievers-vs-super-predators-how-the-racist-love-of-the-model-minority-is-weaponized-against-black-and-asian-american-students/

Au, W., & Apple, M. W. (2009). Neo-Marxism in critical educational theory. In M. W. Apple, W. Au, & L. A. Gandin (Eds.), *The Routledge international handbook of critical education* (pp. 83–95). Routledge.

Au, W., Brown, A. L., & Calderon, D. (2016). *Reclaiming the multicultural roots of U.S. curriculum: Communities of color and official knowledge in education.* Teachers College Press.

Au, W., & Ferrare, J. J. (2014). Sponsors of policy: A network analysis of wealthy elites, their affiliated philanthropies, and charter school reform in Washington State. *Teachers College Record*, *116*(8), 1–24.

Au, W., & Ferrare, J. J. (Eds.). (2015a). *Mapping corporate education reform: Power and policy networks in the neoliberal state.* Routledge.

Au, W., & Ferrare, J. J. (2015b). Other people's policy: Wealthy elites and charter school reform in Washington State. In W. Au & J. J. Ferrare (Eds.), *Mapping corporate education reform: Power and policy networks in the neoliberal state* (pp. 147–164). Routledge.

Au, W., & Hagopian, J. (2017). How one elementary school sparked a citywide movement to make Black students' lives matter. *Rethinking Schools*, *32*(1), 11–18.

Au, W., & Hagopian, J. (2021). Bomb threats and Black Lives Matter at school: Teacing and organizing against white supremacy in K-12 education. In R. Verma & M. W. Apple (Eds.), *Disrupting hate in education: Teacher activists, democracy, and global pedagogies of disruption* (pp. 76–92). Routledge.

Au, W., & Hollar, J. (2016). Opting out of the education reform industry. *Monthly Review*, *67*(10), 29–37.

Au, W., & Lubienski, C. A. (2016). The role of the Gates Foundation and the philanthropic sector in shaping the emerging education market: Lessons from the US on privatization of schools and educational governance. In A. Verger, C. A. Lubienski, & G. Steiner-Khamsi (Eds.), *The global education industry (2016 world yearbook of education* (pp. 27–43). Taylor & Francis.

Baker, B. D. (2016). *Exploring the consequences of charter school expansion in U.S. cities.* Economic Policy Institute. http://epi.org/109218

Baker, E. L., Barton, P. E., Darling-Hammond, L., Haertel, E., Ladd, H. F., Linn, R. L., Ravitch, D., Rothstein, R., Shavelson, R. J., & Shepard, L. A. (2010). *Problems with the use of student test scores to evaluate teachers*. Economic Policy Institute.

Baker, O., & Lang, K. (2013). *The effect of high school exit exams on graduation, employment, wages and incarceration* (Working Paper). National Bureau of Economic Research. http://www.nber.org/papers/w19182.pdf

Balfanz, R., Byrnes, V., & Fox, J. (2015). Sent home and put off track: The antecedents, disproportionalities, and consequences of being suspended in the 9th grade. In D. J. Losen (Ed.), *Closing the school discipline gap: Equitable remedies for excessive exclusion* (pp. 17–30). Teachers College Press.

Ball, S. J. (2012). *Global education Inc.: New policy networks and the neo-liberal imaginary*. Routledge.

Barkan, J. (2011). Got dough?: How billionaires rule our schools. *Dissent*, *58*(1), 49–57.

Barkan, J. (2012). Hired guns on astroturf: How to buy and sell school reform. *Dissent*, *59*(2), 49–57.

Barrow, L., & Rouse, C. E. (2006). The economic value of education by race and ethnicity. *Economic Perspectives*, *30*(2), 14–27.

Beirich, H. (2019, February 20). The year in hate: Rage against change. *Intelligence Report*, *Spring*(166). https://www.splcenter.org/fighting-hate/intelligence-report/2019/year-hate-rage-against-change

Benton, T., & Craib, I. (2011). *Philosophy of social science: The philosophical foundations of social thought* (2nd ed.). PalgraveMacmillan.

Berliner, D. C. (2013). Effects of inequality and poverty vs. teachers and schooling on America's youth. *Teachers College Record*, *115*(12), 1–26. https://doi.org/10.1177/016146811311501203

Bernstein, B. B. (1977). *Class codes and control volume 3: Towards a theory of educational transmissions* (2nd ed., Vol. 3). Routledge and Kegan Paul.

Bernstein, B. B. (1996). *Pedagogy, symbolic control, and identity: Theory, research, critique*. Taylor & Francis.

Bernstein, B. B. (1999). Official knowledge and pedagogic identities. In F. Christie (Ed.), *Pedagogy and the shaping of consciousness: Linguistic and social processes* (pp. 246–261). Cassell.

Beyer, L. E., & Liston, D. P. (1992). Discourse or moral action? A critique of postmodernism. *Educational Theory*, *42*(4), 371–393.

Beyer, L. E., & Liston, D. P. (1996). *Curriculum in conflict: Social visions, educational agendas, and progressive school reform*. Teachers College Press.

Bhaskar, R. (1989). *Reclaiming reality: A critical introduction to contemporary philosophy*. Verso.

Bigelow, B. (2010). Those awful Texas social studies standards: And what about yours? *Rethinking Schools*, *24*(4), 46–48.

Bilge, S. (2020). The fungibility of intersectionality: An Afropessimist reading. *Ethnic and Racial Studies*, *43*(13), 2298–2326. https://doi.org/10.1080/01419870.2020.1740289

Bisseret, N. (1979). *Education, class language and ideology*. Routledge & Kegan Paul.

Black Lives Matter At School. (2019). *About*. Black Lives Matter At School. https://www.blacklivesmatteratschool.com/

Blanc, E. (2019). *Red state revolt: The teachers' strike wave and working-class politics*. Verso.

Blanton, C. K. (2003). From intellectual deficiency to cultural deficiency: Mexican Americans, testing, and public school policy in the American Southwest, 1920–1940. *Pacific Historical Review*, *72*(1), 39–62.

Bloom, C. M., & Erlandson, D. A. (2003). African American women principals in urban schools: Realities, (re)constructions, and resolutions. *Educational Administration Quarterly*, *39*(3), 339–369.

Boal, A. (1990). The cop in the head: Three hypotheses. *The Drama Review*, *34*(3), 35–42.

Bonastia, C. (2015, January 6). *The racist history of the charter school movement: Touted as the cure for what ails public education, charter schools have historical roots that are rarely discussed*. AlterNet. https://www.alternet.org/2012/03/racist-history-charter-school-movement

Bonilla-Silva, E. (2002). We are all Americans!: The Latin Americanization of racial stratification in the USA. *Race & Society*, *5*, 3–16.

Bonilla-Silva, E. (2013). *Racism without racists: Color-blind racism and the persistence of racial inequality in America*. Rowman & Littlefield Publishers Inc.

Bow, L. (2022). *Racist love: Asian abstraction and the pleasures of fantasy*. Duke University Press.

Bowles, S., & Gintis, H. (1976). *Schooling in capitalist America: Educational reform and the contradictions of economic life* (1st ed.). Basic Books.

Bowman, E. (2023, June 30). *Here's what happened when affirmative action ended at California public colleges*. NPR. https://www.npr.org/2023/06/30/1185226895/heres-what-happened-when-affirmative-action-ended-at-california-public-colleges

Bracey, G. W. (2004). *Setting the record straight*. Heinemann.

Brazile, L. (2019, September 5). *"You failed us": Teen author asks 40 students of color to share their experiences at Seattle schools*. Crosscut. https://crosscut.com/2019/09/you-failed-us-teen-author-asks-40-students-color-share-their-experiences-seattle-schools

Brown, A. L. (2010). Counter-memory and race: An examination of African American scholars' challenges to early twentieth century K-12 historical discourses. *The Journal of Negro Education*, *79*(1), 54–65.

Brown, A. L., & Au, W. (2014). Race, memory, and master narratives: A critical essay on U.S. curriculum history. *Curriculum Inquiry*, *44*(3), 358–389. https://doi.org/10.1111/curi.12049

Brown, A. L., & Brown, K. D. (2010). Strange fruit indeed: Interrogating contemporary textbook representations of racial violence toward African Americans. *Teachers College Record*, *112*(1), 31–67.

Brown, A. L., & DeLissovoy, N. (2011). Economies of racism: Grounding educational policy research in the complex dialectic of race, class, and capital. *Journal of Educational Policy*, *26*(5), 595–619. https://doi.org/10.1080/02680939.2010.533289

Brown, E. (2015, May 5). *Why civil rights groups say parents who opt out of tests are hurting kids*. The Washington Post. http://www.washingtonpost.com/local/education/why-civil-rights-groups-say-parents-who-opt-out-of-tests-are-hurting-kids/2015/05/05/59884b9a-f32c-11e4-bcc4-e8141e5eb0c9_story.html

Brown, J. (2015, July 6). *To the honorable Mitch McConnell & the honorable Harry Reid*. http://www.j4jalliance.com/media/openletter/

Budiman, A., & Ruiz, N. G. (2021, April 29). *Key facts about Asian Americans, a diverse and growing population*. Pew Research Center. https://www.pewresearch.org/fact-tank/2021/04/29/key-facts-about-asian-americans/

Buenavista, T. L., Jahakumar, U. M., & Misa-Escalante, K. (2009). Contextualizing Asian American education through critical race theory: An example of U.S. Philipino college student experiences. In S. D. Museus (Ed.), *Conducting research on Asian Americans in higher education* (pp. 69–81). Jossey-Bass.

Burch, P. (2006). The new educational privatization: Educational contracting and high stakes accountability. *Teachers College Record*, *108*(12), 2582–2610.

Burch, P. (2021). *Hidden markets: Public policy and the push to privatized education* (2nd ed.). Routledge.

Burris, C. (2017, April 6). School choice a sham, profits on the taxpayers' dime. *Arizona Capitol Times*. http://azcapitoltimes.com/news/2017/04/06/school-choice-profits-on-the-taxpayers-dime/

Bush, G. W. (1999, October 5). *The future of educational reform*. Manhattan Institute. http://www.manhattan-institute.org/html/bush_speech.htm

Cabrera, N. L. (2014). Beyond Black and white: How white, male, college students see their Asian American peers. *Equity & Excellence in Education*, *47*(2), 133–151. https://doi.org/10.1080/10665684.2014.900427

Carnevale, A., & Quinn, M. C. (2021). *Selective bias: Asian Americans, test scores, and holistic admissions*. Georgetown University, McCourt School of Public Policy, Center on Education and the Workforce. https://cew.georgetown.edu/wp-content/uploads/cew-selective-bias-fr.pdf

Center on Education Policy. (2007). *Choices, changes, and challenges: Curriculum and instruction in the NCLB era* (p. 20). Center on Education Policy. https://www.cep-dc.org/

Center for Popular Democracy, & Integrity in Education. (2014). *Charter school vulnerabilities to waste, fraud, and abuse*. The Center for Popular Democracy, Integrity in Education. https://www.scribd.com/doc/221993993/Charter-School-Vulnerabilities-to-Waste-Fraud-Abuse

Chambers, S. (2014). Ice the ISAT: Boycotting the test under mayor Rahm Emanuel's regime. In J. Hagopian (Ed.), *More than a score: The new uprising against high-stakes testing* (pp. 113–122). Haymarket Books.

Chang, B. (2017). Asian Americans and education. In G. W. Noblit (Ed.), *Oxford research encyclopedia of education* (pp. 1–39). Oxford University Press. https://doi.org/10.1093/acrefore/9780190264093.013.102

Chang, B., & Au, W. (2007). You're Asian, how could you fail math? Unmasking the myth of the model minority. *Rethinking Schools*, *22*(2), 14–19.

Chang, H. (1985). Toward a Marxist theory of racism: Two essays by Harry Chang. *Review of Radical Political Economics*, *17*(3), 34–45.

Chang, J. (2021, March 22). The long history of violence against Asian Americans that led up to Atlanta. *The Washington Post*. https://www.washingtonpost.com/outlook/2021/03/22/atlanta-shooting-history-asians/

Chang, J. (2023, April 13). Asian Americans spent decades seeking fair education. Then the right stole the narrative. *The Guardian*. https://www.theguardian.com/us-news/2023/apr/13/affirmative-action-asian-americans-us-universities

Chapman, P. D. (1988). *Schools as sorters: Lewis M. Terman, applied psychology, and the intelligence testing movement, 1890-1930*. New York University Press.

Chasmar, J. (2017, February 17). *Teachers on leave for "Day Without Immigrants" posts reveling in student absences*. The Washington Times. Retrieved from https://web.archive.org/web/20201112014847/http://www.washingtontimes.com/news/2017/feb/17/teachers-on-leave-for-day-without-immigrants-posts/

Chen, B. X. (2021, June 6). The cost of being an "interchangeable Asian." *The New York Times*. https://www.nytimes.com/2021/06/06/business/the-cost-of-being-an-interchangeable-asian.html

Chen, S., & Doherty, E. (2023, February 25). *Schools unprepared to help Asian American students navigate racial trauma*. Axios. https://www.axios.com/2023/02/25/asian-american-mental-health-schools

Chow, K. (2017, April 19). "Model minority" myth again used as a racial wedge between Asians and blacks. *NPR Code Switch*. https://www.npr.org/sections/codeswitch/2017/04/19/524571669/model-minority-myth-again-used-as-a-racial-wedge-between-asians-and-blacks

Christensen, L. (2014). Putting out the linguistic welcome mat. In W. Au (Ed.), *Rethinking multicultural education: Teaching for racial and cultural justice* (2nd, Revised ed., pp. 137–144). Rethinking Schools Ltd.

CNN. (2002, January 19). *Bush calls education "civil rights issue of our time."* http://edition.cnn.com/2002/ALLPOLITICS/01/19/bush.democrats.radio/

Cokley, K., McClain, S., Enciso, A., & Martinez, M. (2013). An examination of the impact of minority status stress and impostor feelings on the mental health of diverse ethnic minority college students. *Journal of Multicultural Counseling and Development*, *41*(2), 82–95. https://doi.org/10.1002/j.2161-1912.2013.00029.x

Collier County Public Schools. (2017). *District profile*. CCPS. http://www.collierschools.com/Page/349

Coloma, R. S. (2006). Disorienting race and education: Changing paradigms on the schooling of Asian Americans and Pacific Islanders. *Race, Ethnicity, and Education*, *9*(1), 1–15. https://doi.org/10.1080/13613320500490606

Compton, M., & Weiner, L. (Eds.). (2008). *The global assault on teaching, teachers, and their unions: Stories for resistance*. Palgrave Macmillan.

Connell, R. W. (1994). *Schools and social justice*. Temple University Press.

Cooper, C. W. (2005). School choice and the standpoint of African American mothers: Considering the power of positionality. *The Journal of Negro Education*, *74*(2), 174–189.

Cooper, H. (2011, April 6). Obama takes aim at inequality in education. *The New York Times*. http://www.nytimes.com/2011/04/07/us/politics/07obama.html

Corn, S. (2018, January 30). Seattle educators, students primed for "Black Lives Matter At School" week. *South Seattle Emerald*. https://southseattleemerald.org/community/2018/01/31/seattle-educators-students-primed-for-black-lives-matter-at-achool-week

Cornwell, P. (2016a, September 15). Black Men Uniting event at Seattle's John Muir Elementary canceled due to security threat. *The Seattle Times*. http://www.seattletimes.com/seattle-news/education/black-men-uniting-event-at-seattles-john-muir-elementary-cancelled-due-to-security-threat/

Cornwell, P. (2016b, October 19). Seattle teachers hope their cause isn't lost amid noise over Black Lives Matter shirts. *The Seattle Times*. https://www.seattletimes.com/seattle-news/education/seattle-teachers-hope-their-cause-isnt-lost-amid-noise-over-black-lives-matter-shirts/

Costello, M. (2016). *The Trump effect: The impact of the presidential campaign on our nation's schools*. The Southern Poverty Law Center. https://www.splcenter.org/sites/default/files/splc_the_trump_effect.pdf

Coulthard, G. S. (2014). *Red skin, white masks: Rejecting the colonial politics of recognition*. University of Minnesota Press.

CREDO. (2009). *Multiple choice: Charter school performance in 16 states*. Center for Research on Education Outcomes (CREDO). https://credo.stanford.edu/wp-content/uploads/2021/08/multiple_choice_credo.pdf

CREDO. (2013). *National charter school study 2013*. Center for Research on Education Outcomes (CREDO). https://credo.stanford.edu/wp-content/uploads/2021/08/ncss_2013_final_draft.pdf

Cruz, B. C. (2002). Don Juan and rebels under palm trees: Depictions of Latin Americans in US history textbooks. *Critique of Anthropology*, *22*(3), 323–342. https://doi.org/10.1177/0308275X02022003761

Cuauhtin, T., Zavala, M., Sleeter, C., & Au, W. (2019a). Introduction. In T. Cuauhtin, M. Zavala, C. Sleeter, & W. Au (Eds.), *Rethinking Ethnic Studies* (pp. 1–8). Rethinking Schools, Ltd.

Cuauhtin, T., Zavala, M., Sleeter, C., & Au, W. (Eds.). (2019b). *Rethinking Ethnic Studies*. Rethinking Schools Ltd.

Darder, A., & Torres, R. D. (2004). *After race: Racism after multiculturalism*. New York University Press.

Darling-Hammond, L. (2004). From "separate but equal" to "no child left behind": The collision of new standards and old inequalities. In D. Meier & G. Wood (Eds.), *Many children left behind: How the No Child Left Behind Act is damaging our children and our schools* (pp. 3–32). Beacon Press.

Darling-Hammond, L. (2007). Race, inequality and educational accountability: The irony of "No Child Left Behind." *Race, Ethnicity, and Education*, *10*(3), 245–260.

Day, I. (2015). Being or nothingness: Indigeneity, antiblackness, and settler colonial critique. *Critical Ethnic Studies*, *1*(2), 102–121.

Day, I. (2016). *Alien capital: Asian racialization and the logic of settler colonial capitalism*. Duke University Press.

Day, I. (2021, May 13). *Exclusion acts: Iyko Day on Asian hate through the prism of anti-Blackness*. Artforum. https://www.artforum.com/slant/iyko-day-on-asian-hate-through-the-prism-of-anti-blackness-85725

DeLeon, A. P. (2014). "Capitalism is for the body, religion is for the soul": Insurgent social studies for the 22nd century. In E. W. Ross (Ed.), *The social studies curriculum: Purposes, problems, and possibilities* (4th ed., pp. 71–89). SUNY Press.

Delgado, R., & Stefancic, J. (2012). *Critical race theory: An introduction* (2nd ed.). New York University Press.

DeLissovoy, N. (2008). Conceptualizing oppression in educational theory: Toward a compound standpoint. *Cultural Studies ↔ Critical Methodologies*, *8*(1), 82–105. https://doi.org/10.1177/1532708607310794

Denzin, N., & Lincoln, Y. (Eds.). (2000). *Handbook of qualitative research*. Sage.

Devlin, K., Silver, L., & Huang, C. (2021). *U.S. views of China increasingly negative amid coronavirus outbreak*. Pew Research Center. https://www.pewresearch.org/global/2020/04/21/u-s-views-of-china-increasingly-negative-amid-coronavirus-outbreak/

DiMaggio, D. (2010). The loneliness of the long-distance test scorer. *Monthly Review*, *62*(7). https://monthlyreview.org/2010/12/01/the-loneliness-of-the-long-distance-test-scorer/

Dimitriadis, G., & McCarthy, C. (2001). *Reading and teaching the postcolonial: From Baldwin to Basquiat and beyond*. Teachers College Press.

Dingerson, L., Miner, B., Peterson, B., & Walters, S. (Eds.). (2008). *Keeping the promise?: The debate over charter schools*. Rethinking Schools.

Dong, S. (1995). "Too many Asians": The challenge of fighting discrimination against Asian-Americans and preserving affirmative action. *Stanford Law Review*, *47*(5), 1027–1057.

Dumas, M. J. (2008). Theorizing redistribution and recognition in urban education research: "How do we get dictionaries at Cleveland?" In J. Anyon (Ed.), *Theory and educational research: Toward critical social explanation* (pp. 81–103). Routledge.

Dumas, M. J. (2015). My brother as "problem": Neoliberal governmentality and interventions for Black young men and boys. *Educational Policy*, *30*(1), 94–113.

Dumas, M. J. (2016). Against the dark: Antiblackness in education policy and discourse. *Theory Into Practice*, *55*(1), 11–19. https://doi.org/10.1080/00405841.2016.1116852

Dumas, M. J., & Anyon, J. (2006). Toward a critical approach to education policy implementation. In M. I. Honig (Ed.), *New directions in education policy implementation: Confronting complexity* (pp. 149–186). SUNY Press.

Duncan, A. (2011). *The next generation of teachers*. Obama White House archives. https://obamawhitehouse.archives.gov/blog/2011/02/01/next-generation-teachers

Education Data Partnership. (2025). *Rubidoux High Demographi and Socioeconomic Details*. Education Data Partnership. https://www.ed-data.org/school/Riverside/Jurupa-Unified/Rubidoux-High

Eidelson, J. (2014, May 13). *Christie's charter school nightmare: "White flight, and they're bankrupting us."* Salon. http://www.salon.com/2014/03/13/christies_charter_school_nightmare_white_flight_and_they're_bankrupting_us/

Ellis, N. T., & Sanchez, B. (2021, June 24). *Turmoil erupts in school district after claims that critical race theory and transgender policy are pushed*. CNN. https://www.cnn.com/2021/06/24/us/loudoun-county-school-board-meeting/index.html

Erevelles, N. (2005). Understanding curriculum as normalizing text: Disability studies meet curriculum theory. *Journal of Curriculum Studies*, *37*(4), 421–439.

Evans, G. (2018, March 2). The unwelcome revival of "race science." *The Guardian*. https://www.theguardian.com/news/2018/mar/02/the-unwelcome-revival-of-race-science

Ewert, S., Sykes, B. L., & Pettit, B. (2014). The degree of disadvantage: Incarceration and inequality in education. *The ANNALS of the American Academy of Political and Social Science*, *651*, 24–43. https://doi.org/10.1177/0002716213503100

Fabricant, M., & Fine, M. (2013). *The changing politics of education: Privatization and the dispossessed lives left behind*. Paradigm Publishers.

Fang, L. (2014, September 25). Venture capitalists are poised to "disrupt" everything about the education market. *The Nation*. https://www.thenation.com/article/archive/venture-capitalists-are-poised-disrupt-everything-about-education-market/

Farley, T. (2009a). *Making the grades: My misadventures in the standardized testing industry*. Berrett-Koehler Publishers.

Farley, T. (2009b). My misadventures in the standardized testing industry. *The Answer Sheet.* Retrieved from https://web.archive.org/web/20171201124838/http://voices.washingtonpost.com/answer-sheet/standardized-tests/-gerald-martineaupost-today-my.html

Farley, T. (2010). A test scorer's lament. *Rethinking Schools, 23*(2). https://rethinkingschools.org/articles/a-test-scorer-s-lament/

Feinberg, C. (2004, April 29). *Rod Paige offers high praise for No Child Left Behind: Education secretary marks 50th anniversary of* Brown *decision with Kenndey School keynote address.* Harvard University Gazette. https://news.harvard.edu/gazette/story/2004/04/rod-paige-offers-high-praise-for-no-child-left-behind/

Fine, M. (2006). Bearing witness: Methods for researching oppression and resistance—A textbook for critical research. *Social Justice Research, 19*(1), 83–108. https://doi.org/10.1007/s11211-006-0001-0

Fine, M., & Fabricant, M. (2014, October 13). What it takes to unite teachers' unions and communities of color: Overcoming years of tensions and divisions, parents and teachers are linking arms to save public schools. *The Nation.* https://www.thenation.com/article/archive/what-it-takes-unite-teachers-unions-and-communities-color/

Fine, M., & Ruglis, J. (2009). Circuits and consequences of dispossession: The racialized realignment of the public sphere for U.S. youth. *Transforming Anthropology, 17*(1), 20–33. https://doi.org/10.1111/j.1548-7466.2009.01037.x

Foley, D. A., Levinson, B. A., & Hurtig, J. (2000). Chapter 2: Anthropology goes inside: The new educational ethnography of ethnicity and gender. *Review of Research in Education, 25,* 37–98. https://doi.org/10.3102/0091732X025001037

Foner, E. (2010, April 5). Twisting history in Texas. *The Nation, 290,* 4–6.

Foote, M. (2007). Keeping accountability systems accountable. *Phi Delta Kappan, 88*(5), 359-363. https://doi.org/10.1177/003172170708800506

Foster, J. B. (2016). The opt out revolt: Democracy and education. *Monthly Review, 67*(10). https://monthlyreview.org/2016/03/01/the-opt-out-revolt/

Foucault, M. (1995). *Discipline and punish: The birth of the prison* (A. Sheridan, Trans.; second Vintage Books). Vintage Books.

Frankenberg, E., Siegel-Hawley, G., & Wang, J. (2013). Choice without equity: Charter school segregation. *Educational Policy Analysis Archives, 19*(1). http://epaa.asu.edu/ojs/article/view/779

Fraser, N. (1995). From redistribution to recognition? Dilemmas of justice in a "post-Socialist" age. *New Left Review, 212,* 68–93.

Fraser, N. (2017, January 2). The end of progressive neoliberalism. *Dissent.* https://www.dissentmagazine.org/online_articles/progressive-neoliberalism-reactionary-populism-nancy-fraser

Freeman, E. (2019). Feminist theory and its use in qualitative research in education. In *Oxford research encyclopedia of education.* Oxford. https://oxfordre.com/education/view/10.1093/acrefore/9780190264093.001.0001/acrefore-9780190264093-e-1193

Freire, P. (1974). *Pedagogy of the oppressed* (M. B. Ramos, Trans.). Seabury Press.

French, E. (2005, July 10). Uniting China to speak Mandarin, the one official language: Easier said than done. *The New York Times.* https://www.nytimes.com/2005/07/10/world/asia/uniting-china-to-speak-mandarin-the-one-official-language-easier.html

Galeano, E. (1998). *Open veins of Latin America: Five centuries of the pillage of a continent.* New York University Press.

Gates Jr., B. (2009, July 21). *Speech delivered to the National Conference of State Legislatures*. National Conference of State Legislatures. http://www.gatesfoundation.org/media-center/speeches/2009/07/bill-gates-national-conference-of-state-legislatures-ncsl

Gee, J. P. (2008). *Social linguistics and literacies: Ideology in discourses* (3rd ed.). Routledge/Falmer.

Gelman, S. A., & Roberts, S. O. (2017). How language shapes the cultural inheritance of categories. *Proceedings of the National Academy of Sciences of the United States of America*, *114*(30), 7900–7907. https://doi.org/10.1073/pnas.1621073114

Gewertz, C. (2019, October 14). Seattle Schools lead controversial push to "rehumanize" math. *Education Week*. https://www.edweek.org/ew/articles/2019/10/11/seattle-schools-lead-controversial-push-to-rehumanize.html

Gillborn, D. (2013). Interest-divergence and the colour of cutbacks: Race, recession and the undeclared war on Black children. *Discourse: Studies in the Cultural Politics of Education*, *34*(4), 477–491. https://doi.org/10.1080/01596306.2013.822616

Giordano, G. (2005). *How testing came to dominate American schools: The history of educational assessment*. Peter Lang.

Giroux, H. A. (1993). The politics of insurgent multiculturalism in the era of the Los Angeles Uprising. *The Journal of the Midwest Modern Language Association*, *26*(1), 12–30.

Glasser, H. M., & Smith III, J. P. (2008). On the vague meaning of "gender" in education research: The problem, its sources, and recommendations for practice. *Educational Researcher*, *37*(6), 343–350.

Gold, J. (2016). *Shifting out of neutral: A history teacher leaves the struggle for objectivity behind*. Learning for Justice. https://www.learningforjustice.org/magazine/spring-2016/shifting-out-of-neutral

Gorman, M. (2021, April 1). *"We're not fungible": Asian American attys on racism at work*. Law360. https://www.law360.com/articles/1370961

Gottesman, I. (2016). *The critical turn in education: From Marxist critique to poststructuralist feminism to critical theories of race*. Routledge.

Gould, S. J. (1996). *The mismeasure of man* (rev. and expanded ed.). Norton.

Gramsci, A. (1971). *Selections from the prison notebooks* (Q. Hoare, Trans.). International Publishers.

Greene, M. (1994). Chapter 10: Epistemology and educational research: The influence of recent approaches to knowledge. *Review of Research in Education*, *20*, 423–464. https://doi.org/10.3102/0091732X020001423

Groeger, L. V., Waldman, A., & Eads, D. (2018, October 16). *Miseducation: Is there racial inequality at your school?* ProPublica: Miseducation. https://projects.propublica.org/miseducation/

Gupta, A., Szymanski, D. M., & Leong, F. T. L. (2011). The "Model Minority myth": Internalized racialism of positive stereotypes as correlates of psychological distress, and attitudes towark help-seeking. *Asian American Journal of Psychology*, *2*(2), 101–114. https://doi.org/10.1037/a0024183

Gupta, P. (2023). *They called us exceptional: And other lies that raised us*. Crown.

Guthrie, R. V. (1998). *Even the rat was white: A historical view of psychology* (2nd ed.). Allyn and Bacon.

Gutstein, E. (2009). Math, SATs, and racial profiling. In W. Au (Ed.), *Rethinking multicultural education: Teaching for racial and cultural justice* (pp. 341–347). Rethinking Schools Ltd.

Hagopian, J. (Ed.). (2014a). *More than a score: The new uprising against high-stakes testing*. Haymarket Books.

Hagopian, J. (2014b). Our destination is not on the MAP. In *More than a score: The new uprising against high-stakes testing* (pp. 31–47). Haymarket Books.

Hagopian, J. (2014c). Salt of the Earth School: "They can't break us." Interview with Jia Lee. In J. Hagopian (Ed.), *More than a score: The new uprising against high-stakes testing* (pp. 107–112). Haymarket Books.

Hagopian, J. (2014d). Seattle test boycott: Our destination is not on the MAP. *Rethinking Schools*, *27*(3). http://www.rethinkingschools.org/archive/27_03/27_03_hagopian .shtml

Hagopian, J. (2015, October 30). *Obama regrets "taking the joy out of teaching and learning" with too much testing*. CommonDreams. http://www.commondreams.org /views/2015/10/30/obama-regrets-taking-joy-out-teaching-and-learning-too-much -testing

Hagopian, J. (2016, October 17). *Solidarity with #BlackLivesMatterAtSchool: Hundreds of professors across the country support Seattle educators in their day of action*. I Am an Educator. https://iamaneducator.com/2016/10/17/solidarity-with -blacklivesmatteratschool-hundreds-of-professors-across-the-country-support -seattle-educators-in-their-day-of-action/

Hagopian, J. (2020). Making Black Lives Matter at school. In D. Jones & J. Hagopian (Eds.), *Black Lives Matter at school: An uprising for educational justice* (pp. 1–24). Haymarket Books.

Hagopian, J., & Network for Public Education. (2015, May 5). Resistance to high stakes tests serves the cause of equity in education: A reply to "We oppose anti-testing efforts." *Truthout*. https://truthout.org/articles/resistance-to-high-stakes-tests-serves -the-cause-of-equity-in-education/

Hall, S. (1979). The great moving right show. *Marxism Today, January*, 14–19.

Haney, W. (1984). Testing reasoning and reasoning about testing. *Review of Educational Research*, *54*(4), 597–654.

Hanson, A. F. (2000). How tests create what they are intended to measure. In A. Filer (Ed.), *Assessment: Social practice and social product* (pp. 67–81). RoutledgeFalmer.

Harding, S. (2004a). How standpoint methodology informs philosophy of science. In S. N. Hesse-Biber & P. Leavy (Eds.), *Approaches to qualitative research* (pp. 62–80). Oxford University Press.

Harding, S. (2004b). Rethinking standpoint epistemology: What is "strong objectivity"? In S. Harding (Ed.), *The feminist standpoint reader* (pp. 127–140). Routledge.

Harris, P., Smith, B. M., & Harris, J. (2011). *The myths of standardized tests: Why they don't tell you what you think they do*. Rowman & Littlefield Publishers, Inc.

Hart, R., Casserly, M., Uzzell, R., Palacios, M., Corcoran, A., & Spurgeon, L. (2015). *Student testing in America's Great City Schools: An inventory and preliminary analysis*. Council of the Great City Schools. https://www.cgcs.org/cms/lib/DC00 001581/Centricity/Domain/87/Testing%20Report.pdf

Hartlep, N. D., & Scott, D. P. (2016). *Asian/American curricular epistemicide*. Sense Publishers.

Hartsock, N. C. M. (1983). The feminist standpoint: Developing the ground for a specifically feminist historical materialism. In S. Harding & M. B. Hintikka (Eds.), *Discovering reality: Feminist perspectives on epistemology, metaphysics, methodology, and philosophy of science* (pp. 283–310). D. Reidel.

Hartsock, N. C. M. (1998a). Marxist feminist dialectics for the 21st century. *Science & Society*, *62*(3), 400–413.

Hartsock, N. C. M. (1998b). *The feminist standpoint revisited & other essays*. Westview Press.

Harvey, D. (2004). The "new" imperialism: Accumulation by dispossession. *Socialist Register*, *40*, 63–87.

Harvey, D. (2007). Neoliberalism as creative destruction. *Annals of the American Academy of Political and Social Science*, *610*, 22–44.

Henry, A. (1996). Five Black women teachers critique child-centered pedagogy: Possibilities and limitations of oppositional standpoints. *Curriculum Inquiry*, *26*(4), 363–384.

Herrera, D. R. (2015). The Philippines: An overview of the colonial era. *Education About ASIA*, *20*(1), 14–19.

Herrnstein, R. J., & Murray, C. A. (1996). *The bell curve: Intelligence and class structure in American life* (1st Free Press pbk.). Simon & Schuster.

Hess, D. (2009). *Controversy in the classroom: The democratic power of discussion.* Routledge.

Heubert, J. P. (2001). High stakes testing and civil rights: Standards of appropriate test use and a strategy for enforcing them. In G. Orfield & M. L. Kornhaber (Eds.), *Raising standards or raising barriers?: Inequality and high-stakes testing in public education* (pp. 179–194). New Century Press.

Hibbett, M. (2019). In their fight to stop a new US military base, Okinawans confront two colonizers. *The Nation*. https://www.thenation.com/article/archive/okinawa-japan-us-military/

Higgins, S. (2013). *Charter school scandals*. http://charterschoolscandals.blogspot.com/

Hill Collins, P. (1989). The social construction of Black feminist thought. *Signs*, *14*(4), 745–773.

Hill, K., & Dreher, A. (2021, June 13). What's behind Eastern Washington's low coronavirus vaccine rates? The answer may not be simple. *Spokesman Review*. https://www.spokesman.com/stories/2021/jun/13/whats-behind-eastern-washingtons-low-coronavirus-v/

HiPointDem. (2012, June 18). *Bill Gates tells us why "his" high school was a great learning environment*. Seattle Education. https://seattleducation2010.wordpress.com/2012/06/18/bill-gates-tells-us-why-his-high-school-was-a-great-learning-environment/

Hlebowitsh, P. S. (1993). *Radical curriculum theory reconsidered: A historical approach*. Teachers College Press.

Hlebowitsh, P. S. (2005). Generational ideas in curriculum: A historical triangulation. *Curriculum Inquiry*, *35*(1), 73–87.

Ho, C., & Jackson, J. W. (2001). Attitudes toward Asian Americans: Theory and measurment. *Journal of Applied Social Psychology*, *31*, 1553–1581.

Hong, C. P. (2020). *Minor feelings: An Asian American reckoning*. One World.

Horn, J. (2012, December 12). *Paul Tough, KIPP, and the character con: A review of "How children succeed: Grit, curiousity, and the hidden power of character."* Substance News. http://www.substancenews.net/articles.php?page=3831&section=Article

Howe, K. R. (2009). Positivist dogmas, rhetoric, and the education science question. *Educational Researcher*, *38*(6), 428–440. https://doi.org/10.3102/0013189X09342003

Huebner, D. E. (1976). The moribund curriculum field: Its wake and our work. *Curriculum Inquiry*, *6*(2), 153–167.

Huggins, N. I. (1991). The deforming mirror of truth: Slavery and the master narrative of American history. *Radical History Review*, *49*, 25–48.

Hwang, W.-C. (2021). Demystifying and addressing internalized racism and oppression among Asian Americans. *American Psychologist*, *76*(4), 596–610. https://doi.org/10.1037/amp0000798

Iftikar, J. S., & Museus, S. D. (2018). On the utility of Asian critical (AsianCrit) theory in the field of education. *International Journal of Qualitative Studies in Education*, *31*(10), 935–949. https://doi.org/10.1080/09518398.2018.1522008

Ishizuka, K. (2016). *Serve the people: Making Asian America in the long sixties*. Verso.

Iyengar, M. M. (2014). Not mere abstractions: Language policies and language ideologies in U.S. settler colonialism. *Decolonization: Indigeneity, Education, & Society*, *3*(2), 33–59.

Jackson, K. B. (2023). "A tragedy for us all": Ketanji Jackson's impassioned affirmative action dissent. *The Guardian*. https://www.theguardian.com/commentisfree/2023/jun/29/kentanji-brown-jackson-affirmative-action-dissent

Jackson, P. W. (1980). Curriculum and its discontents. *Curriculum Inquiry*, *10*(2), 159–172.

Jackson, P. W. (1996). Conceptions of curriculum and curriculum specialists. In P. W. Jackson (Ed.), *Handbook of research on curriculum: A project of the American Educational Research Association* (pp. 3–40). Simon & Schuster Macmillan.

James, G. G. M. (1995). *Stolen legacy: Greek philosophy is stolen Egyptian philosophy*. Africa World Press. (Originally published in 1954)

Jeung, R., Yellow Horse, A., & Cayanan, C. (2021). *Stop AAPI hate national report*. Stop AAPI Hate. https://stopaapihate.org/wp-content/uploads/2021/08/Stop-AAPI-Hate-Report-National-v2-210830.pdf

Jiang, Y., Granja, M. R., & Koball, H. (2017). *Basic facts about low-income children: Children under 18 years, 2015* [Fact Sheet]. National Center for Children in Poverty, Columbia University. http://www.nccp.org/publications/pdf/text_1170.pdf

Jimenez, T. R., & Horowitz, A. L. (2013). When white is just alright: How immigrants redefine achievement and reconfigure the ethnoracial hierarchy. *American Sociological Review*, *78*(5), 849–871. https://doi.org/10.1177/0003122413497012

Jones, B. (2015). Keys to the schoolhouse: Black teachers, privatization, and the future of teacher unions. In B. Picower & E. Mayorga (Eds.), *What's race got to do with it?: How current school reform policy maintains racial and economic inequality* (Vol. 2, pp. 81–102). Peter Lang.

Jones, D., & Hagopian, J. (Eds.). (2020). *Black Lives Matter at school: An uprising for educational justice*. Haymarket Books.

Joseph, G. (2016). Where charter-school suspensions are concentrated. *The Atlantic*. https://www.theatlantic.com/education/archive/2016/09/the-racism-of-charter-school-discipline/500240/

Joseph, G. (2017, January 19). *What Betsy DeVos didn't say about school choice*. CityLab. http://www.citylab.com/politics/2017/01/what-betsy-devos-didnt-say-about-school-choice/513269/

Journey for Justice Alliance. (2016). *The Journey for Justice Alliance education platform: An equitable and just school system now!* The Journey for Justice Alliance. https://j4jalliance.com/projects/

Jun, H. (2011). *Race for citizenship: Black Orientalism and Asian uplift from pre-emancipation to neoliberal America*. NYU Press.

Jung, M.-H. (2008). *Coolies and cane: Race, labor, and sugar in the age of emancipation.* Johns Hopkins University Press.

Kafala, T., & Cary, L. (2006). Postmodern moments in curriculum theory: The logic and paradox of dissensus. *Journal of Curriculum Theorizing*, *22*(1), 25–43.

Kamenetz, A. (2017, March 9). *"I have children crying in the classroom."* NPREd: How Learning Happens. http://www.npr.org/sections/ed/2017/03/09/518996780/i-have-children-crying-in-the-classroom

Kang, J. (1996). Negative action against Asian Americans: The internal instability of Dworkin's defense of affirmative action. *Harvard Civil Rights-Civil Liberties Law Review*, *31*(1), 1–47.

Kane, T. J., & Staiger, D. O. (2002). Volatility in school test scores: Implications for test-based accountability systems. In D. Ravitch (Ed.), *Brookings papers on education policy 2002* (1st ed., pp. 235–284). The Brookings Institution.

Kang, J. C. (2022, November 4). The sad death of affirmative action. *The New Yorker*. https://www.newyorker.com/news/our-columnists/the-sad-death-of-affirmative-action

Karier, C. J. (1972). Testing for order and control in the corporate liberal state. *Educational Theory*, *22*(Spring), 159–180.

Karp, S. (2003). Let them eat tests: NCLB and federal education policy. In L. Christensen & S. Karp (Eds.), *Rethinking school reform* (pp. 199–213). Rethinking Schools.

Karp, S. (2012). School reform we can't believe in. *Rethinking Schools*, *24*(3). https://rethinkingschools.org/articles/school-reform-we-can-t-believe-in/

Karp, S. (2013). Charter schools and the future of public education: It's time to refocus public policy on providing excellent public schools for all. *Rethinking Schools*, *28*(1). https://rethinkingschools.org/articles/charter-schools-and-the-future-of-public-education/

Kelleher, J. S., Tang, T., & Rodriguez, O. R. (2021, August 21). *Mask, vaccine conflicts descend into violence and harassment.* AP News. https://apnews.com/article/health-coronavirus-pandemic-2eba81ebe3bd54b3bcde890b8cf11c70

Kelleher, K. (2019, February 13). Gilded Age 2.0: U.S. income inequality increases to pre-great depression levels. *Fortune*. https://fortune.com/2019/02/13/us-income-inequality-bad-great-depression/

Kelley, A. (2021, June 17). *Texas passes law banning critical race theory in schools.* The Hill. https://thehill.com/changing-america/respect/equality/558927-texas-passes-law-banning-critical-race-theory-in-schools/

Kelley, R. D. G. (2017, November 7). *What is racial capitalism and why does it matter?* Katz Distinguished Lecture in the Humanities, University of Washington. https://youtu.be/REo_gHIpvJc

Kim, C. J. (1999). The racial triangulation of Asian Americans. *Politics & Society*, *27*, 105–138. https://doi.org/10.1177/0032329299027001005

Kim, C. J. (2018). Are Asians the new Blacks?: Affirmative Actions, anti-Blackness, and the "sociometry" of race. *Du Bois Review*, *15*(2), 1–28. https://doi.org/10.1017/S1742058X18000243

Kim, P.-G., & Marshall, J. D. (2006). Synoptic curriculum texts: Representation of contemporary curriculum scholarship. *Journal of Curriculum Studies*, *38*(3), 327–349.

Kim, P. Y., & Lee, D. (2014). Internalized model minority myth, Asian values, and help-seeking attitudes among Asian American students. *Cultural Diversity and Ethnic Minority Psychology*, *20*(1), 98–106. https://doi.org/10.1037/a0033351

King, L. J. (2014). When lions write history. *Multicultural Education*, *22*(1), 2–11.

King, L. J., Davis, C., & Brown, A. L. (2012). African American history, race and textbooks: An examination of the works of Harold O. Rugg and Carter G. Woodson. *The Journal of Social Studies Research*, *36*(4), 359–386.

King, L. J., & Simmons, C. (2018). Narratives of Black history in textbooks: Canada and the United States. In S. A. Metzger & L. M. Harris (Eds.), *The Wiley international handbook of history teaching and learning* (pp. 93–116). John Wiley & Sons, Inc.

Kingkade, T., Zadrozny, B., & Collins, B. (2021, June 15). *Critial race theory battle invades school boards—With help from conservative groups*. NBC News. https://www.nbcnews.com/news/us-news/critical-race-theory-invades-school-boards-help-conservative-groups-n1270794

Kirchner, L. (2017, May 3). Don't believe the FBI's most recent hate crime statistics. *Pacific Standard*. https://psmag.com/news/hate-crime-trends-hard-track-98345

Kirst, M. W. (2002). *Mayoral influence, new regimes, and public school governance* (p. 18). Consortium for Policy Research in Education, University of Pennsylvania. http://www.cpre.org/Publications/rr49.pdf

Klonsky, M. (2011). Power philanthropy: Taking the public out of public education. In P. E. Kovacs (Ed.), *The Gates Foundation and the future of U.S. "public" schools* (pp. 21–38). Routledge.

Kochhar, R., & Cilluffo, A. (2018). *Income inequality in the U.S. is rising most rapidly among Asians*. Pew Research Center. https://www.pewresearch.org/social-trends/2018/07/12/income-inequality-in-the-u-s-is-rising-most-rapidly-among-asians/

KrazyTA. (2014, March 19). *KrazyTA explains what Bill Gates wants for his own children*. Diane Ravitch's Blog. https://dianeravitch.net/2014/03/19/krazyta-explains-what-bill-gates-wants-for-his-own-children/

Kretchmar, K., Sondel, B., & Ferrare, J. J. (2014). Mapping the terrain: Teach For America, charter school reform, and corporate sponsorship. *Journal of Education Policy*, *29*(6), 742–759. https://doi.org/10.1080/02680939.2014.880812

Kroman, D. (2019, May 9). *Reports of hate crimes and bias have surged in Seattle since 2012*. Crosscut. https://crosscut.com/2019/05/reports-hate-crimes-and-bias-have-surged-seattle-2012

Kwong, P. (1996). *The new Chinatown*. Hill and Wang.

Ladd, H. F., Clotfelter, C. T., & Holbein, J. B. (2017). The growing segmentation of the charter school sector in North Carolina. *Education Finance and Policy*, *19*(55), 1–28. https://doi.org/10.1162/edfp_a_00226

Ladson-Billings, G. (2006). From the achievement gap to the education debt: Understanding achievement in U.S. schools. *Educational Researcher*, *35*(7), 3–12.

Ladson-Billings, G. (2017). "Makes me wanna holler": Refuting the "culture of poverty" discourse in urban schooling. *The ANNALS of the American Academy of Political and Social Science*, *673*(1), 80–90. https://doi.org/10.1177/0002716217718793

Ladson-Billings, G., & Tate IV, W. F. (1995). Towards a critical race theory of education. *Teachers College Record*, *97*(1), 47–68.

Lake, R. J. (2008). In the eye of the beholder: Charter schools and innovation. *Journal of School Choice*, *2*(2), 115–127. http://dx.doi.org/10.1080/15582150802136090

Lan, S. (2011). *Diaspora and class consciousness: Chinese immigrant workers in multiracial Chicago*. Routledge.

Landau, I. (2008). Problems with feminist standpoint theory in science education. *Science & Education*, *17*, 1081–1088. https://doi.org/10.1007/s11191-007-9131-5

Lane, A. (2016, August 24). *The Trump campaign: A white revolt against "neoliberal multiculturalism."* Counterpunch. https://www.counterpunch.org/2016/08/24/the-trump-campaign-a-white-revolt-against-neoliberal-multiculturalism/

Lapp, D., Lin, J., Dolson, E., & Moran, D. (2017). *The fiscal impact of charter school expansion: Calculation in six Pennsylvania school districts*. Research for Action. https://www.researchforaction.org/publications/fiscal-impact-charter-school-expansion-calculations-six-pennsylvania-school-districts/

Layton, L. (2014, June 7). How Bill Gates pulled off the swift Common Core revolution. *The Washington Post*. http://www.washingtonpost.com/politics/how-bill-gates-pulled-off-the-swift-common-core-revolution/2014/06/07/a830e32e-ec34-11e3-9f5c-9075d5508f0a_story.html

Lazarin, M. (2014). *Testing overload in America's schools*. Center for American Progress. https://cdn.americanprogress.org/wp-content/uploads/2014/10/LazarinOvertestingReport.pdf

Lee, E. (2015). *The making of Asian America: A history*. Simon & Schuster.

Lee, J. (2006). *Tracking achievement gaps and assessing the impact of NCLB on the gaps: An in-depth look into national and state reading and math outcome trends* (p. 80). Harvard Civil Rights Project. https://files.eric.ed.gov/fulltext/ED491807.pdf

Lee, J., Wong, J., & Ramakrishnan, K. (2021). Asian Americans Support for Affirmative Action Increased Since 2016—Data Bits. *AAPI Data 2021*. http://aapidata.com/blog/affirmative-action-increase/

Lee, R. E. (1999). *Orientals: Asian Americans in popular culture*. Temple University Press.

Lee, S. J. (2005). *Up against whiteness: Race, school and immigrant youth*. Teachers College Press.

Lee, S. J. (2006). Additional complexities: Social class, ethnicity, generation, and gender in Asian American student experiences. *Race Ethnicity and Education*, *9*(1), 17–28. https://doi.org/10.1080/13613320500490630

Lee, S. J. (2009). *Unraveling the "model minority" stereotype: Listening to Asian American youth*. Teachers College Press.

Lemann, N. (1999). *The big test: The secret history of the American meritocracy*. Farrar, Straus, and Giroux.

Leonardo, Z. (2009). *Race, whiteness, and education*. Routledge.

Leonardo, Z. (2011). After the glow: Race ambivalence and other educational prognoses. *Educational Philosophy and Theory*, *43*(6), 675–698. https://doi.org/10.1111/j.1469-5812.2010.00645.x

Leonardo, Z. (2012). The race for class: Reflections on a critical raceclass theory of education. *Educational Studies*, *58*(5), 427–449.

Lew, J. (2006). *Asian Americans in class: Charting the achievement gap among Korean American youth*. Teachers College Press.

Lieb, D. A. (2025, May 15). *As Trump targets DEI, Republican-led states intensify efforts to stamp it out*. ABC News. https://abcnews.go.com/Politics/wireStory/trump-targets-dei-republican-led-states-intensify-efforts-121862885

Lin, M. H., Kwan, V. S. Y., Cheung, A., & Fiske, S. T. (2005). Stereotype content model explains prejudice for an envied outgroup: Scale of anti-Asian American stereotypes. *Personality and Social Psychology Bulletin*, *31*(1), 34–47. https://doi.org/10.1177/0146167204271320

Lindsay, J. M. (2020, December 15). *The 2020 election by the numbers*. The Water's Edge (Council on Foreign Relations). https://www.cfr.org/blog/2020-election-numbers

Lipman, P. (2011). *The new political economy of urban education: Neoliberalism, race, and the right to the city*. Routledge.

Liu, M., Geron, K., & Lai, T. (2008). *The snake dance of Asian American activism: Community, vision, and power*. Lexington Books.

Lomawaima, K. T. (1999). The unnatural history of American Indian education. In K. Swisher & J. Tippeconnic III (Eds.), *Next steps: Research and practice to advance Indian education* (pp. 1–32). ERIC Clearinghouse on Rural Education and Small Schools.

Losen, D. J., Keith, M. A., II, Hodson, C. L., & Martinez, T. E. (2016). *Charter schools, civil rights and schools discipline: A comprehensive review*. The Center for Civil Rights Remedies (at The Civil Rights Project). https://civilrightsproject.ucla.edu/resources/projects/center-for-civil-rights-remedies/school-to-prison-folder/federal-reports/charter-schools-civil-rights-and-school-discipline-a-comprehensive-review/losen-et-al-charter-school-discipline-review-2016.pdf

Louie, V. (2001). Parents' aspirations and investment: The role of social class in the educational experience of 1.5 and second generation Chinese Americans. *Harvard Educational Review*, *71*, 438–474.

Love, B. (2019, February 12). "Grit is in our DNA": Why teaching grit is inherently anti-Black. *Education Week*. https://www.edweek.org/leadership/opinion-grit-is-in-our-dna-why-teaching-grit-is-inherently-anti-black/2019/02

Love, B. (2023). *Punished for dreaming: How school reform harms Black children and how we heal*. St. Martin's Press.

Lukacs, G. (1971). *History and class consciousness*. MIT Press.

Luke, C., & Gore, J. (Eds.). (1992). *Feminisms and critical pedagogy*. Routledge.

Lurie, J. (2015, April 17). Just how racist are schoolteachers? *Mother Jones*. http://www.motherjones.com/kevin-drum/2015/04/teachers-racism-bias-stanford

Luthar, S. S., Ebbert, A. M., & Kumar, N. L. (2021). Risk and resilience among Asian American youth: Ramification of Discrimination and low authenticity in self-presentations. *American Psychologist*, *76*(4), 643–657. https://doi.org/10.1037/amp0000764

Lye, C. (2005). *America's Asia: Racial form and American literature, 1893–1945*. Princeton University Press.

Lye, C. (2008). The Afro-Asian analogy. *PMLA*, *123*(5), 1732–1736.

Madaus, G. F., & Clarke, M. (2001). The adverse impact of high-stakes testing on minority students: Evidence from one hundred years of test data. In G. Orfield & M. L. Kornhaber (Eds.), *Raising standards or raising barriers?: Inequality and high-stakes testing in public education* (pp. 85–106). Century Foundation Press.

Maeda, D. J. (2009). *Chains of Babylon: The rise of Asian America*. University of Minnesota Press.

Malewski, E. (Ed.). (2009). *Curriculum studies handbook: The next movement*. Routledge.

Manicom, A. (1992). Feminist pedagogy: Transformations, standpoints, and politics. *Canadian Journal of Education*, *17*(3), 365–389.

Marx, K. (1967). *Capital: A critique of political economy* (S. M. and E. Aveling, Trans.; Vol. 1). International Publishers.

Mayorga, E., Aggarwal, U., & Picower, B. (Eds.). (2020). *What's race got to do with it: How current school reform policy maintains racial and economic inequality* (2nd ed.). Peter Lang.

McAlevey, J. (2019, October 15). *Chicago's teachers are making history. Again*. The Nation. https://www.thenation.com/article/archive/union-strike-chicago-teachers/

McCoy, S. (2017). *Texts that teach: Curriculum, affect, and critical pedagogy in the neoliberal university* [Dissertation, University of Washington]. https://search.proquest.com/openview/97bbcec10a9dff3ebea9f37410fcbf6c/1?pq-origsite=gscholar&cbl=18750&diss=y

McGee, E. (2018). "Black genius, Asian fail": The detriment of stereotype lift and stereotype threat in high-achieving Asian and Black STEM students. *AERA Open*, *4*(4), 1–16. https://doi.org/10.1177/2332858418816658

McGee, K. (2021, June 15). *Texas "critical race theory" bill limiting teaching of current events signed into law*. The Texas Tribune. https://www.texastribune.org/2021/06/15/abbott-critical-race-theory-law/

McLaren, P., & Farahmandpur, R. (2005). Marx after post-Marxism: Reclaiming critical pedagogy for the left. In P. McLaren (Ed.), *Red seminars: Radical excursions into educational theory, cultural poliitcs, and pedagogy* (pp. 3–24). Hampton Press, Inc.

McNeil, L. M. (2000). *Contradictions of school reform: Educational costs of standardized testing*. Routledge.

Meier, D., & Knoester, M. (2017). *Beyond testing: Seven assessments of students and schools more effective than standardized tests*. Teachers College Press.

Melamed, J. (2011). *Represent and destroy: Rationalizing violence in the new racial capitalism*. University of Minnesota Press.

Merriam-Webster. (2019). *Insurgent*. Merriam-Webster Dictionary. https://www.merriam-webster.com/dictionary/insurgent

Miller, J. L. (2005). The American curriculum field and its worldly encounters. *Journal of Curriculum Theorizing*, *21*(2), 9–24.

Mills, C. (2014). *The racial contract*. Cornell University Press.

Miron, G., & Urschel, J. (2012). The impact of school choice reforms on student achievement. In K. G. Welner, P. H. Hinchey, & W. J. Mathis (Eds.), *Exploring the school choice universe: Evidence and recommendations* (pp. 211–236). Information Age Publishing.

Miron, G., Urschel, J. L., Mathis, W. J., & Tornquist, E. (2010). *Schools without diversity: Education management organizations, charter schools, and the demographic stratification of the American school system*. Education and the Public Interest Center and Education Policy Research Unit. http://nepc.colorado.edu/files/EMO-Seg.pdf

Mockaitis, T. (2021, October 19). *Teaching "opposing views" of the Holocaust is the latest effort to rewrite history*. The Hill. https://thehill.com/opinion/education/577351-opposing-views-of-the-holocaust-is-the-latest-effort-to-rewrite-history?rl=1

Montefiore, C. S. (2013, December 15). *How China distorts its minorities through propaganda*. BBC News. https://www.bbc.com/culture/article/20131215-how-china-portrays-its-minorities

Morrison, K. R. B. (2004). The poverty of curriculum theory: A critique of Wraga and Hlebowitsh. *Journal of Curriculum Studies*, *36*(4), 487–494.

Murphy, P., Regenstein, E., & McNamara, K. (2012). *Putting a price tag on the Common Core: How much will smart implementation cost?* Thomas B. Fordham Institute. http://www.edexcellence.net/publications/putting-a-price-tag-on-the-common-core.html

Murphy-Shigematsu, S. (2004). Expanding the borders of the nation: Ethnic diversity and citizenship in Japan. In J. A. Banks (Ed.), *Diversity and citizenship education: Global perspectives* (pp. 303–332). Jossey-Bass.

Myers, L. L. (2013, March 7). *U.S. probes racial disparities in Seattle school discipline*. Reuters. https://www.reuters.com/article/us-usa-schools-seattle/u-s-probes-racial-disparities-in-seattle-school-discipline-idUSBRE9260KJ20130307

NAACP. (2016, October 15). *Statement regarding the NAACP's resolution on a moratorium on charter schools*. NAACP.org. http://www.naacp.org/latest/statement-regarding-naacps-resolution-moratorium-charter-schools/

National Poverty Center. (2017). *Poverty in the United States: Frequently asked questions*. Retrieved from https://web.archive.org/web/20170122222646/http://www.npc.umich.edu/poverty/

National Research Council. (2011). *Incentives and test-based accountability in education*. Committee on Incentives and Test-Based Accountability in Public Education, M. Hout & S.W. Elliott (Eds.). Board on Testing and Assessment, Division of Behavioral and Social Sciences and Education.

Nesterova, Y. (2019). Teaching Indigenous children in Taiwan: Tensions, complexities and opportunities. *Global Studies of Childhood*, *9*(2), 156–166. https://doi.org/10.1177/2043610619846349

Ng, J. C., Lee, S. S., & Pak, Y. K. (2007). Contesting the model minority and perpetual foreigner stereotypes: A critical review of literature on Asian Americans in education. *Review of Research in Education*, *31*, 95–130. https://doi.org/10.3102/0091732X06298015

Ngai, M. M. (2000). American Orientalism. *Reviews in American History*, *28*(3), 408–415.

Nguyen, V. T. (2024, January 23). Palestine is in Asia: An Asian American argument. *The Nation*. https://www.thenation.com/article/world/palestine-asia-orientalism-expansive-solidarity/

Ngũgĩ, wa T. (1986). *Decolonising the mind: The politics of language in African literature*. Heinemann.

Nichols, S. L., & Berliner, D. C. (2007). *Collateral damage: How high-stakes testing corrupts America's schools*. Harvard Education Press.

Nichols, S. L., Glass, G. V., & Berliner, D. C. (2005). *High-stakes testing and student achievement: Problems for the No Child Left Behind Act* (EPSL-0509-105-EPRU). Education Policy Research Unit, Education Policy Studies Laboratory, College of Education, Division of Educational Leadership and Policy Studies, Arizona State University. https://nepc.colorado.edu/publication/high-stakes-testing-and-student-achievement-problems-no-child-left-behind-act

Ninh, E. K. (2021). *Passing for perfect: College impostors and other model minorities*. Temple University Press.

Noltemeyer, A. L., Ward, R. M., & Mcloughlin, C. (2015). Relationship between school suspension and student outcomes: A meta-analysis. *School Psychology Review*, *44*(2), 224–240. https://doi.org/10.17105/spr-14-0008.1

Office of Superintendent of Public Instruction. (2017a). *John Muir Elementary School*. Washington State Report Card. https://reportcard.ospi.k12.wa.us/ReportCard/ViewSchoolOrDistrict/101058

Office of Superintendent of Public Instruction. (2017b). *Prosser School District*. Washington State Report Card. https://reportcard.ospi.k12.wa.us/ReportCard/ViewSchoolOrDistrict/100205

Office of Superintendent of Public Instruction. (2019). *Washington State Report Card: Seattle School District #1*. https://reportcard.ospi.k12.wa.us/ReportCard/ViewSchoolOrDistrict/100229

Okamura, J. Y., & Fujikane, C. (Eds.). (2013). *Asian settler colonialism: From local governance to the habits of everyday life in Hawaii*. University of Hawaii Press.

Okihiro, G. Y. (2014). *Margins and mainstreams: Asians in American history and culture*. University of Washington Press.

Omi, M., & Winant, H. (2015). *Racial formations in the United States*. Routledge.

Ong, A. (1996). Cultural citizenship as subject-making: Immigrants negotiate racial and cultural boundaries in the United States. *Current Anthropology*, *37*(5), 737–762.

Ong, A. (2016). *Fungible life: Experiment in the Asian city of life*. Duke University Press.

Oommen, T. K. (2004). Crisis of citizenship education in the Indian republic: Contestation between cultural monists and pluralists. In J. A. Banks (Ed.), *Diversity and citizenship education: Global perspectives* (pp. 333–354). Jossey-Bass.

Orfield, M., & Luce, T. (2016). An analysis of student performance in Chicago's charter schools. *Education Policy Analysis Archives*, *24*(111). http://dx.doi.org/10.14507/epaa.24.2203

Osajima, K. (1988). Asian Americans as the model minority: An analysis of the popular press image in the 1960s and 1980s. In G. Y. Okihiro, S. Hune, A. A. Hansen, & J. M. Liu (Eds.), *Reflections on shattered windows: Promises and prospects for Asian American studies* (pp. 165–174). Washington State University Press.

Osajima, K. (2005). Asian Americans as the model minority: An analysis of the popular press image in the 1960s and 1980s. In K. A. Ono (Ed.), *A companion to Asian American studies* (pp. 215–225). Blackwell Publishing Ltd.

Pang, V. O., Kiang, P. N., & Pak, Y. (2003). Asian Pacific American students: Challenging a biased educational system. In J. A. Banks (Ed.), *Handbook of research on multicultural education* (2nd ed., pp. 542–563). Jossey-Bass.

Patel, L. (2016). *Decolonizing educational research: From ownership to answerability*. Routledge.

Pelzer, J. (2015). *Charter school operator owns property bought with public money, Ohio Supreme Court rules*. Cleveland.com. http://www.cleveland.com/open/index.ssf/2015/09/charter_school_operator_owns_p.html

Perry, M. (2002). *Marxism and history*. Palgrave.

Petersen, W. (1966, January 9). Success story, Japanese-American style. *The New York Times*, 21, 33, 36, 38, 40–41, 43.

Pfannenstiel, B. (2021, October 7). *Sen. Chuck Grassley's compliment to Korean American judge Lucy Koh sparks backlash for racial stereotype*. USA Today. https://www.usatoday.com/story/news/politics/2021/10/07/chuck-grassley-compliment-lucy-koh-korean-american-judge-echoes-racial-stereotype/6032593001/

Pinar, W. F. (Ed.). (1975). *Curriculum theorizing: The reconceptualists*. McCutchan Publishing.

Pinar, W. F. (1978). The reconceptualization of curriculum studies. *Curriculum Studies*, *10*(3), 205–214.

Pinar, W. F. (2006). Relocating cultural studies into curriculum studies. *Journal of Curriculum Theorizing*, *22*(2), 55–72.

Pinnick, C. L. (2008). Science education for women: Situated cognition, feminist standpoint theory, and the status of women in science. *Science & Education*, *17*, 1055–1063. https://doi.org/10.1007/s11191-008-9153-7

Pondiscio, R. (2015, March 25). *Opting out, race, and reform*. Common Core Watch. https://edexcellence.net/articles/opting-out-race-and-reform

Poon, O., & Segoshi, M. S. (2018). The racial mascot speaks: A critical race discourse analysis of Asian Americans and *Fisher vs. University of Texas*. *The Review of Higher Education*, *42*(1), 235–267.

Poon, O., Segoshi, M. S., Tang, L., Surla, K. L., Nguyen, C., & Squire, D. D. (2019). Asian Americans, affirmative action, and the political economy of racism: A multidimensional model of raceclass frames. *Harvard Educational Review*, *89*(2), 201–226. https://doi.org/10.17763/1943-5045-89.2.201

Poon, O., Squire, D., Kodama, C., Byrd, A., Chan, J., Manzano, L., Furr, S., & Bishundat, D. (2016). A critical review of the model minority myth in selected literature on Asian Americans and Pacific Islanders in higher education. *Review of Educational Resesarch*, *86*(2), 469–502. https://doi.org/10.3102/0034654315612205

Popkewitz, T. S., & Fendler, L. (Eds.). (1999). *Critical theories in education: Changing terrains of knowledge and politics*. Routledge.

Prashad, V. (2000). *The karma of brown folk*. University of Minnesota Press.

Preston, C., Goldring, E., Berends, M., & Cannata, M. (2012). School innovation in district context: Comparing traditional public schools and charter schools. *Economics of Education Review*, *31*(2), 318–330. https://doi.org/10.1016/j.econedurev.2011.07.016

Probert, C. (2017, February 18). *Teacher placed on leave after her Facebook post urges reporting illegal residents*. The Sacramento Bee. http://www.sacbee.com/news/nation-world/national/article133574239.html

Prothero, A. (2017, August 16). *Public support for charter school plummets, poll finds*. Education Week. http://www.edweek.org/ew/articles/2017/08/15/public-support-for-charter-schools-plummets-poll.html

Raftery, I. (2017, June 16). *To understand white liberal racism, read these private emails*. KUOW. http://archive.kuow.org/post/understand-white-liberal-racism-read-these-private-emails

Ravitch, D. (2010). *The death and life of the great American school system: How testing and choice are undermining education* (e-book). Basic Books.

Ravitch, D. (2013). *Reign of error: The hoax of the privatization movement and the danger to America's public schools*. Alfred A. Knopf.

Rawls, K. (2013). *Who is profiting from charters?: The big bucks behind charter school secrecy, financial scandal and corruption*. AlterNet. https://www.alternet.org/2013/05/who-profiting-charters-big-bucks-behind-charter-school-secrecy-financial-scandal-and

Renter, D. S., Scott, C., Kober, N., Chudowsky, N., Joftus, S., & Zabala, D. (2006). *From the capital to the classroom: Year 4 of the No Child Left Behind Act* (p. 214). Center on Education Policy. http://www.cep-dc.org/nclb/Year4/Press/

Renzulli, L. A., & Evans, L. (2005). School choice, charter schools, and white flight. *Social Problems*, *52*(3), 398–418.

Resmovits, J. (2011, July 15). *Murdoch education affiliate's $2.7 million consulting contract approved by New York City*. Huffington Post. http://www.huffingtonpost.com/2011/07/15/murdoch-education-affiliate-contract-approved_n_900379.html

Rethinking Schools. (2013, January 21). *Leading educators support teacher test boycott*. Rethinking Schools Blog. https://rethinkingschoolsblog.wordpress.com/2013/01/21/leading-educators-support-teacher-test-boycott/

Rethinking Schools. (2014). The gathering resistance to standardized tests. *Rethinking Schools*, *28*(3). https://rethinkingschools.org/articles/the-gathering-resistance-to-standardized-tests/

Rich, M. (2013, April 30). NewSchools fund attracts more capital. *The New York Times*. http://www.nytimes.com/2013/05/01/education/newschools-venture-fund-links-with-rethink-education.html?ref=education&_r=1&

Rodriguez, K. (2016, September 14). *Grade school teachers to wear Black Lives Matter shirts to class to protest "systemic oppression."* Breitbart. http://www.breitbart.com/big-government/2016/09/14/grade-school-teachers-wear-black-lives-matter-shirts-class-protest-systemic-oppression/

Rodriguez, M., Barthelemy, R., & McCormick, M. (2022). Critical race and feminist standpoint theories in physics education research: A historical review and potential applications. *Physical Review Physics Education Research*, *18*(1). https://doi.org/10.1103/PhysRevPhysEducRes.18.013101

Rodriguez, N. N., An, S., & Kim, E. J. (2024). *Teaching Asian America in elementary classrooms*. Routledge.

Rogers, J. A. (2015). *From superman to man*. Merchant Books. (Originally published in 1917)

Rogers, J., Franke, M., Yun, J.-E. E., Ishimoto, M., Diera, C., Geller, R. C., Berryman, A., & Brenes, T. (2017). *Teaching and learning in the age of Trump: Increasing stress and hostility in America's high schools*. UCLA Institute for Democracy, Education, and Access. https://idea.gseis.ucla.edu/publications/teaching-and-learning-in-age-of-trump

Rosenbaum, J. E. (1976). *Making inequality: The hidden curriculum of high school tracking* (1st ed.). John Wiley & Sons.

Rosenbusch, M. H. (2005). The No Child Left Behind Act and teaching and learning languages in U.S. schools. *The Modern Language Journal*, *89*(2), 250–261.

Ross, E. W. (1998). Social studies education and the pursuit of social justice. *Theory and Research in Social Education*, *26*(4), 457–460.

Ross, E. W. (2000). Redrawing the lines: The case against traditional social studies education. In D. W. Hursh, E. W. Ross, & J. L. Kincheloe (Eds.), *Democratic social education: Social studies for social change* (pp. 43–63). Falmer Press.

Ross, E. W. (2015, October 25). *Teaching and the ideology of neutrality*. Critical Education. https://blogs.ubc.ca/criticaleducation/2015/10/25/teaching-and-the-ideology-of-neutrality/

Rushton, P. J., & Jensen, A. R. (2005). Thirty years of research on race differences in cognitive ability. *Psychology, Public Policy, and Law*, *11*(2), 234–294.

Sabzalian, L., Shear, S. B., & Snyder, J. (2021). Standardizing Indigenous erasure: A TribalCrit and QuantCrit analysis of K-12 U.S. civics and government standards. *Theory & Research in Social Education*, *49*(3), 321–359. https://doi.org/10.1080/00933104.2021.1922322

Sacks, P. (1999). *Standardized minds: The high price of America's testing culture and what we can do to change it*. Perseus Books.

Said, E. W. (1978). *Orientalism*. Pantheon Books.

Salcedo, A. (2021, March 19). *Racist anti-Asian hashtags spiked after Trump first tweeted "Chinese virus," study finds*. The Washington Post. https://www.washingtonpost.com/nation/2021/03/19/trump-tweets-chinese-virus-racist/

Saltman, K. J. (2011). From Carnegie to Gates: The Bill and Melinda Gates Foundation and the venture philanthropy agenda for public education. In P. E. Kovacs (Ed.), *The Gates Foundation and the future of U.S. "public" schools* (pp. 1–20). Routledge.

Saltman, K. J. (2012). *The failure of corporate school reform*. Paradigm Publishers.

Sanchez, A. (2021, August 9). *Outlawing the truth*. The Progressive Magazine. https://progressive.org/magazine/outlawing-the-truth-sanchez/

Sandoval, C. (2000). *Methodology of the oppressed*. University of Minnesota Press.

Sanjoy, C. (2016). *The other one percent: Indians in America*. Oxford University Press.

Santana, L. M., & Singh, C. (2024). Importance of accounting for student identities and intersectionality for creating equitable and inclusive physics learning environments. *Physical Review Physics Education Research*, *20*(2). https://doi.org/10.1103/PhysRevPhysEducRes.20.020142

Saranillio, D. I. (2013). Why Asian settler colonialism matters: A thought piece on critiques, debates, and Indigenous difference. *Settler Colonial Studies*, *2*(3–4), 280–294. https://doi.org/10.1080/2201473X.2013.810697

Sass, T. R. (2008). *The stability of value-added measures of teacher quality and implication for teacher compensation* [Policy Brief]. National Center for Analysis of Longitudinal Data in Educational Research.

Schochet, P. Z., & Chiang, H. S. (2010). *Error rates in measuring teacher and school performance based on test score gains* (NCEE 2010–4004; p. 59). U.S. Department of Education, Institute of Educational Sciences, National Center for Educational Evaluation and Regional Assistance. http://ies.ed.gov/ncee/pubs/20104004/pdf/20104004.pdf

Schwab, J. J. (1969). The practical: A language for curriculum. *School Review*, *78*(1), 1–23.

Schwartz, S. (2021, February 3). *Lawmakers push to ban "1619 Project" from schools*. Education Week. https://www.edweek.org/teaching-learning/lawmakers-push-to-ban-1619-project-from-schools/2021/02

Scott, J. T. (2013). Rosa Parks moment? School choice and the marketization of civil rights. *Critical Studies in Education*, *54*(1), 5–18. http://dx.doi.org/10.1080/17508487.2013.739570

Scott, J. T., & Jabbar, H. (2014). The hub and the spokes: Foundations, intermediary organizations, incentivist reforms, and the politics of research evidence. *Educational Policy*, *28*(2), 233–257.

SEARAC & AAJC Los Angeles. (2020). *Southeast Asian American journeys: A national snapshot of our communities*. The Southeast Asian Resource Action Center & Asian Americans Advancing Justice—Los Angeles. https://www.searac.org/wp-content/uploads/2020/02/SEARAC_NationalSnapshot_PrinterFriendly.pdf

Selden, S. (1999). *Inheriting shame: The story of eugenics and racism in America*. Teachers College Press.

Shear, S. B. (2015). Cultural genocide masked as education: U.S. history textbooks' coverage of indigenous education policies. In P. T. Chandler (Ed.), *Doing race in social studies: Critical perspectives* (pp. 13–40). Information Age Publishing.

Shear, S. B., Knowles, R. T., Soden, G. J., & Castro, A. J. (2015). Manifesting destiny: Re/presentations of Indigenous peoples in K–12 U.S. history standards. *Theory & Research in Social Education*, *43*(1), 68–101. https://doi.org/10.1080/00933104.2014.999849

Shollenberger, T. L. (2015). Racial disparities in school suspension and subsequent outcomes: Evidence from the National Longitudinal Survey of Youth. In D. J. Losen (Ed.), *Closing the school discipline gap: Equitable remedies for excessive exclusion* (pp. 31–43). Teachers College Press.

Shor, I. (1986). *Culture wars: School and society in the conservative restoration 1969–1984*. Routledge & Kegan Paul.

Siegel, H. (2006). Epistemological diversity and educational research: Much ado about nothing much? *Educational Researcher*, *35*(3), 3–12. https://doi.org/10.3102/0013189X035002003

Silva, D. (2019, September 30). *Study on Harvard find 43 percent of white students are legacy, athletes, related to donors or staff*. NBC News. https://www.nbcnews.com/news/us-news/study-harvard-finds-43-percent-white-students-are-legacy-athletes-n1060361

Simon, S. (2013). *Special report: Class struggle—How charter schools get the students they want*. Reuters. http://www.reuters.com/article/2013/02/15/us-usa-charters-admissions-idUSBRE91E0HF20130215

Slabbert, J. A., & Hattingh, A. (2006). "Where is the post-modern truth we have lost in reductionist knowledge?": A curriculum's epitaph. *Journal of Curriculum Studies*, *38*(6), 701–718.

Slattery, P. (2006). *Curriculum development in the postmodern era* (2nd ed.). Routledge.

Sleeter, C. (2000). Epistemological diversity in research on preservice teacher preparation for historically underserved children. *Review of Research in Education*, *25*, 209–250.

Sleeter, C. (2002). State curriculum standards and the shaping of student consciousness. *Social Justice*, *29*(4), 8–25.

Smith, L. T. (1999). *Decolonizing methodologies*. Zed Books.

Smitherman, G. (1997). Black language and the education of black children: One mo once. *The Black Scholar*, *27*(1), 28–35.

Snaza, N. (2014). The death of curriculum studies and its ghosts. *Journal of Curriculum and Pedagogy*, *11*(2), 154–173. https://doi.org/10.1080/15505170.2014.966932

Sommeiller, E., Price, M., & Wazeter, E. (2016). *Income inequality in the U.S. by state, metropolitan area, and county*. Economic Policy Institute. http://www.epi.org/files/pdf/107100.pdf

Spatig, L. (2005). Feminist critique of developmentalism: What's in it for teachers? *Theory and Research in Education*, *3*(3), 299–326. https://doi.org/10.1177/1477878505057431

Spence, L. K. (2013). The neoliberal turn in Black politics. *Souls: A Critical Journal of Black Politics, Culture, and Society*, *14*(3–4), 139–159. http://dx.doi.org/10.1080/10999949.2012.763682

Stapleton, S. R. (2020). Toward critical environmental education: A standpoint analysis of race in the American environmental context. *Environmental Education Research*, *26*(2), 155–170. https://doi.org/10.1080/13504622.2019.1648768

Stith, J., Rivera, H., & Tutashinda, C. (2016). *A vision for Black lives: Policy demands for Black power, freedom, & justice: An end to the privatization of education and real community control by parents, students and community members of schools including democratic school boards and community control of curriculum, hiring, firing, and discipline policies*. #BlackLivesMatter. https://m4bl.org/wp-content/uploads/2020/06/12-End-Militarization-of-Law-Enforcement.pdf

Stoskopf, A. (1999). The forgotten history of eugenics. *Rethinking Schools*, *13*(3). https://rethinkingschools.org/articles/the-forgotten-history-of-eugenics/

Stovall, D. (2016). *Born out of struggle: Critical race theory, school creation, and the politics of interruption*. SUNY Press.

Stovall, D. (2020). Mayoral control: Reform, whiteness, and critical race analysis of neoliberal educational policy. In E. Mayorga, U. Aggarwal, & B. Picower (Eds.), *What's race got to do with it?: How current school reform policy maintains racial and economic inequality* (2nd ed., pp. 113–128). Peter Lang.

Strauss, V. (2013). *Bill Gates: 'It would be great if our education stuff worked but. . . .'* Washington Post: The Answer Sheet. http://www.washingtonpost.com/blogs/answer-sheet/wp/2013/09/27/bill-gates-it-would-be-great-if-our-education-stuff-worked-but/

Sullivan, A. (2017, April 4). Why do Democrats feel sorry for Hillary Clinton? *New York Magazine*. https://nymag.com/intelligencer/2017/04/why-do-democrats-feel-sorry-for-hillary-clinton.html

Suzuki, B. H. (1977). Education and the socialization of Asian Americans: A revisionist analysis of the "model minority" thesis. *Amerasia*, *4*(2), 23–51. https://doi.org/10.17953/amer.4.2.x203l74863857108

Takacs, D. (2002). Positionality, epistemology, and social justice in the classroom. *Social Justice*, *29*(4), 168–181.

Takeda, O. (2015). A forgotten minority?: A content analysis of Asian Pacific Americans in introductory American government textbooks. *Political Science & Politics*, *48*(3), 430–439. https://doi.org/10.1017/S1049096515000190

Tan, X., & Michel, R. (2011). Why do standardized testing programs report scaled scores?: Why not just report the raw or precent-correct scores? *ETS R&D Connections*, *16*. https://www.ets.org/Media/Research/pdf/RD_Connections16.pdf

Taylor, D. (2016, October 11). *Teachers in Seattle affirm that Black Lives Matter in public schools*. Seattle Education. https://seattleducation2010.wordpress.com/2016/10/11/teachers-in-seattle-affirm-that-black-lives-matter-in-public-schools/

Taylor, S. (1997). Critical policy analysis: Exploring contexts, texts, and consequences. *Discourse: Studies in the Cultural Politics of Education*, *18*(1), 23–35.

Thomas, P. L. (2014, December 4). *Grit, education narratives veneer for white, wealth privilege*. The Becoming Radical. https://radicalscholarship.wordpress.com/2014/12/04/grit-education-narratives-veneer-for-white-wealth-privilege/

Tran, D. X. (2014). Forget teaching to the test–Castle Bridge boycotts it! In J. Hagopian (Ed.), *More than a score: The new uprising against high-stakes testing* (pp. 211–218). Haymarket Books.

Tuck, E., & Yang, K. W. (2012). Decolonization is not a metaphor. *Decolonization: Indigeneity, Education, & Society*, *1*(1), 1–40.

Tyack, D. (1974). *The one best system: A history of American urban education*. Harvard University Press.

U.S. Department of Education. (2009). *Race to the Top Program Executive Summary*. U.S. Department of Education.

U.S. Department of Education. (2025, January 23). *U.S. Department of Education takes action to eliminate DEI*. U.S. Department of Education. https://www.whitehouse.gov/fact-sheets/2025/04/fact-sheet-president-donald-j-trump-reinstates-commonsense-school-discipline-policies/

U.S. News & World Report. (1966, December 26). Success story of one minority group in U.S. *U.S. News & World Report*, *61*(26), 73–76.

United Sikhs. (2019, September 11). *United Sikhs release timeline of attacks against Sikhs across America since Sept. 11, 2001*. Intrado: Global Newswire. https://www.globenewswire.com/news-release/2019/09/12/1914493/0/en/UNITED-SIKHS-RELEASE-TIMELINE-OF-ATTACKS-AGAINST-SIKHS-ACROSS-AMERICA-SINCE-SEPT-11-2001.html

United States Census Bureau. (2020). *U.S. Census Bureau releases new educational attainment data*. United States Census Bureau. https://www.census.gov/newsroom/press-releases/2020/educational-attainment.html

Vasquez Heilig, J., Jellison Holme, J., LeClair, A. V., Redd, L. D., & Ward, D. (2016). The problematic segregation of special populations in charter schools relative to traditional public schools. *Stanford Law & Policy Review*, 27, 251–294.

Vetterkind, R. (2021, September 29). *Wisconsin assembly passes ban on teaching critical race theory*. Wisconsin State Journal. https://madison.com/wsj/news/local/govt-and-politics/wisconsin-assembly-passes-ban-on-teaching-critical-race-theory/article_1e53044a-8047-58c7-9560-368ae54fb588.html

Vicens, A. J. (2014, September 4). *Bill Gates spent more than $200 million to promote Common Core. Here's where it went: The Gates foundation has bankrolled a sprawling network of groups to advance the standards*. MotherJones. http://www.motherjones.com/politics/2014/09/bill-melinda-gates-foundation-common-core/

Vinson, K. D., & Ross, E. W. (2003). Controlling images: The power of high-stakes testing. In K. J. Saltman & D. A. Gabbard (Eds.), *Education as enforcement: The militarization and corporatization of schools* (pp. 241–258). RoutledgeFalmer.

von Zastrow, C. (2004). *Academic atrophy: The condition of the liberal arts in America's public schools* (p. 40). Council for Basic Education. http://www.ecs.org/html/Document.asp?chouseid=5058

Walker, A., Shafer, J., & Liams, M. (2004). "Not in my classroom": Teacher attitudes towards English language learners in the mainstream classroom. *NABE Journal of Research and Practice*, 2(1), 130–160.

Wallace, K., & Lamotte, S. (2016, November 30). *Harassment in schools skyrockets after election, teachers report*. CNN. http://www.cnn.com/2016/11/29/health/school-survey-post-election-negative-incidents/

Wang, L. L. (2007). Model minority, high-tech coolies, and foreign spies: Asian Americans in science and technology, with special reference to the case of Dr. Wen Ho Lee. *Amerasia Journal*, *33*(1), 49–62. https://doi.org/10.17953/amer.33.1.t086q80881t36t16

Warikoo, N. (2022). *Race at the top: Asian Americans and whites in pursuit of the American dream in suburban school*. University of Chicago Press.

Watsky, C., Ishimatsu, J., Harrison, A., & Nieves, E. (2020). *The economic reality of the Asian American Pacific Islander community is marked by diversity and inequality, not universal success* [FactFile]. Prosperity Now & the National Coalition for Asian Pacific Americans Community Development. https://learninghub.prospercanada.org/knowledge/the-economic-reality-of-the-asian-american-pacific-islander-community-is-marked-by-diversity-and-inequality-not-universal-success/

Watson, D., Hagopian, J., & Au, W. (Eds.). (2018). *Teaching for Black Lives*. Rethinking Schools, Ltd.

Waxman, O. B. (2023, April 6). Exclusive: New data shows the anti-critical race theory movement is "far from over." *Time*. https://time.com/6266865/critical-race-theory-data-exclusive/

Weber, M. (2013a, April 24). *How every kid could go to Bill Gates's private school*. Jersey Jazzman. http://jerseyjazzman.blogspot.com/2013/04/how-every-kid-could-go-to-bill-gatess.html

Weber, M. (2013b, May 27). Steve Perry: The final debunk. *Jersey Jazzman*. http://jerseyjazzman.blogspot.com/2013/05/dr-steve-perry-final-debunk.html

Weber, M. (2015, May 24). *Standardized tests: Symptoms, not causes*. Jersey Jazzman. http://jerseyjazzman.blogspot.com/2015/05/standardized-tests-symptoms-not-causes.html

Weiler, K. (1991). Freire and a feminist pedagogy of difference. *Harvard Educational Review*, *61*(4), 449–474.

Welner, K. G. (2013). The dirty dozen: How charter schools influence student enrollment. *Teachers College Record*. http://www.tcrecord.org/Content.asp?ContentID=17104

Whelan, L. (2015, September 15). Seattle teacher strike is the latest front line in America's public school wars: It's about much more than a wage dispute. *Mother Jones*. http://www.motherjones.com/politics/2015/09/heres-why-seattle-teacheres-are-strike/

White House. (2025, January 29). *Ending radical indoctrination in K–12 schooling*. https://www.whitehouse.gov/presidential-actions/2025/01/ending-radical-indoctrination-in-k-12-schooling/

Wing, J. Y. (2007). Beyond Black and white: The model minority myth and the invisibility of Asian American students. *The Urban Review*, *39*(4), 455–487. https://doi.org/10.1007/s11256-007-0058-6

Winnubst, S. (2020). The many lives of fungibility: Anti-blackness in neoliberal times. *Journal of Gender Studies*, *29*(1), 102–112. https://doi.org/10.1080/09589236.2019.1692193

Wolff, D. (2009, September 25). *Speculating on education*. Counterpunch. http://www.counterpunch.org/2009/09/25/speculating-on-education/

Wong, A. (2019, January 23). *America's teachers are furious: From West Virginia to Los Angeles, educators are ushering in a new era of labor activism*. The Atlantic. https://www.theatlantic.com/education/archive/2019/01/teachers-are-launching-a-rebellion/580975/

Wong, K. K., & Shen, F. X. (2005). When mayors lead urban schools: Assessing the effects of mayoral takeovers. In W. G. Howell (Ed.), *Besieged: School boards and the future of education politics* (pp. 81–101). Brookings Institutions Press.

Wraga, W. G. (1998). Interesting, if true: Historical perspectives on the "reconceptualization" of curriculum studies. *Journal of Curriculum and Supervision*, *14*(1), 5–28.

Wraga, W. G. (1999). "Extracting sun-beams out of cucumbers": The retreat from practice in reconceptualized curriculum studies. *Educational Researcher*, *28*(1), 4–13.

Wraga, W. G., & Hlebowitsh, P. S. (2003). Toward a renaissance in curriculum theory and development in the USA. *Journal of Curriculum Studies*, *35*(4), 425–437.

Yam, K. (2022, November 1). *Behind the vocal Asian Amerian minority railing against affirmative action*. NBC News. https://www.nbcnews.com/news/asian-america/vocal-asian-american-minority-railing-affirmative-action-rcna55082

Yang, A. A. (2015, October 19). Colonialism and imperialism in Asia. *Henry M. Jackson School of International Studies & Newspapers in Education: Global Asia:*

Yesterday, Today and Tomorrow. https://jsis.washington.edu/nie/wp-content/uploads/sites/16/2016/05/NIE-2015_Teacher-Guide.pdf

Yee, A. (2021, March 2). *It's a myth that Asian-Americans are doing well in the pandemic*. Scientific American. https://www.scientificamerican.com/article/its-a-myth-that-asian-americans-are-doing-well-in-the-pandemic/

Yellow Horse, A., Jeung, R., & Matriano, R. (2022). *Stop AAPI hate national report*. Stop AAPI Hate. https://stopaapihate.org/wp-content/uploads/2022/03/22-SAH-NationalReport-3.1.22-v9.pdf

Yi, J., & Todd, N. R. (2021). Internalized model minority myth among Asian Americans: Links to anti-Black attitudes and opposition to affirmative action. *Cultural Diversity and Ethnic Minority Psychology*, *27*(2). https://doi.org/10.1037/cdp0000448

Yi, V., Mac, J., Na, V. S., Venturanza, R. J., Museus, S. D., Buenavista, T. L., & Pendakur, S. L. (2020). Toward an anti-imperialistic critical race analysis of the model minority myth. *Review of Educational Research*, *90*(4), 542–579. https://doi.org/10.3102/0034654320933532

Yonezawa, S. (2000). Unpacking the black box of tracking decisions: Critical tales of families navigating the course placement process. In M. G. Sanders (Ed.), *Schooling students placed at risk: Research, policy, and practice in the education of poor and minority adolescents* (pp. 109–137). Lawrence Erlbaum.

Zabala, D. (2007). *State high school exit exams: Gaps persist in high school exit exam pass rates—Policy brief 3* (p. 2). Center on Education Policy.

Zehr, H. (2011, March 10). *Restorative or transformative justice?* Zehr Institute. https://www.zehr-institute.org/resources/restorative-or-transformative-justice

Zeichner, K. M., & Pena-Sandoval, C. (2015). Venture philanthropy and teacher education policy in the U.S.: The role of the New Schools Venture Fund. *Teachers College Record*, *117*(6). 1–44. https://doi.org/10.1177/016146811511700508

Zinn, H. (1995). *A people's history of the United States: 1492-present* (rev. and updated). HarperPerennial.

Zinn Education Project. (2021, August 11). *Pledge to teach the truth*. Zinn Education Project. https://www.zinnedproject.org/news/pledge-to-teach-truth

Zinn Education Project. (2023). *Zinn Education Project: Teaching people's history*. Zinn Education Project. https://zinnedproject.org

Index

About the Author

Wayne Au is professor in the School of Educational Studies at the University of Washington Bothell. A long-time educational activist and scholar, his work critically examines issues of power and justice in educational policy and practice.